WORLD BANK TECHNICAL PAPER NO. 399

Finance, Private Sector, and Infrastructure Network

Concessions for Infrastructure

A Guide to Their Design and Award

Michel Kerf
with
R. David Gray
Timothy Irwin
Céline Lévesque
Robert R. Taylor

under the direction of Michael Klein

The World Bank
Washington, D.C.

Technical Papers are published to communicate the results of the Bank's work to the development community with the least possible delay. The typescript of this paper therefore has not been prepared in accordance with the procedures appropriate to formal printed texts, and the World Bank accepts no responsibility for errors. Some sources cited in this paper may be informal documents that are not readily available.

The findings, interpretations, and conclusions expressed in this paper are entirely those of the author(s) and should not be attributed in any manner to the World Bank, to its affiliated organizations, or to members of its Board of Executive Directors or the countries they represent. The World Bank does not guarantee the accuracy of the data included in this publication and accepts no responsibility for any consequence of their use. The boundaries, colors, denominations, and other information shown on any map in this volume do not imply on the part of the World Bank Group any judgment on the legal status of any territory or the endorsement or acceptance of such boundaries.

The material in this publication is copyrighted. Requests for permission to reproduce portions of it should be sent to the Office of the Publisher at the address shown in the copyright notice above. The World Bank encourages dissemination of its work and will normally give permission promptly and, when the reproduction is for noncommercial purposes, without asking a fee. Permission to copy portions for classroom use is granted through the Copyright Clearance Center, Inc., Suite 910, 222 Rosewood Drive, Danvers, Massachusetts 01923, U.S.A.

ISSN: 0253-7494

Michel Kerf is a private sector development specialist in the Private Sector Development and Finance Group of the World Bank's Middle East and North Africa Region. R. David Gray is a consultant, Timothy Irwin is an economist, Céline Lévesque is a consultant, and Robert R. Taylor is a principal financial analyst, all in the Private Participation in Infrastructure Group of the World Bank's Private Sector Development Department.

Library of Congress Cataloging-in-Publication Data

Concessions for infrastructure : a guide to their design and award /
    Michel Kerf . . . [et al].
        p.   cm. — (World Bank technical papers ; no. 399)
    ISBN 0-8213-4165-0
    1. Infrastructure (Economics).   2. Privatization.   3. Concessions.
I. Kerf, Michel, 1965–   . II. World Bank.   III. Series.
HC79.C3C66   1998
363—dc21   97-50066
                                                            CIP

Contents

Foreword

In recent years countries around the world have met the challenge of developing and maintaining critical infrastructure by restructuring public utilities and expanding private sector participation in the infrastructure sectors. Recognizing the importance of adequate infrastructure services, such as power, telecommunications, transport, water supply, and sanitation, for the development of industry and the quality of life, and given the constraints on public budgets to finance these growing infrastructure needs, governments have sought to shift part of the burden of new infrastructure investment to the private sector. In addition, private sector involvement can bring increased efficiency in investment, management, and operation. And restructuring utilities along competitive lines has demonstrated the enormous potential benefits to governments and consumers of unshackling competition for improving and expanding infrastructure services.

Many countries have enlisted private sector participation in infrastructure through the use of concession contracts with private operators and developers. A concession, broadly defined, is a legal arrangement in which a firm obtains from the government the right to provide a particular service. Concessions can be used to create competition for the market under conditions in which the service provider has significant market power. Concession arrangements can take any number of forms involving the shifting of risks and responsibilities from the public to the private sector.

Concession arrangements entail a myriad of legal and economic issues, including the organization of government entities responsible for concession programs and the adequacy of the broader legal and regulatory environment. The design and implementation of concession contracts that allocate risks and responsibilities and the mechanisms for evaluating and awarding projects are also of paramount importance. The government's role as regulator and as a provider of support for infrastructure concessions must also be assessed. While some countries have established extensive concession programs, others are just beginning to develop these programs. This report provides a guide to the complex range of issues and options involved in the implementation of concession arrangements, drawing on the experience of both industrial and developing countries.

Nemat Shafik
Director
Private Sector Development and Finance Group
Middle East and North Africa Region

Bernardo Frydman
Deputy Manager
Private Sector Department
Inter-American Development Bank

Acknowledgments

This report was conceived jointly by the Inter-American Development Bank and the World Bank. It was prepared by the Private Participation in Infrastructure (PPI) Group of the World Bank's Private Sector Development Department and benefited greatly from comments provided at several stages by Bernardo Frydman, Ezequiel Machado, Terry Powers, and John Cahillane of the Inter-American Development Bank. Valuable assistance and comments were also given by Penelope Brook Cowen, Pierre Guislain, Neil Roger, and Warrick Smith. Chapters 5 and 6 of this report draw extensively on previous work by Michael Klein and Warrick Smith.

Abstract

This report is not a step-by-step guide on how to negotiate concessions. Nor is it an attempt to identify model contracts or clauses. Rather, it aims at helping policymakers and their advisers to better understand some of the most important and difficult issues related to the design, award, implementation, monitoring, and modification of concessions. Here, we broadly define concessions as any arrangements in which a firm obtains from the government the right to provide a particular service under conditions of significant market power.

While it is impossible to succinctly summarize the multiple issues discussed in the report, and while in many cases there is no single "best" answer to a particular question, some key recommendations emerge. They deserve to be emphasized. The following ten recommendations constitute a nonexhaustive list:

The main rationale for concessions is that they can facilitate the regulation of natural monopolies. In markets that are naturally competitive, direct competition between firms can usually work well without recourse to concessions. Before awarding concessions, governments should therefore first determine whether competition can be made to work in the relevant activities, possibly through reforming the market structure.

Governments often grant exclusive rights to the concessionaire. But, in many cases, this may not be desirable. Permitting entry by new competitors helps ensure that direct competition will take place wherever possible and can pressure the incumbent to maintain good performance. In addition, many of the objectives pursued through the granting of exclusive rights—such as making deals more attractive to private operators or ensuring that some redistributive social goals are met—can often be achieved through other means.

While many aspects of a concession are transaction- or sector-specific, several key principles related to the award, design, or monitoring of concessions are substantially identical across sectors. There will often be important advantages in clearly specifying such principles in cross-sectoral laws or regulations applicable to private infrastructure schemes in general.

The allocation of risks between the involved parties is at the core of concession design. While theoretical principles are well-known—risks should be borne by the party best able to control, manage, or hedge against them—their application in practice often raises numerous difficulties. A careful analysis will often be necessary to distinguish between costs that are truly exogenous to the operator (that is, those against which the company cannot protect itself) and those that are not. Only exogenous costs should be passed on to other parties such as consumers, suppliers, or the conceding authority.

Striking an adequate balance between certainty and flexibility is another main challenge of concession design. Performance targets, for example, can be designed so as to allow for renegotiations under specific, preestablished procedures. Usually, they should focus on the end results to be achieved rather than on the means to be used in order to preserve the flexibility of the concessionaire's operational arrangements.

Protecting the poorest users is often a major objective of the tariff regime. Cross-subsidies, which are widely used to pursue this objective, tend to be distortionary, anticompetitive, and nontransparent. International experience demonstrates that there are numerous alternatives, such as financing such subsidies through the budget or through special funds, which present fewer drawbacks.

Competitive award mechanisms are generally preferred. In some circumstances, however, negotiated procedures may be more suitable. In such cases it will be important that some safeguards, such as benchmarking or allowing other developers to better the proposed terms, be built in to ensure transparency and efficiency.

Even when concessions incorporate detailed and specific rules, there is still a need for at least some degree of regulatory discretion. The challenge, then, is to protect the regulatory process from both industry and short-term political pressures and to ensure that the regulator has access to people with sufficient technical capabilities. Establishing specialized, cross-sectoral regulatory bodies that are independent of the government is often advantageous in this respect. When such solutions are politically unacceptable, a range of incremental or alternative approaches can be considered.

The fact that the financial cost of raising capital is lower for the government than for private investors is often presented as an argument in favor of government participation in infrastructure projects. But, the argument is flawed for a number of reasons. First, the government's lower cost of capital reflects its ability to resort to taxation to repay its debts, not the inherently lower economic costs of government-funded projects. Second, civil servants often have less incentive to invest wisely than private project managers. Finally, government participation in infrastructure projects alongside private investors might distort these investors' incentives to maximize overall project returns.

Concessioning infrastructure services is always a complex exercise that raises new sets of questions and problems for the administration. It is absolutely essential for governments to retain qualified and experienced experts who are able to provide sound advice on the range of issues discussed in this report.

CHAPTER 1

Introduction

The past 15 years have witnessed a fundamental change in the way governments think about infrastructure. In rich and poor countries alike private ownership and operation have been replacing public provision, while monopoly has been giving way to competition. Concessions have played a central role in these changes. The concession documents themselves have been used to specify the rights and obligations of the private firms, while the bidding processes that have been used to award concessions have brought competitive pressures to bear in previously sheltered industries.

1.1 Defining Concessions

Throughout the report we use *concession* broadly to refer to any arrangement in which a firm obtains from the government the right to provide a particular service under conditions of significant market power. A concession is thus a device that can be used to create competition for a market, when competition in the market is not operating. Indeed, for the purposes of this report, concessions can be thought of as legal arrangements suitable for creating competition for a market.

According to this definition, concessions need not involve the private sector, since governments can award concessions to public enterprises. Concessions are typically given to privately owned companies, however, and concessions to private firms are the focus of this report.

For our purposes the following arrangements may be counted as concessions: leases, affermages (a form of lease used widely in France), build-operate-transfer contracts (BOTs), and divestitures with revocable licenses to operate. When we refer to concessions in the narrower sense, in which the concessionaire has investment responsibilities, we use *pure concession* or *concession stricto sensu*. At the same time there may be arrangements commonly called concessions that fall outside the scope of this report: *concession* might be used to refer to the rights to operate in a market, even when those rights are not limited in number and thus confer no market power.

1.2 Early Concessions

Concessions have gained in popularity recently, but they are an old innovation. The modern theory dates back at least to the nineteenth century and Edwin Chadwick's (1859) discussion of competition for the market. The famous nineteenth century economist Alfred Marshall outlined the case for concessions as follows:

> A public authority may be able to own the franchise and, in some cases, part of the fixed capital of a semi-public undertaking, and to lease them for a limited number of years to a Corporation who shall be bound to perform services, or deliver goods, at a certain price and subject to certain other regulations ... the special point of the proposal is that, where

1

possible, the competition for the franchise shall turn on the price or the quality, or both, of the services or the goods, rather than on the annual sum paid for the lease. (quoted in Ekelund and Hébert 1981: 471)

The practice of concessions dates back even further, however, to the middle ages (see Bezançon 1995). Moreover, in the past two centuries infrastructure networks in water, power, gas, and rail were often developed by private firms that, incidentally, bore substantial market risk with limited protection from competition. We mention a few early concessions below without trying to be comprehensive or necessarily representative.

Private companies developed much of the early water infrastructure in France, Britain, and the United States. In 1777, for example, the French government gave the Perrier brothers a 15-year concession to collect and distribute water to households in parts of Paris. They took the water from the Seine using English-made pumps, transported it through pipes of wood and steel, and then delivered it in barrels—that is, until they ran into financial trouble and their firm was nationalized (Benzançon 1995). The next century saw the founding of the well-known French firms, Compagnie Générale des Eaux and Lyonnaise des Eaux.

In London there were as many as six private water companies operating by the 1820s (Foreman-Peck and Millward 1994). And in the United States at the dawn of the nineteenth century, 15 of the 16 waterworks that had been constructed were private. By the end of the century, however, governments had become the dominant force in water supply, at least in the cities (Jacobson and Tarr 1995:11).

Local private firms were responsible for developing most of the electricity utilities in Brazil, Chile, Costa Rica, and Mexico—Colombia being the only exception among a group of five reviewed in one study of the development of the industry (Cavers and Nelson 1959). The same was true of the United States. The early power companies were privately owned and they operated in competitive, largely unregulated, commercially risky environments. They had franchises, but no exclusive rights to serve. Although they were subsequently regulated and protected from competition, they remained private. In the gas sector in the United Kingdom, to take another example, exclusive franchises were never legalized, and by 1850, 14 separate private gas companies were operating over the whole London metropolis (Foreman-Peck and Millward 1994).

The transport sector offers many early examples of private infrastructure construction and operation. In France the king concessioned roads and bridges. The concessionaires collected tolls in return for maintaining the routes—often being criticized for doing the former with more zeal than the latter. Canals were also built in France under concessions as early as the seventeenth century. The concession document established the tariff that could be charged and the timetable for construction; the entrepreneurs building the canal bore market risk. Later, in many Latin American countries such as Argentina, Brazil, and Uruguay, private developers from Britain, France, and the United States built many of the early railways. The history of rail in Mexico illustrates the common cycle of public and private ownership:

The Díaz regime undertook initially to promote railways either directly or through subsidies to state governments; but the results were slow to appear. So after 1880 policy shifted to subsidies to private companies, partly in the form of land grants, which attracted substantial amounts of British and American capital. Private construction by numerous companies produced a rather disorganized network with considerable duplication of routes. So government gradually attempted to consolidate companies and buy out part of their capital. The eventual result was a national railway system (Ferrocarriles Nacional de México, formed in 1909), with majority government ownership but continuing private participation from the United States and Great Britain (Reynolds 1985: 99–100).

Later, the Mexican railways were completely nationalized. Now, they are being privatized again. In the United States a similar story emerges. Most of the public transit systems built in the late nineteenth century were private, as were many roads. According to one account, the "heyday of privately owned and operated roads supported by user fees came during the early decades of the nineteenth century. Many roads were built and maintained by state-chartered turnpike companies. . . [But] partly as a result of competition from canals and railroads by the 1860s, most private toll roads had been turned over to states and counties for operation from general tax revenues" (Jacobson and Tarr 1995:3).[1]

1.3 The Rationale for Concessions

Concessions should be used in areas where they are most likely to aid development. Although they can be used in any industry and were, for example, used in France to license butchers and bakers in the Middle Ages, they are most likely to help development when they are used to regulate natural monopolies—that is, services that can be provided more cheaply by a single firm than by two or more.

1.3.1 Natural Monopoly

When markets can be served efficiently by several firms—when they are naturally competitive—ordinary competition usually works well. But when they are naturally monopolistic ordinary, head-to-head competition does not operate. Competitively auctioned concessions in these industries allow some of the benefits of competition to be brought to bear in the absence of direct competition between firms. That is, they substitute competition *for* the market for competition *in* the market.

Take, for example, a water concession awarded to the bidder offering to supply water at the lowest price to consumers. If it is well-designed, it encourages efficiency in two ways that parallel the effects of competition in the market. First, it leads firms to offer to sell water at a price that covers their costs but not much more— just as ordinary competitive pressures keep prices

down and limit profits. Moreover, the government does not need to estimate the lowest profitable water price and then regulate to prevent the monopoly supplier from charging a higher price; through competitive bidding, the firms reveal that price themselves. Since firms usually have better information than regulators, the price that arises from competitive bidding is probably the best available estimate of the appropriate price. Second, a concession encourages firms to produce water cheaply, since inefficient firms cannot win the bidding and remain profitable. To win, firms are forced to offer a price for water not much higher than their cost of supplying it. The firm that wins is therefore likely to be one of the most efficient.[2]

What about industries that are neither natural monopolies nor highly competitive but are most efficiently served by, say, just two firms? If the government knew the industry was best served by just two firms and knew that these firms would charge high markups in the absence of regulation, it might be beneficial to award two concessions for the industry. The award of the concession could then be used to create competition for the market, where competition in the market would operate but not very effectively. This reasoning may underlie the award of a small number of licenses in mobile telecommunications. Concessioning seems less likely to improve on free entry and unregulated prices in such cases than in naturally monopolistic industries, however, since the market failure is smaller and more likely to be outweighed by regulatory failure.

1.3.2 Natural Monopoly and Infrastructure

The following infrastructure sectors are usually considered natural monopolies and are therefore the most suitable candidates for concessioning:

- Water distribution.
- Power transmission and distribution (as opposed to power retailing or "supply").
- Gas transmission and distribution (as opposed to gas retailing).

- Railway infrastructure (the tracks and stations, for example).
- Roads.

Other infrastructure businesses, however, are potentially competitive, and concessions may not be the best solution for them:

- Power generation.
- Gas production.
- The retail supply of both gas and power.
- Long-distance and mobile telecommunications.
- Rail services (as distinct from the tracks).

Concessions are not necessarily the wrong option in these sectors. Although power generation is potentially competitive in most countries, for example, some electricity markets may be too small to support effective competition in the market. In those markets, a competitively awarded concession may be the best option. But in the potentially competitive industries listed above governments should think carefully about whether ordinary competition can be made to work by reforming market structure before turn-ing to a concession.

1.3.3 Concessions and the Reform of Market Structure

Since one infrastructure sector may contain poten-tially competitive and inherently monopolistic seg-ments, it is sometimes useful to unbundle the segments (see table 1.1 for some examples). Then, competition in the market may work more effec-tively in the competitive sectors, while competition for the market is used for the naturally monopolis-tic sectors. Within the potentially competitive sec-tors an existing company may also be broken up into several competing firms.

Before awarding concessions in an infrastructure sector, therefore, governments should consider what is the best structure for that industry. Does it make sense to unbundle the industry vertically—separat-ing an upstream segment, such as generation, from a downstream segment, such as transmission? Does it make sense to unbundle some of the segments hor-izontally—creating, for example, several generation companies out of one? Only when these questions have been answered should concessioning begin.

Table 1.1 Examples of Market Structure Reform

Sector	Reform	Country examples
Power	Separating generation from transmission and creating competition in generation	Argentina, Australia, Colombia, New Zealand, United Kingdom
	Permitting free entry in generation	The countries above plus the United States
Gas	Separating production and supply from transmission and distribution	Argentina, Colombia, Mexico
	Permitting free entry in gas transmission	Chile, Germany, New Zealand
Telecommunications	Separating local from long-distance service	Argentina, Hong Kong, United States
	Permitting free entry in basic services	Australia, Chile, New Zealand, United Kingdom
Rail	Separating infrastructure (track) from rolling stock	Sweden, United Kingdom
	Separating railway lines by geographical region	Argentina, Mexico

Source: World Bank staff.

1.3.4 Reputation

Concessions generally have a limited term, at the end of which they are put out to bid again. When the incumbent concessionaire has the opportunity to compete in the rebidding, it has an extra incentive to perform well during the term of the original concession, since by performing well, it improves its chances of being awarded the concession again.[3] If one firm competes for many concessions, it has a further incentive to perform well in order to qualify as a bidder for other concessions. Governments can therefore better harness the benefits of reputation by awarding several concessions in a single industry, each for a different region, and permitting international firms to compete for local concessions, since these companies have valuable reputations they want to protect.[4]

1.3.5 Exclusivity

Concessions are best suited, we have said, to industries that are natural monopolies. A question that arises is whether concessions for natural monopolies should confer a legal monopoly.

1.3.5.1 What happens in practice? Most often, concessions give the winning firm the exclusive right to provide the service in question, and this legal monopoly typically endures for the length of the concession. There are, however, exceptions.

First, the period of exclusivity sometimes ends before the concession. One example is the Venezuelan telecommunications concession, in which the holder of a 30-year concession has exclusive rights for just 9 years. Another is the Abidjan–Ougadougou (Côte d'Ivoire–Burkina Faso) railway concession, which gives the concessionaire the exclusive right to run trains on the tracks for the first 7 years of the 15-year concession, after which other operators must be permitted to enter (Mitchell and Budin 1995).

Second, some concessions give no legal monopoly at all. In addition to the early power franchises in the United States, Compañía de Teléfonos in Chile was awarded a 50-year nonexclusive concession in the 1930s (Guislain 1997: 210). And there are several modern instances of firms in naturally monopolistic infrastructure industries that do not enjoy legal protection from competition. In Germany and Chile gas transmission companies have no legal monopoly. In New Zealand exclusive legal franchises have now been removed for most infrastructure services, including the transportation of gas and electricity, at both the transmission and distribution levels.

1.3.5.2 Should governments grant exclusivity? Although it is common for governments to grant exclusivity, it is not clear whether governments aid development by doing so.[5] The arguments for not granting exclusivity are, on the face of it, strong. Even in natural monopolies the threat of entry can sometimes spur an incumbent monopolist to perform better. (Technically, the threat of entry will be more valuable the more contestable is the market—or the smaller are the sunk costs of entry into the market.) New firms may choose not to enter, but their ability to do so if the incumbent offers poor value for money keeps the latter on its toes. Similarly, the possibility of entry by other firms can encourage an incumbent to extend service to unserved areas within the franchise boundary more quickly than it would otherwise—to ensure that it does not lose business.

Moreover, permitting entry reduces the costs of mistakenly concessioning an industry that turns out to have been—or because of technological change becomes—naturally competitive. If the industry really is naturally monopolistic, exclusivity may make no difference. But if the industry turns out to be potentially competitive, exclusivity prevents helpful competition.

What are the arguments for granting exclusivity? At least three can be made.

- Sometimes concessionaires are required to offer services at low prices to households but can charge businesses more. Other times, they are required to charge everyone the same price, even if the costs of service differ—as may happen when remote rural customers pay the same as city dwellers. At still other times existing customers may subsidize the cost of expanding the network to reach new customers. In all of these cases exclusivity prevents new firms from undercutting the prices paid by the overcharged customers and thereby depriving the concessionaire of the revenue needed to subsidize the others. Using the jargon, it prevents cherry-picking or cream-skimming.

- Because competition tends both to lower firms' profits and introduce new risks, exclusivity rights make concessions more attractive to potential bidders and their financiers. The government can therefore concession an exclusive business more easily or get more money for it. When other circumstances are unfavorable—because of severe political risk, for example—exclusivity might make or break a deal.
- Finally, exclusivity can prevent second and third firms from inefficiently entering industries that are naturally monopolistic (that is, most efficiently served by just one firm). Although the threat of entry may be helpful, its occurrence may be wasteful. In the nineteenth century, for example, competing companies laid parallel water pipes in the United Kingdom and parallel railway lines in Germany, which on the face of it seems inefficient.[6]

These arguments are correct, as far as they go. Yet they do not by themselves imply that concessionaires should have exclusive rights to serve. Although exclusivity can resolve certain problems, there may be better solutions. Legal monopolies are only one way of permitting one class of customers to subsidize another in order to achieve redistributive goals; there are others that are generally less costly (see section 3.3.5). Similarly, there may be other ways of increasing the attractiveness of a concession to bidders that are less harmful than exclusivity—such as improving the regulatory regime and eliminating costly investment obligations. And although there may be cases in which inefficient entry would occur without exclusivity, the government needs to weigh this risk against the risk of stifling beneficial competition. Some inefficient entry and duplication may be a price worth paying for the benefits of competitive pressure.

1.4 A Comparison of Different Types of Concessions

Concessions in the broad sense used here come in different guises. As well as pure concessions (*concessions stricto sensu*), there are arrangements called franchises, operating concessions, management contracts, leases, affermages, BOTs, and so on. The names are not always applied consistently, nor are they always helpful. What really matter are the incentives and opportunities created by the contracts.

1.4.1 *Types of Concessions*

One key difference among various concession arrangements is the nature and extent of the risk they transfer from the government to the concessionaire, and we can classify them accordingly.

- *Management contracts with incentive payments.* When management contracts provide for a performance-related payment, part of the operating risk of the business may be transferred from the government to the concessionaire, since the concessionaire's profits may vary with the operating performance of the company. But significant operating risk remains with the government as long as the government's financial returns still depend on the firm's operating profits.
- *Leases.* In a lease, as we use the term, the concessionaire is paid no fee by the government. The concessionaire's profits depend directly on the operating profits of the firm. Operating risk is thus fully transferred to the concessionaire. The government still maintains responsibility for investment and thus bears investment risk.
- *Pure concessions, BOTs, and rehabilitate-operate-transfers (ROTs).* In these arrangements the concessionaire undertakes investments as well, and both operating and investment risks are substantially transferred to the concessionaire.[7]

There is also a distinction between retail and wholesale concessions. In a retail concession the concessionaire sells services to the public.

Distribution concessions in electricity, water, telecommunications, and gas are examples. In a wholesale concession the concessionaire sells to another entity (often a government agency or state-owned enterprise), which in turn sells to the public. Concessions for independent power projects and for bulk water supply are examples. The concessionaire's rights and obligations and the risks it bears tend to vary systematically between retail and wholesale concessions.

1.4.2 Similarities and Differences

Because the detailed contractual provisions concerning risk transfer, duration, exclusivity, and so on are what matters, contracts with different names can have similar effects. A contract called a *concession*, for example, may closely resemble one called a *management contract* in its incentive effects if its contractual clauses effectively guarantee the concessionaire revenue and compensate it for cost increases.

Further, a divested business needing a license to operate may be in much the same position as a firm with a fixed-term lease. British and French water policies illustrate the point nicely. Although the British system is described as a *divestiture* and the French as *concessioning,* the two regimes may have similar economic effects. In Britain the government sold water-distribution assets to private companies, whereas in France local governments remain the legal owners of the assets and lease them to private water companies for limited periods of time. When the lease expires, typically after 15 to 30 years, the local government re-awards it, possibly to a different company. On the surface, the two policies may thus seem quite different.

Yet in practice the French companies seldom lose their concessions when they are rebid, and the British companies have no guarantee of continued operation. The divested British firms need a license to operate, and the licenses they were given at the time of privatization will expire after 25 years, in 2014. After that date the government can revoke a company's license, as long as it has given

10 years' notice, even if the company has done nothing wrong.[8] The two systems are thus much more similar than they might seem.

The possible resemblance between divestiture and concession raises another issue. Sometimes governments believe that the best policy would be to "fully privatize" a given public enterprise, but fear that "privatization" would be too unpopular. As a result, they may choose to lease or concession the business instead. As the previous discussion suggests, however, there may be little practical difference between policies described as divestitures and those described as concessions. What both the government and its critics should be concerned about are the details of arrangements.

Finally, contracts that go under a single name may have quite different effects. Contracts described as concessions, for example, typically transfer investment risk to the concessionaire. But not all operators of concessions have investment obligations.

These possibilities imply that in designing or analyzing a concession one must look beyond the arrangement's name and consider the details of its provisions relating to rights, obligations, and the allocation of risk. It does not imply, however, that the legal instrument used to concession infrastructure is irrelevant. A country's laws may treat differently two arrangements with seemingly similar functions. Some arrangements, for example, may be governed by administrative law, others by the law of private contracts, with significant implications for the modification or enforcement of the contract. In Turkey the government wanted contract law to govern its BOT contracts with private power producers, but was frustrated by a finding of the Turkish courts that the arrangements were concessions under the Turkish constitution and therefore subject to administrative law.

1.4.3 Differences between Concessions and Other Rights

Concessions must be distinguished from other rights that business may need in order to operate. For example, a power concessionaire must

ng wires over land that it does not
ter concessionaire must lay pipes
ople's land. Similarly, companies
town-planning, resource-use, or other
environmental permits to carry out their business
efficiently. These permissions may require
approval from a government agency distinct
from the conceding authority. They are discussed
in section 2.2.

Notes

1. For a historical perspective of the cycle of public
and private ownership in infrastructure see Klein and
Roger (1994).

2. For more on the rationale for concessions, see
Dnes (1995).

3. For more on the award and re-award of concessions see chapter 4 and section 3.8, respectively.

4. For more on reputation and concessions see
Zupan (1989).

5. If the government expects firms to bid for a concession, it must give them something of value.
Frequently that thing is an existing business. But if the
government has no existing business to give to the
winning bidder, it is hard to see how a concession is
possible without exclusivity. A concession to supply
electricity to a currently unserved town could not be
awarded, for example, unless it conferred exclusive
rights upon the winner. Otherwise, interested firms
would have no need for the concession and instead of
bidding for it would simply start up business. The
question that arises in this case is whether the government should award an exclusive concession or instead
rely on free entry.

6. Economists have shown theoretically that in certain circumstances more than one firm will be able
profitably to enter a naturally monopolistic industry,
even though provision by just one firm would be
cheaper. See Train (1991).

7. For more on these different types of contracts,
see Guislain and Kerf (1995).

8. See http://www.open.gov.uk:80/ofwat/appt.htm.

CHAPTER 2

The Broad Environment for Concessions

The success of a concession depends not only on the details of the contract or license but also on the adequacy of the broader legal and institutional environment governing the concession's design, award, and operation. This chapter looks first at how governments can best organize themselves to manage the process of designing and awarding concessions, and then at laws and regulations that affect the operation of concessions.

2.1 Government Organization

The interface between the government and the private sector is key to the success of private infrastructure arrangements. Governments need to perform numerous tasks when planning, designing, implementing, and regulating concessions. And inefficient organization can result in substantial cost to the government, developers, and consumers.

2.1.1 Government Responsibilities for Concessions

The functions that governments must perform regarding concessions span a wide range, from the establishment of an enabling environment to the award of specific concessions and their regulation (box 2.1).

2.1.2 Costs of Government Disorganization and Guiding Principles for Improved Operations

A lack of definition and transparency in government processes can increase uncertainty for investors and developers and thus multiply costs or stop projects from going ahead. For example, unclear assignment of authority to grant concessions and adopt related support measures or overly complicated and undefined approval processes can prevent concessions from developing smoothly (box 2.2).

Governments should try to implement the following principles in order to improve the way they manage concessions:

- Effective coordination of relevant government policies and approvals.
- Clarification of roles and responsibilities with respect to private investors.
- Acquiring access to the expertise required to design and implement complex transactions.

The design and implementation of concessions requires the coordination of several governmental actors. Sectoral ministries will usually be responsible for developing overall sectoral policy, finance ministries will usually have a close interest in the public revenue or liability implications of particular projects, and environmental ministries or authorities may have an interest in projects, as may ministries of justice, competition authorities, and others. Some coordination will often also be necessary between actors at central, provincial, and municipal governments regarding, for example, necessary approvals or the granting of guarantees.

When the government does not effectively coordinate all relevant actors, it risks sending mixed signals to private investors and causing delays,

---

Box 2.1 A Sample of Government Responsibilities for Concessions

Framework
- Adopting legal provisions to enable the granting of concessions.
- Establishing or identifying regulatory authorities.
- Managing government support to infrastructure projects.
- Managing public relations and information.

Project identification and analysis
- Identifying projects amenable to concessions (including in-house and unsolicited proposals).
- Prioritizing projects amenable to concessions.
- Hiring advisers.
- Performing a preliminary review of the costs and benefits of the project (without duplicating the analysis to be performed by the private sector), especially in cases where the government will be assuming part of the market risk.
- Reviewing legal and regulatory issues.
- Determining preliminary selection criteria.
- Granting permission for the project to go ahead (for example, for the opening of the bidding process).
- Setting a timetable for the project.

Enabling and supporting measures for specific projects
- Granting permits and other necessary authorizations (such as environmental permits, rights of way).

- Determining the form of government support for the project.

Design of the concession arrangements
- Choosing legal instruments.
- Allocating responsibilities.
- Choosing and designing pricing rules and performance targets.
- Determining bonuses and penalties.
- Determining duration and termination.
- Designing adaptation mechanisms to new or unforeseen circumstances.
- Choosing and designing a dispute settlement mechanism.

Concession award
- Choosing the method of award.
- Making decisions regarding prequalification and shortlisting.
- Determining bid structure and evaluation method.
- Determining bidding rules and procedures.
- Proceeding with the bidding.
- Negotiating.

Exercise of regulatory function
- Implementing regulatory rules.
- Supervising and monitoring.
- Enforcing rules (for example, imposing penalties).

Source: Klein, So, and Shin (1996); Fishbein and Babbar (1996); and World Bank staff.

---

either of which can deter investors or increase development costs substantially. When several large transactions are envisaged, governments should consider establishing an explicit sequencing plan to help in marketing the projects and to avoid overburdening local financial markets.

Investors will want to know what entities are responsible for providing what approvals and against what criteria. This knowledge is essential to effective coordination within government, but it is also important to guide and give confidence to potential investors. In addition, it is a prerequisite for transparent approval and bidding procedures.

Governments need expertise in a range of new areas to design and implement concessions. In addition to the technical engineering requirements of particular projects, new skills will be required in financing, regulating, and marketing to potential investors and consumers. Inadequate expertise in

these areas can prevent the establishment of mutually beneficial and sustainable private infrastructure arrangements.

All countries undertaking major private infrastructure arrangements—industrial and developing countries alike—must hire outside expertise from investment bankers, lawyers, and others. While detailed technical expertise can be contracted out in this way, governments still require staff with relevant expertise to hire and oversee the consultants, and to incorporate the lessons of experience for future transactions (box 2.3).

2.1.3 Degree of Decentralization in Government Organization

In order to manage their concession programs, governments may organize themselves in a more or less decentralized manner. Government activities

---

Box 2.2 One Measure of the Cost of Government Disorganization

One measure of the effectiveness of government organization in the design and award of concessions is the amount of transaction costs incurred by participants in the process. Developing an infrastructure project with private sector participation is a complex task requiring firms and governments to prepare proposals, conduct bidding, negotiate deals, and arrange funding. These activities may generate high transaction costs, including travel costs, staff costs, time delays, and advisory fees for investment bankers, lawyers, and consultants. In general, the weaker is the policy framework and institutional capacity of the government, the higher these transaction costs are likely to be.

On average, transaction costs may amount to as much as 5 to 10 percent of total project costs. But there can be wide variations depending on the stability of the policy environment. Where there is a well-developed policy framework, costs average 3 to 5 percent, whereas they may be as much as 10 to 12 percent in untested environments. Interestingly, empirical evidence suggests that transaction costs have little to do with project size. Rather, they stem from a lack of definition and transparency in government processes, which increase uncertainty for investors and developers and thus multiply costs. Unclear lines of authority between national and local entities and an onerous approval process can delay projects, sometimes for years, or even cause them to be abandoned. China, for example, is notorious for its tortuous bureaucratic processes: any project valued over $30 million requires review and approval by the central government, in addition to authorization by the concerned province, and must pass twice through the State Planning Council.

While the transaction costs incurred in private projects are often more apparent than in public projects, private projects do not necessarily generate higher overall costs. Greater attention to project parameters and better monitoring may avoid the time and cost overruns that are common in executing public sector projects. Also, as governments gain more experience with such projects and clarify the policy framework—resulting in speedier processes—these costs tend to fall.

Source: Klein, So, and Shin (1996).

---

regarding the design and award of concessions in Chile, for example, are much more centralized than those in Brazil. How does this difference affect the design and implementation of concessions?

First, decentralization is used here in two situations. The first is vertical decentralization, in which the authority to grant and administer concessions has been transferred to local governments. The second is horizontal decentralization, in which the functions regarding concessions have been dispersed within one level of government. For example, responsibilities for concessions in transport, water, or electricity could be assigned to sector departments or ministries within a single tier or level of government—this would be horizontal decentralization. On the other hand, a single unit or entity (within a single tier or level of government) could be assigned the administration of all concessions in transport, water, and electricity—this would be horizontal centralization.

Second, one has to keep in mind that organizations for concessions combine centralization and decentralization in different ways. For example, a country's administration of concessions can be vertically decentralized at the same time as being horizontally centralized. Take the case of Brazil. There, some responsibilities for concessions belong to the state of Rio de Janeiro—meaning that functions are vertically decentralized (although not all the way to the municipal level). On the other hand, Rio de Janeiro uses a central unit to manage its concessions; which means that its functions are horizontally centralized. Similarly, the organization can be vertically centralized but horizontally decentralized. This is the case in New Zealand, where the central government has the main responsibility for concessions (vertically centralized), but sectoral departments have the lead (horizontally decentralized). Further, in some countries certain sectors are the responsibility of vertically decentralized authorities while other sectors remain vertically centralized. For example, in France water is vertically decentralized but telecommunications and electricity are vertically centralized.

Box 2.3 Hiring Advisers

In hiring advisers, governments must address a number of issues:

- *What type of consultants are needed?* Concession advisory services can require economic and regulatory consultants, legal advisers, technical consultants and engineers, environmental consultants, investment bankers, and others.
- *How should the advisory work be packaged?* If a range of advisory services is needed, governments have the option of hiring a consortium (with a lead firm, which can be easier to manage and can result in more uniform advice) or hiring separate advisers (which provides access to a range of advice on complex issues and can promote a more informed discussion).
- *How should the advisers be hired?* As a general principle governments should use competitive bidding to select advisory firms, as competition will generally enhance the quality of proposals, enable governments to choose from a number of proposals, and increase transparency in the process. Direct hiring may be justifiable, but governments

should use it judiciously and follow a transparent process that stands up to public scrutiny.
- *On what basis should advisers be remunerated?* Establishing appropriate fee structures for advisers is a complex but important task, as the fee structure may affect the type of advice given. For example, investment banks frequently are paid on the basis of a success fee for completing a transaction. Thus the advisory firm will benefit if a public enterprise is sold as a legal monopoly (that is, it will fetch a higher market price), but the sector as a whole and the economy may suffer as a consequence.
- *How should advisers be managed?* Governments can enhance the effectiveness of advisers during the assignment by having a strong counterpart on their side, ensuring that advisers have access to all pertinent information on a timely basis, and making timely decisions throughout the process to provide continued clear direction to the advisers. Otherwise, advisers will work in a vacuum, with high cost and little return to the client government.

Source: World Bank staff.

Third, it is important to remember that much depends on the political system and traditions of the country in question. One should not, however, give up trying to tailor or improve the system in place. Even in cases where the jurisdiction and organization of different tiers of governments, or entities within them, have clearly been defined in the constitution, most systems will have room for some improvement in the conduct of government business.

2.1.3.1 Vertical decentralization. There is no universally good or bad way of making changes. There are common trade-offs, however, between vertical centralization and decentralization (table 2.1), as well as between horizontal centralization and decentralization (table 2.2). An analysis of such trade-offs shows the strengths and weaknesses of each approach and indicates how an organization can be improved in these regards.

Most systems are not perfectly centralized or decentralized. In practice, intermediate solutions can be devised in order to strike a more optimum balance between the two extremes. For example, policy determination and implementation can be separated and assigned to different tiers of government. Different tiers of government can also deal with different policy questions. And different levels of government might cooperate on certain matters.

In a system that emphasizes vertical centralization one of the main challenges is to take into account specific local conditions. Consultation mechanisms could be useful to achieve this. In a system that emphasizes vertical decentralization one of the main challenges is to deal with constrained technical capabilities. Expertise can be enhanced through the use of a central unit staffed with skilled individuals that are at the disposal of local authorities for guidance, advice, and training.

Table 2.1 Trade-Offs in Vertical Decentralization

Criterion	Centralized approach	Decentralized approach
Provides flexibility to adapt to local conditions, priorities, and preferences	–	+
Promotes consistent policies	+	–
Promotes experimentation with different approaches	–	+
Favors learning between jurisdictions	+	–
Helps the development of expertise that is specific to local conditions	–	+
Uses economies of scale to deal with the problem of constrained capacities	+	–
Provides decisionmakers with better information	–	+
Enables decisionmakers to take into account the effect of local policies on other jurisdictions	+	–
Promotes the accountability of decisionmakers	–	+
Facilitates the consideration of how decisions regarding concessions can affect trade between jurisdictions (such as standards, subsidies)	+	–

Source: World Bank staff.

2.1.3.2 Horizontal decentralization. There are similar trade-offs between horizontally centralized and decentralized approaches (table 2.2).

Most governments do not take an approach to concessions that is totally centralized or decentralized horizontally. Intermediate solutions can, in fact, be better. Responsibilities regarding budgetary commitments may, for example, remain entirely centralized within the finance ministry to ensure control, while sectoral policymaking can be decentralized toward individual sector ministries.

In a system that emphasizes horizontal centralization one of the main challenges is to take into account sectoral specifics. The formation of sectoral departments within a centralized entity can serve this purpose. In a system that emphasizes

Table 2.2 Trade-Offs in Horizontal Decentralization

Criterion	Centralized approach	Decentralized approach
Enables a focus on sectoral specifics	–	+
Promotes consistent policies across sectors (that is, reduces the risk of distortions arising from inconsistent approaches to common issues)	+	–
Promotes experimentation with different approaches	–	+
Favors learning among sectors	+	–
Helps the development of sector-specific expertise	–	+
Uses economies of scale to deal with the problem of constrained capacities	+	–
Minimizes the impact of sectoral politics	–	+
Improves resistance to improper influences from particular industries or political authorities	+	–
Decreases the opportunity to inappropriately apply precedents from one sector to other sectors	–	+
Improves the ability to deal with blurring industry boundaries	+	–

Source: World Bank staff.

decentralization one of the main challenges is to maintain coherence among sectors. Establishing coordination mechanisms between sectors will be important in this regard. The adoption of cross-sectoral regulatory frameworks can also play a significant role (see section 2.1.4 below).

Most of the new institutional models being adopted around the world reflect some balance between extreme cases of centralization and decentralization and exhibit different ways of tackling the challenges mentioned above. Section 2.1.5 presents some country illustrations.

2.1.4 The Use of Cross-Sectoral Regulatory Frameworks

All concessions contain many project-specific details. In addition, some issues are unique to a particular industry and hence require attention on a sector-specific basis. Examples include technical and safety standards and market structure arrangements. But many of the issues associated with the awarding of contracts and some other key principles are nearly identical across sectors. For these issues there are a number of potential advantages to adopting common rules across sectors, including economies of scale, common interpretations, avoidance of the rule-making process being captured by industry-specific interest groups, and the sending of a clear signal by government authorities

that they are committed to promoting private sector participation in infrastructure (box 2.4).

2.1.5 Government Organization: Illustrations

Governments around the world are working to improve and reform their organization in order to facilitate the development and execution of private infrastructure projects. A few cases are presented here. These examples demonstrate how some governments have applied the guiding principles presented in section 2.1.2 and have met some of the challenges presented by centralization and decentralization (section 2.1.3).

2.1.5.1 Bolivia. In 1994, to implement its bold Capitalization Program, Bolivia created the position of minister for capitalization. The Minister was made responsible for all aspects of government programs covering telecommunications, electricity, railways, airlines, airports, hydrocarbons, and water. Sector-specific working groups were formed within the Capitalization Ministry, drawing on relevant expertise from state-owned entities, sector ministries, and the private sector. A central procurement unit was formed and made responsible for handling the large number of contracts for consultants and advisers. Having accomplished its objectives, the ministry closed its doors in the summer of 1997.

Box 2.4 The Role of Cross-Sectoral Regulatory Frameworks

A growing number of countries are adopting cross-sectoral frameworks for private infrastructure, including Brazil, Bulgaria, Chile, China, Colombia, Hungary, the Philippines, and Vietnam.

While details vary among countries, the key elements of cross-sectoral frameworks include clear rules on:

- Which infrastructure sectors are open to private participation.
- Which agencies are responsible for approving private projects or contracts.
- Tariff adjustment.

- Contract amendment and termination.
- Competitive bidding, including the scope of exceptions.
- Availability of international arbitration.
- Other issues important to private infrastructure arrangements that are not dealt with adequately in other laws. Examples vary from country to country but include the treatment of security interests in private projects and rules on liquidated damages (that is rules regarding setting in advance of the amount of compensation to be paid in case of certain breaches of obligations).

Source: Kerf and Smith (1996).

2.1.5.2 Peru. Privatization of state-owned enterprises was the first stage of the Peruvian government's endeavor to develop private participation in infrastructure. Initially, the Private Investment Promotion Commission (COPRI) was responsible for the entire privatization program, including divestiture of state enterprises. COPRI is an interministerial commission composed of six members of the government and assisted by a small technical secretariat. Various special committees were set up to privatize individual state-owned enterprises chosen by COPRI (Guislain 1997: 156).

With many infrastructure assets now divested to the private sector, Peru is entering the second stage of its strategy, focusing its attention on concessions, including many greenfield projects. The Private Concessions Promotion Commission (PROMCEPRI) was created in December 1996 for this purpose. Modeled after COPRI, PROMCEPRI is meant to be the only agency in charge of promoting private investment within the area of public infrastructure and utilities. PROMCEPRI will also use special committees to implement its concession program.

2.1.5.3 Mexico. Mexico uses a relatively decentralized approach to support its infrastructure privatization program. Sectoral ministries primarily design and implement the projects, while the cabinet, supported by an interministerial commission, does the high-level policy coordination. The secretariat to the interministerial commission, located in the Ministry of Finance, is not directly involved with specific concessions but is used as a channel for managing concessional loans and donor support to the program.

2.1.5.4 The Philippines. The government of the Philippines created a novel institutional structure to support the country's large private infrastructure program (under the 1989 BOT Law and Regulations). Each sectoral agency has a specialist "BOT Unit" responsible for coordinating the design and implementation of its projects. National, provincial, and municipal authorities

select and award projects under the framework. The authorities prepare a list of priority projects, which must be approved by either the Investment Coordination Committee (ICC) of the National Economic Development Authority (NEDA), the NEDA Board, or by local or regional councils, depending on the conceding jurisdiction and the cost of proposed projects, as specified in the Implementing Regulations to the Law. Projects undertaken on a build-own-operate (BOO) basis, or through contractual arrangements other than those defined under the Law, require presidential approval.

As part of its program, the government created a BOT Center. The Center has about 14 professional staff members and performs the following tasks:

- Keeping an updated national inventory of all nominated projects that are eligible for development under the BOT framework.
- Providing general advice to foreign investors doing business in the Philippines.
- Developing infrastructure projects.
- Providing technical assistance and training to central and local government officials on the design and implementation of projects.
- Spearheading promotional activities for the Philippine BOT program and specific projects through brochures and roadshows.

Initially, the Center was mainly involved in marketing the BOT concept to private investors. As the concept has become better known, most marketing and similar tasks have been devolved to the BOT units in each sectoral agency. The BOT Center now spends more time training national and local government officials.

2.1.5.5 Australia—State of Victoria. State governments in Australia have the main responsibility for most infrastructure sectors. In the State of Victoria individual government departments are ultimately responsible for concession design and award. Project responsibility is assigned to a single minister in each case. This minister is then responsible for facilitating consultation with the other government departments involved in the project. The minister will also work with the Department of Treasury and Finance. In order to provide guidance and promote consistency in analysis and procedures, the Victorian government has formulated an "Infrastructure Investment Policy for Victoria," a description of which was published in June 1994 by the Department of Treasury and Finance. That department also acts as a reference center when guidance is required by other government entities (see Department of Treasury and Finance 1994, 1996).

2.2 The Broader Legal and Regulatory Environment

One of the first things investors will want to check before becoming involved in a concession is whether the country's legal and regulatory environment is favorable to concession operations. A concession agreement cannot unilaterally modify or override the provisions of a law or the country's constitution. Thus one cannot assume that all issues or problems can be handled within the boundaries of a concession agreement.

In order to create a legal environment that is conducive to concession arrangements, governments may have to amend or repeal some laws and regulations. They may also have to adopt new legal provisions to permit the granting of certain rights. While the overall legal framework should be reviewed, it would be pointless in the context of a specific concession to document and remedy all the shortcomings that can be found in a country's legal environment. Efforts must be focused on the core part of the legal framework that must be in place for the concession program to succeed (Guislain 1997: 46, 87). This section identifies the main issues that should be tackled.

2.2.1 Threshold Legal Impediments to Private Participation

Governments must remove impediments that prohibit private participation in infrastructure. Two of the most important obstacles regarding concessions are laws and regulations that prohibit the private ownership and operation of public services and foreign investment in infrastructure sectors. Sometimes, although they do not prohibit the participation of the private sector or foreigners in infrastructure, governments impose conditions on participation. Investors will want to be aware of these conditions, as they may severely limit the scope of private involvement.

The following questions regarding limitations on private participation must be answered:

- Does the law permit the private provision of infrastructure services? In some cases the constitution or a law must be amended in order to abolish the legal monopoly of state-owned enterprises.
- Does the law permit the sale of certain infrastructure assets to the private sector?
- Does a specific law need to be adopted to transfer infrastructure assets to the private sector? This is not necessary in most common-law countries, unless there is specific legislation to the contrary, but it is often required in civil-law countries.
- Are there limits or conditions for participation? For example, is the concessionaire obliged to form a joint venture with a public entity or to incorporate itself locally?

Likewise, the following questions on participation by foreign investors must be addressed:

- Are foreigners legally entitled to hold concessions?
- Are there limits to the foreign operation of public utilities? For example, do foreigners need to partner with local firms? Are foreigners limited to a maximum number of shares?
- Are foreigners excluded from certain sectors? For example, foreigners are sometimes excluded from "strategic" sectors.
- Are there other forms of discrimination against foreigners? For example, are domestic firms preferred in the bidding terms?

2.2.2 *Property and Land-Use Rights*

To attract private investment at a reasonable cost, governments must make credible commitments to rules that safeguard property rights. Investors need adequate protection against unwarranted government expropriation and want to know that the land rights they hold can be exercised and protected.

2.2.2.1 Legal provisions and restraints on expropriation. All countries reserve the right to expropriate property for public purposes. In some countries such powers will be found in the legislation on the "eminent domain" right of the state (which describes the government's expropriation powers). Such powers can also be found in the Constitution. Many Latin American countries (for example, Colombia, Brazil, Bolivia, and Peru) have adopted new constitutions in the 1980s that include rights and obligations on expropriation.

Investors will want to know the conditions for expropriation. For example:

- Are investors compensated, and which standards apply to compensation?
- Are the rights to expropriate limited in scope?
- Are the rights to expropriate subject to judicial review?

2.2.2.2 Land law. Concession operations often require the use and ownership of land. Investors are likely to find answers to their questions regarding property rights in the country's legal system.[1]

- Does the constitution recognize private ownership (of land, for example)? Many constitutions had to be amended in Eastern Europe and countries of the former Soviet Union (1989–90) and in some countries like Vietnam (1992) in order to allow privatization.
- How are ownership rights defined, recognized, and protected in the host country?
- What restrictions, if any, are placed on the transferability of those rights?

- How do titling and registration function in the host country (or in what ways are they deficient)? This information is important for determining the availability of title, for example.
- What enforcement mechanisms protect property rights?
- What restrictions may be placed on foreigners with respect to the acquisition and exercise of ownership rights for land or other real estate assets?

Concessionaires often need to acquire rights of way, for example for electricity transmission, fuel supply, or roads. They will also want to know:

- What are the rules applicable to the acquisition of rights of way? Can titles be secured and transferred in a timely manner?
- Who has the legal authority to acquire rights of way?
- If the government has this authority, can the exercise of those rights be delegated?
- How will the cost be apportioned?

Building infrastructure often requires that numerous people move to a different location (box 2.5). Many people have had to be resettled because of hydro dam projects and because of railway projects (such as in Mexico). Some of the issues concerning resettlement are similar to those raised by expropriation, while others are specific, they include:[2]

- What is the scope of the power of eminent domain?
- What is the nature of compensation associated with it? For example, what valuation method will be used? What is the timing of payment?
- Which legal and administrative procedures are applicable? For example, which appeal processes are available? What is the normal time frame for such procedures?
- What is the legal framework for land titling and registration procedures?
- Which laws and regulations apply to the agencies responsible for implementing resettlement?

Box 2.5 Resettlement Issues in Chile

A dam being built on the Bio Bio River in Chile, with financing from the International Finance Corporation (IFC), has caused resettlement and environmental problems and shows how the breach of an indigenous law can hinder a private infrastructure project.

   The dam has caused the river to rise in some areas, flooding the ancestral lands of the native Pehuenche Indians living there. Groups opposing the dam have claimed that the program to aid and resettle inhabitants has been inadequate and that the rights of the Pehuenche to remain on the land under a new Indigenous Law in Chile are being violated. The IFC withdrew its support from the project amid claims that the developer had failed to meet the conditions of the loan with regard to the resettlement of inhabitants.

Source: Inter Press Service (1997).

- Which laws and regulations apply to the agencies responsible for land use, environment, water use, and social welfare?

2.2.3 *Environmental and Safety Laws*

Concessions are often conferred for projects that can have significant environmental impacts in sectors such as electricity transmission, ports, hydropower, airports, railways, and roads (box 2.6). Safety and health standards can also affect the planning and operation of the concession (in, for example, water and power plants). Investors will want to know:[3]

- Does the law require environmental impact studies, environmental permits, or licenses?
- What procedures are used? For example, does the concessionaire need to submit a project summary? What assessments must be performed?
- Does the law affect the construction and operation of facilities? For example, what conditions apply to the preservation of the natural environment, to temporary facilities, and to the use of pollutants?

- Will the concessionaire be liable for past environmental damages?
- Will the concessionaire be liable for future environmental damages?
- What are the standards of environmental compliance and reporting?
- What laws and regulations apply to wildlife, health, water, and land use? Who is responsible for applying them?
- What safety regulations apply to the concession?

2.2.4 *Labor and Immigration Laws*

Labor and immigration laws will present the concessionaire with a more or less conducive environment for operation:

- Does the law mandate the use of local employees?
- Are there restrictions on the use of foreign managers?
- What are the visa requirements for foreign personnel?

   Issues also arise when the employees of a state-owned enterprise slated to be privatized are to

---

Box 2.6 Environmental Issues in Malaysia

The breach of an environmental law can delay and seriously disrupt a project. In Malaysia, for example, local people initially won a court case to stop Erkan, the main contractor of the 2,400 megawatt Bakun hydroelectric dam, from starting work on the project.

A breach of the Environmental Quality Act was the basis for the decision. On February 17, 1997, however, the ruling was overturned on the grounds that the Act referred to in the original decision was not applicable in Sarawak, where the dam is located.

Source: Oxford Analytica (1997).

become employees of the concessionaire. These include questions regarding whether the labor regime applicable to the personnel of state-owned enterprises continues to apply under the concession (that is, does the employment relationship continue?). In Morocco, for example, there is a legal presumption of continuity of the employment relationship, despite changes in the employer's status, be it as a result of succession, sale, merger, split-up, absorption, transformation, or otherwise: "all labor contracts in effect on the day of such change remain in force between the new employer and the staff of the enterprise" (article 754 of the Obligations and Contracts Code, quoted in Guislain 1997: 74).

Table 2.3 Business Operation Provisions and their Potential Impact on Concessions

Accounting rules	• Standards applied for purposes of taxation and regulatory oversight • Accounting and auditing procedures (for example, is audit by a public agency mandatory?)
Bankruptcy law	• Conditions and procedures for liquidation, bankruptcy, and insolvency • Protection afforded to the project company's creditors
Contract law	• Conditions for the formation of contracts (for example, contractual capacity of key customers and suppliers)
Company law	• Provisions on the establishment of companies • Limits to ownership forms (for example, with or without limited liability, and joint stock companies) • Ability to "unbundle" control and voting rights from the rights to dividends and income • Provisions for minimum capital requirements, on the conditions of sale or transfer of shares and on the protection of minority shareholders
Financial law	• Ability to get financing from local banks, pension funds, and other financing sources
Foreign exchange rules	• Conditions of money convertibility, repatriation of profits, and so on
Import/export law	• Right to import materials and liabilities for import duties • Submission to export controls
Intellectual property rights law	• Protection of patent, know-how, and business secrets • Ratification of international conventions
International law	• Ratification of international conventions, for example on trade and investment, which affect other areas of the law (such as expropriation and currency convertibility)
Public procurement law	• Conditions of publicity, access, and competition (for example, is there a preferential treatment for state-owned enterprises?)
Securities law	• Conditions for the issuance and trading of shares and operation of financial intermediaries • Existence of a securities exchange market and regulatory body • Creation, perfection, and enforcement of collateral interests (see section 6.1.)
Tax law	• Application of corporate income tax, real estate tax, value-added tax (for example, regarding tax withholding treatment, standards applied to transfer pricing, depreciation norms, tax exemptions, double taxation) • Tax administration procedures

Source: Guislain (1997) and World Bank staff.

2.2.5 Competition Law and Policy

Especially in network industries, concessionaires will be concerned with the conditions and terms of their access to the network. If private operators rely on a state enterprise for access, and if the state enterprise is also a competitor in the market, concerns may arise about the abuse of market power. Rules regarding mergers and acquisitions can also affect a concessionaire's business strategy.

Competition rules can be found in individual agreements, sectoral laws, general competition laws and regulations, and possibly in all such instruments at once. It is important to know:

- Does the country have an economy-wide competition law?
- Do sectoral laws contain competition provisions?
- In case of conflict, which law takes precedence?
- Which bodies have jurisdiction over competition matters?
- In case of conflict, which body takes precedence, the utility regulatory body or the competition authorities?
- What rules apply to mergers and acquisitions? How do these affect the concessionaire?

2.2.6 Business Operation Provisions

Many laws and regulations affecting business operations can have an important impact on concessions (table 2.3). Investors must understand what benefits can be found in the law (for example tax benefits) and what obstacles must be alleviated or how the project can be modified to accommodate obstacles.

Some questions will be more important than others for certain concessions. For example, foreign exchange rules might be especially crucial to investors when project revenues are in local currency. A number of questions then arise:

- Does the concessionaire have the ability to exchange local currency into foreign currency?
- How will the rate be determined? Is the rate different for foreigners?
- Can project revenues be transferred to offshore revenue accounts and retention accounts?
- Can profits be repatriated? Under what conditions?
- What types of approvals are required?

2.2.7 Enforcement Provisions

Finally, investors will want to make sure that all the rights they benefit from under the law can be enforced. Investors should be aware of these facts and assess in each case how the host country's court system functions. In some cases alternative dispute settlements mechanisms can be considered. Important questions include:

- How well do courts perform their functions (in terms of delays, costs, expertise, problems of corruption)?
- What alternative dispute settlement mechanisms are available in the country?
- Are public parties able to submit disputes to international arbitration?
- Will international arbitral awards be recognized in the country?
- Can these awards be enforced in practice?

Dispute settlement mechanisms are discussed in more detail in section 3.10.

Notes

1. This list of questions is derived from Guislain (1997: 47).

2. This list of questions is derived from World Bank (1990).

3. This list of questions is derived from World Bank (1989) and Guislain (1997: 81–83).

CHAPTER 3

Concession Design

3.1 Introduction

3.1.1 Striking a Balance

Public and private parties in concessions come to the negotiating table with differing concerns and objectives. Private operators and their financiers seek to reap adequate returns in sufficiently stable environments. In the infrastructure field they are likely to be concerned about the large and immobile nature of required investments and about the length of payback periods—once in the market, they might be at the mercy of political authorities. In addition, infrastructure tariffs tend to be subject to political pressures, and risks of nonpayment, especially by public users, can be substantial. In some sectors revenues are raised exclusively in local currency, thereby also raising concerns over convertibility and the transfer of revenues.

Public parties, on the other side, will want to limit possible abuses of monopoly power by the private operator. They will seek to maximize productive efficiency (production at lowest possible costs) as well as allocative efficiency (the producer will supply an extra unit of a good or service to all users willing to pay the costs of producing that extra unit). They will also want to ensure that appropriate quality, environmental, and health standards are maintained. Finally, they are likely to impose certain conditions (related to tariffs, coverage, and so on) in the pursuit of social objectives.

Clearly, some trade-offs will have to be made among these various objectives. Compromises are necessary, for example, between creating incentives for productive efficiency (which increases the risks borne by the concessionaire) and providing sufficient comfort to investors to ensure that desirable projects are undertaken. Efforts to promote allocative efficiency might have to be reconciled with the requirement that some users receive subsidized services. Assuaging, to the greatest extent, the concerns of the parties involved and striking an appropriate balance between the different objectives pursued are the ultimate goals of concession design.

3.1.2 General Overview of Concession Contracts

There are model contracts, such as the model water lease contract, published by Decree in the *Official Journal of the French Republic* in March 1980 and summarized in table 3.1.[1] No two concession agreements are exactly the same, however. Technical provisions do, of course, vary by sector. The scope of the private operator's responsibilities can also vary with different types of contracts, as was mentioned in section 1.4.1. Substantial differences also appear between contracts of the same type (leases, for example, or concessions *stricto sensu*) concluded in the same sector, as the parties tailor each agreement to their specific situation and needs. Finally, the form of the contractual agreement depends on the specific features of the overall legal framework. Cross-sectoral concession laws, where they exist, may contain provisions that do not have to be repeated in individual contracts (see section 2.1.4). Some countries, such as France, have developed a wide body of case law on concessions; consequently, contracts can be kept relatively short, since key provisions and principles have been interpreted and defined by the courts. In fact, a range of legal instruments—including contractual agreements, as well as constitutions, laws, ministerial decrees, and decisions by the courts or by regulatory entities—can be used to embody the rules relating to a given private investment scheme (see annex 1 on the choice of regulatory instruments).

Despite the wide variations found in the contents of different concession arrangements, there is a set of core issues or topics that must be dealt with in most contracts of this type. It is mainly with these issues or topics that we will be concerned.

In the process of designing a concession-type contract, the government will need to ask and answer a variety of questions about the best feasible means of meeting its service objectives. Some of these questions will concern facts; some will require excursions into theory. Some will appear routine; others, at least for first-time concessions, may come as a surprise. Even apparently straightforward issues may require more careful consideration than is apparent at first, as the following two examples show.

3.1.2.1 Identifying the Contracting Parties. Especially in municipal-level projects, it may not be clear who has the right to grant the concession. Then, the government needs to ask itself such questions as:

- Is the conceding authority the government itself, a state-controlled body, a government ministry, a municipality or a number of municipalities, an association of municipalities, or some other body? How many of these bodies should be parties to the contract? For example, in some Latin American jurisdictions the municipalities will need to form a *mancomunidad,* which is not only an association representing the municipalities, but also an entity with a separate legal personality.
- Are the relevant assets, or use rights, to be trans-

ferred under the concession owned by different parties? If so, should two or more parties be granting the concession? In one proposed Latin American water concession, assets that were controlled by the state water company had come from a variety of sources. But, the transfer of title had not been properly registered. In order to ensure that no disputes would arise at a later date regarding the transfer of the assets from the state water company granting the concession to the concessionaire, the parties that had originally transferred their assets to the state company (in this case, the government and certain municipalities) became parties to the concession contract and agreed to waive any claims or rights they may have had to these transferred assets.
- Does the identified conceding authority have the legal power to grant the concession, enter into the project documents, and perform its obligations?

And on the concessionaire's side:

- What type of entity should be used as the concession vehicle (local companies, partnerships, limited partnerships, joint ventures)?
- If a sponsor is not a party to the concession contract, what other kinds of sponsor support may be required, such as comfort letters, undertakings, guarantees, letters of credit, or subordinated loans?[2]

3.1.2.2 The purpose and extent of the concession. The government must have worked out its position on the degree of exclusivity (if any) to be conferred on the concessionaire (see section 1.3.5). The contractual arrangements for the concession may have to address such questions as:

- Will exclusivity be granted to the concessionaire? If not, will the conceding authority undertake not to grant similar concessions or prevent third parties from acquiring similar rights during the lifetime of the concession?
- Will the conceding authority undertake not to supply services itself?

- Will exclusivity lapse after a specified period or if specified services are not provided?
- Can the operator unilaterally expand the service area during the lifetime of the concession?
- What are the rights and obligations of the concessionaire with respect to other utilities or community groups engaged in the production of their own services?

This brief checklist suggests that even the apparently straightforward entries in table 3.1 can be spelled out only after careful thought and study of local legal and physical conditions.[3]

The primary focus of this chapter, however, is on some of the more complicated issues that must be resolved in order to write a satisfactory concession contract—how to provide for price adjustments over time, for example, or how to credibly provide for fair compensation in the event of early termination. This discussion will draw on practical experience from countries that have already established concessions and, where necessary, on elements of theory that illuminate the trade-offs implied by different policy and contractual choices.

Two main questions will determine, to a large extent, the design of the more complex provisions of concession agreements: how risks should be shared between parties and how rules should be designed so as to leave some flexibility in interpretation.

3.1.3 The Main Principles of Risk Allocation

A variety of risks are inherent to infrastructure projects. The criteria for risk allocation are simple to present in theory. Risks should normally be borne by the party best able to assess, control, and manage them or by the party with the best access to hedging instruments, the greatest ability to diversify the risks, or the lowest cost of the risks bearing. The aim is to ensure that the party with the ability to reduce risks has incentives to do so and that remaining risks are borne by the party for which it is least costly.

In practice, however, it is often very difficult, for a variety of reasons, to determine exactly who should bear some types of risks:

- It is not always easy to determine unambiguously the extent to which a party is in a position to adopt appropriate risk mitigation measures. To what extent, for example, can a company protect itself against the risk of exchange rate fluctuations? A company might be unable to control or hedge against those risks, and some might argue that the risks should therefore be passed on to consumers. But a company might in fact be able to determine, up to a point, the extent of its exposure to exchange rate risks. If that is the case, the company might more appropriately bear those risks itself. Indeed, only exogenous costs (that is, costs against which the company cannot protect itself) should normally be passed on in order to preserve the operator's incentives to function efficiently and reduce excessive risk exposure.
- In some cases different parties can adopt different risk mitigation measures, and the question of who is in a better position to deal with risk might be complex. It is generally agreed, for example, that the risk that new laws or regulations might discriminate against the project should be borne by the government because the government is in a position to prevent discrimination, while the operator will often be unable to protect itself (especially since there might be very little opposition from the rest of society against measures that affect only the project). But what about the risk of changes in the general legal framework that are unfavorable to the project but that affect many different businesses in the same way (a rise in taxes, for example)? Again, the government is, to a certain extent, in a position to directly control that risk (less so than in the previous case, however, because the government cannot commit to leave the legal framework unchanged for 20 or 30 years). But this time it can be argued that the operator should bear the risk because it has to expect that the general framework will change over the duration of the contract and will be able, in some cases at least, to adopt commercial decisions that will minimize exposure to such risk.[4]

Table 3.1 French Model Contract for a Water Lease

Headings	Provisions
General provisions	
Introduction	Contracting parties
General economics of the contract	Description of the lease, its duration, and the responsibilities of the lessee
Purpose and extent of lease	Definition of the service, exclusivity of service, definition of leased area, revision of leased area, utilization of public and private roads
Operation of service	Regulation of service, requests for connection, obligation to connect, user contract, control by the municipality, contracts concluded with third parties
Personnel	Status of personnel, secondments (elective clause), rights, and obligations of the personnel of the lessee
Works	General principles, maintenance and large repairs, forced execution of maintenance work, connections, metering, renewals, construction and extensions, extensions requested by users, control of the lessee, and integration of private networks
Financing	Fees for use of public facilities, surcharge collected on behalf of the municipality, basic tariff, indexation of basic tariff, price reductions for some categories of users, sale price to public users, new works, price indexation for new works, price indexation for maintenance work, verification of financial statements
Revision of price and indexation formulas	Revision of price and indexation provisions, revision of indexation formula for new works and maintenance, revision procedure
Fiscal provisions	Taxes, transfer of value-added tax (elective clause)
Guarantees, sanctions, and disputes	Performance bonds, financial penalties, step-in rights, termination, choice of residence, dispute resolution
End of lease	Transfer of lease, continuity of service, transfer of assets, acquisition of assets, personnel of the lessee
Technical provisions	
Definition of service	Inventory of real estate assigned to lessee, transfer of installations at beginning of contract, transfer of new installations during course of contract, import-export transit of water
Operation	Health provisions, production and conveyance installation, water source, quantity, quality, pressure, meters, verification and reading of meters, individual connections, firefighting, cut-offs
Works	Quality standards, distinction between maintenance and renewals, pipeworks passing under public roads, works on municipal facilities, role of the lessee in awarding works contracts, control of works undertaken by the lessee
Financial and accounting provisions	
Application of financial provisions	Payment of user charges to the lessee, price schedule for works, maintenance of municipal facilities, payment for special extensions, time frame for the settlement of work expenses to be reimbursed by the municipality
Production of accounts	Annual reports, technical reports, financial statements, operating accounts, verification by the municipality
Miscellaneous clauses	List of annexes

Source: République Française (1980) and World Bank staff.

- In addition to the parties' abilities to adopt risk mitigation measures, their level of risk aversion should also be taken into account. If investors are highly risk averse, for example, some risk-sharing arrangements with the government might be justified, even if, as a result of such an agreement, investors are protected against risks in situations where they could have reduced their exposure. The gain from protecting risk-averse investors must be weighed against the loss resulting from the fact that investors will have weaker incentives to protect themselves or that they might adopt other types of uneconomic behavior (the incentive properties of risk- sharing arrangements are discussed further in section 6.2.3.2). On the other hand, risk- sharing arrangements might also encourage more investors to take part in a bidding process, thereby increasing competition for the market.
- Authorities' monitoring capabilities will also determine how risks should be shared between the parties. If output quality cannot be properly monitored, for example, one might choose a price regime that limits the incentives of the operator to lower costs by reducing quality, even if it might mean that the operator will be less vigilant about keeping costs under control.[5]
- Monitoring capabilities will also vary with the type of investor, and this is also likely to influence the optimum risk-sharing arrangement. It can be argued, for example, that private investors are often able to monitor project managers more closely than taxpayers can monitor civil servants, and that it might therefore be advisable to limit the types of risks that the government can bear and the maximum value of the government's contingent liabilities.[6]
- Finally, transaction costs must be taken into account. The risk-sharing arrangement that seems best independent of transaction costs might not be desirable in practice: indeed, tailoring risk-sharing arrangements to specific situations might prove to be extremely expensive, and standard solutions might have to be adopted in some cases.

Table 3.2 summarizes the main types of risks encountered in infrastructure projects and the way in which they should normally be allocated, not only between public authorities and concessionaires, but also between other parties, such as contractors, suppliers, insurers, and users. As mentioned above, appropriate allocation of risk is very complex and exceptions to the solutions recommended in the table might be justified in some cases.[7]

3.1.4 Certainty Versus Flexibility

Concessions can be designed so as to leave more or less discretion to those in charge of interpreting and implementing them. At one extreme, rules can be very specific and can eliminate almost all scope for discretion. At the other, rules can be designed so as to leave a large degree of discretion to the contracting parties themselves or to third parties responsible for regulating the arrangement.

Three main factors will influence the amount of discretion to be retained:

- *Level of country risk.* The more stable a country and the greater its reputation for respecting private property rights and regulatory commitments, the more discretion can be retained without significantly increasing investors' perceptions of risks and, therefore, the cost of capital (figure 3.1).
- *Reputation of the private firm.* When an operator has a reputation to preserve and when bad performance would seriously undermine that reputation, an argument can be made in favor of more flexible rules, as there might be less need to tightly control the operator's behavior.
- *Characteristics of the regulated industry.* Flexible rules will be more important when rapid technological evolution substantially modifies the costs of the activity or calls for changing the structure of the sector (for example, because the scope for competition is increased).

To the extent that discretion is retained on issues that are of concern to investors, such as prices, the

Table 3.2 Identification and Allocation of Risks

What is the risk?	*How does it arise?*	*How should it be allocated?*
Design/development risk		
Design defect	Design fault in tender specifications	Public sector to bear risk
	Contractor design fault	Liquidated damages to be paid by contractor; once liquidated damages are exhausted, erosion of project company's returns
Construction risk		
Cost overrun	Within construction consortium's control (inefficient construction practices, wastages, and so on)	Contractor to bear risk through fixed-price construction contract plus liquidated damages; once liquidated damages are exhausted, erosion of project company's returns
	Outside construction consortium's control: changes in the overall legal framework (changes of laws, increased taxes, and so on)	Insurer risk if insurance is available; once insurance proceeds are exhausted, erosion of project company's returns
	Outside construction consortium's control: actions of government that specifically affect the project (delays in obtaining approvals or permits, and so on)	Public sector to bear risk
Delay in completion	Within construction consortium's control (lack of coordination of subcontractors, and so on)	Liquidated damages to be paid by constructor; once liquidated damages are exhausted, erosion of project company's returns
	Outside construction consortium's control (force majeure, and so on)	Insurer risk, if risk was insured; once insurance proceeds are exhausted, erosion of project company's returns
Failure of project to meet performance criteria at completion	Quality shortfall, defects in construction, and so on	Liquidated damages to be paid by constructor; once liquidated damages are exhausted, erosion of project company's returns
Operating cost risk		
Operating cost overruns	Change in practice of operator at project company's request	Project company to bear risk
	Operator failure	Liquidated damages to be paid by operator to the project company; once liquidated damages are exhausted, erosion of project company's returns
Failure or delay in obtaining permissions, consents, and approvals	Public sector discretion	Public authorities to bear risk
Changes in prices of supplies	Increased prices	Allocation of risk to the party best able to control, manage, or bear it (supplier, project company, or users)
Nondelivery of supplies on the part of public authorities	Public sector failure	Public authorities to bear risk

Table 3.2 Identification and Allocation of Risks *(continued)*

What is the risk?	*How does it arise?*	*How should it be allocated?*
Revenue risk		
Changes in tariffs	In accordance with the terms of the contract (for example, indexation of tariffs leads to reduced demand)	Project company to bear risk
	Government breach of the terms of the contract	Public sector to bear risk
Changes in demand	Decreased demand	Project company to bear risk
Shortfall in quantity, or shortfall in quality leading to reduced demand	Operator's fault	Liquidated damages to be paid by the operator; once liquidated damages are exhausted, erosion of project company's returns
	Project company's fault	Liquidated damages to be paid by the project company to public authority
Financial risk		
Exchange rates; interest rates	Devaluation of local currency; fluctuations	Project company to bear risk (hedging facilities might be put in place)
Foreign exchange	Nonconvertibility or nontransferability	Public sector to bear risk; in case of contract termination, compensation to be paid by government
Force majeure risk		
Acts of God	Floods, earthquakes, riots, strikes, and so on	Insurer risk, if risk was insured; otherwise, risk to be borne by project company
Changes in law	Changes in general legal framework (taxes, environmental standards, and so on)	Normally, project company to bear risk (public sector could bear risk when changes are fundamental and completely unforeseeable; for example, switch from free market to central planning)
	Changes in legal or contractual framework directly and specifically affecting the project company	Public sector to bear risk
Performance risk		
Political force majeure	Breach or cancellation of contract; expropriation, creeping expropriation, failure to obtain or renew approvals	Insurer's risk, if risk was insured; otherwise risk to be borne by public sector; in case of contract termination, compensation to be paid by government
Environmental risk		
Environmental incidents	Operator's fault	Liquidated damages to be paid by the operator; once liquidated damages are exhausted, erosion of project company's returns
	Pre-existing environmental liability	Public sector to bear risk

Source: World Bank (1997: 46–50).

Figure 3.1 Regulatory Engineering—A Decision Tree

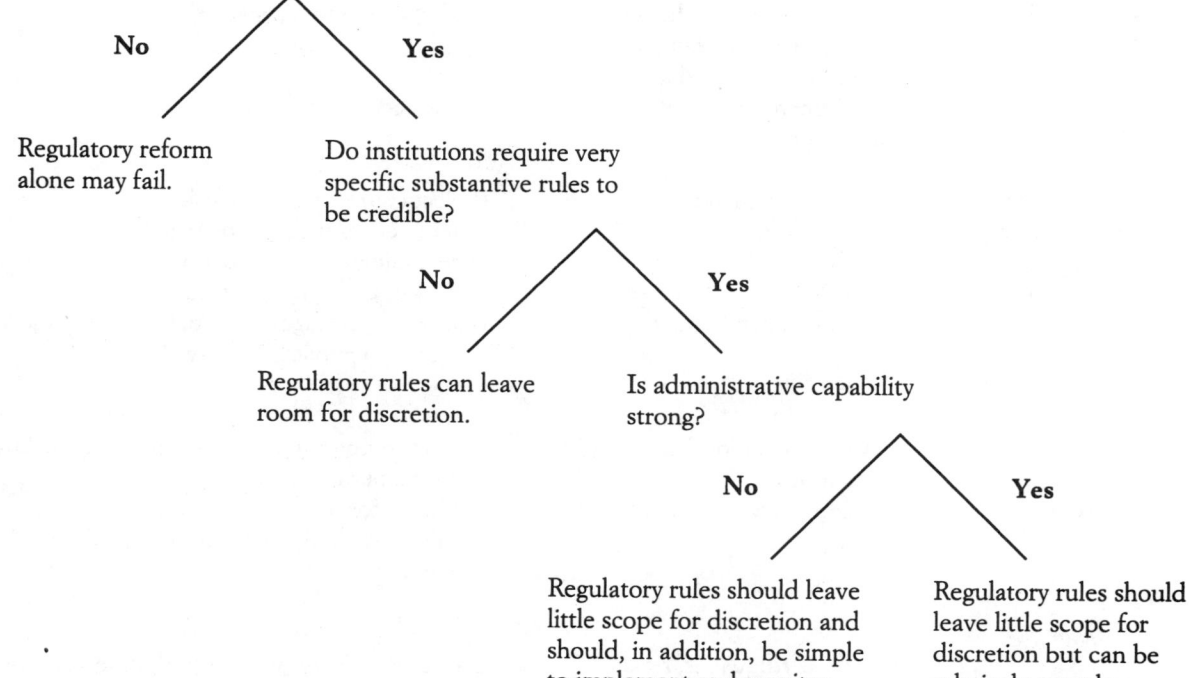

Are domestic institutions capable of credible commitment (adhering to and implementing prespecified rules)?

No — Regulatory reform alone may fail.

Yes — Do institutions require very specific substantive rules to be credible?

No — Regulatory rules can leave room for discretion.

Yes — Is administrative capability strong?

No — Regulatory rules should leave little scope for discretion and should, in addition, be simple to implement and monitor.

Yes — Regulatory rules should leave little scope for discretion but can be relatively complex.

Source: Levy and Spiller (1993).

challenge is to minimize the risk that the discretion might be misused. This subject is dealt with in chapter 5.

3.2 Allocation of Responsibilities

3.2.1 Main Design Issues

In most contracts allocation of responsibilities between parties will be specified in the provisions defining the service to be provided, conditions of operation of the service, and works to be undertaken (see, for example, table 3.1 and articles 2.1, 2.2 and IV of the *IFC Guide to Power Purchase Agreements* in annex 2).

Questions to be addressed while designing these provisions include:

- Who is responsible for tariff collection? Who bears the risk of nonpayment?

- Is the conceding authority responsible for supplying some inputs to the private operator? Is such supply guaranteed?
- Who is responsible for maintenance? Who is responsible for renewals? How can the distinction be made between maintenance and renewals?
- Who is responsible for upgrades? How are upgrades defined?
- Who is responsible for new investments?[8]

3.2.2 Some Lessons of International Experience

International experience reveals the importance of the following points:

- *Minimizing problems of overlapping or undefined responsibilities.* This problem is one of the most pervasive in concession arrangements. Leases in particular too often suffer from poor distinction between maintenance (which is the responsibility of the lessee) and renewals (which must be carried out by the public party). Special efforts have been made in the design of some recently concluded agreements to tackle that problem. For example, the Senegal water distribution lease, concluded in April 1996, distinguishes between maintenance and renewals on the basis of the length of the amortizing periods for each asset, which is defined in the contract.

- *Avoiding an allocation of responsibilities that hinders operational efficiency.* Responsibilities of the parties might be clearly defined, but in such a way as to make the provision of the service unnecessarily difficult. This is the case, for example, in the lease contract concluded in Guinea in the electricity sector. The renewal of certain small items, including vehicles, tools, office supplies, computer equipment, and small generating sets is the responsibility of the lessee. All other renewals must be carried out by the state holding company, which also must, at the beginning of the contract, rehabilitate some of the small items to be later renewed by the lessee. The arrangement proves extremely difficult to implement in practice, as responsibility for maintenance is, in effect, split between the state holding company and the lessee. More generally, the efficient coordination of new investments with operations and maintenance often proves difficult under lease arrangements, since the public party remains the principal financier of works that contribute to the operational efficiency of the lessee.

- *Allowing the operator to adopt appropriate measures to obtain payment from public and private users when the operator bears the risk of tariff collection.* The problem of nonpayment constitutes one of the biggest obstacles to the implementation of private participation in infrastructure schemes and one of the main causes of failure in some of the deals that are implemented. The private operator of the water and electricity system in Gambia, for example, was expropriated by the government in early 1995, after it started

disconnecting large numbers of small customers who were not paying their bills. In many cases disconnecting service to public agencies is explicitly or implicitly forbidden. There are several possible measures that private operators can be empowered to adopt to effectively tackle the problem (box 3.1).

3.3 Price Setting

3.3.1 Main Design Issues

Provisions determining the price at which services can be sold are, of course, central to concessions. Concession contracts, or in some cases other legal instruments such as laws or regulations controlling the prices of infrastructure services, will comprise provisions establishing the basic tariff, possibly differentiating between types of services, categories of consumers, and so on. In addition, special provisions might, for example, provide for tariffs benefiting public entities or poor users. (See, for example, table 3.1, and Article 2.2, paragraph 2, in the *Guide to Power Purchase Agreements* in annex 2). Provisions dealing with the adjustment of tariffs, as opposed to the structure of prices, are examined in section 3.4.

Some of the main issues related to the price structure include:

- Are the rules for establishing the tariff level and structure clear?
- Does the concessionaire have the freedom to vary the tariff structure and cost allocation across the customers within certain limits?
- Does the concessionaire have the freedom to introduce tariff surcharges in times of high demand?
- Does the concessionaire have the freedom to propose contracts to users, according to which service might be interrupted in times of high demand?
- Should some users benefit from preferential tariffs? If such tariffs create a shortfall in revenue, how should that shortfall be compensated?

Box 3.1 Tackling Nonpayment by Private and Public Users of Infrastructure Services

Nonpayment by users of infrastructure services (stemming from refusal to pay bills or from fraudulent connections) is a major problem in many countries. The problem is especially prevalent where the services have been heavily subsidized for long periods of time, thus leading to a perception among the population that such services should be free.

Many private providers have considered this situation to be an opportunity, seeing a possibility of raising collection rates considerably. But, the opportunity exists only to the extent that the service providers are free to adopt a series of measures designed to deal effectively with the issue. Such measures might include:

With respect to private customers:

- *Disconnection in case of nonpayment.* This is clearly the most important tool with which to obtain payment.
- *Installing hard-to-tamper-with and prepayment meters.* This increases the cost of service provision, but might be justified in some circumstances.
- *Promoting self-policing among the user community.* One such solution recently adopted in the electricity sector in Argentina involves disconnecting neighborhoods where consumption levels indicate large-scale thefts, so as to give incentives to users in the area to prevent such thefts. Entrusting responsibility for the operation of water fountains to private operators is based on

a similar idea, since operators must pay the utility and are left to collect revenues from individual users whom they presumably know well and on whom they are usually able to exert some pressure in case of nonpayment. Concluding concessions not with one operator but with the user community itself, as is sometimes done for small water distribution systems, for instance, might constitute yet another way of achieving the same objective.

- *Public awareness campaigns.* In several instances such campaigns have proven effective in reducing wasteful consumption and in increasing willingness to pay.

With respect to public users:

- *Disconnection of nonessential services.* Ideally, this should be combined with progressively narrower definitions of essential services.
- *Insisting on separate accounts for different government departments and parastatals.* The objective is to make it easier to disconnect individual nonpayers.
- *Requiring payment from central budget authorities.* Such authorities are usually in a better position to require and obtain payment from other public users.
- *Insisting that funding be specifically earmarked for utility bills, with prohibition of disbursement for any other purpose.*

Source: Kerf and Smith (1996).

- More generally, does the tariff provide incentives to the operator to ensure proper maintenance or expansion of the system? And does the tariff enable users to take into account the economic value of the service, while making consumption decisions?

3.3.2 The Role of Prices

Prices provide signals to suppliers about how much to supply and to consumers about how much to consume. In order to maximize the overall welfare of society, the price of a good or service should reflect the costs incurred in the production of that good or service. These costs should include not only

the suppliers' direct costs of production, but also the costs that production might impose on others (through pollution, for example). On the other hand, prices should also reflect demand conditions. Goods or services for which users are willing to pay a lot should be priced higher than those for which users are willing to pay a little. At any given price suppliers are willing to supply a certain quantity of goods or services, and consumers are willing to consume a certain quantity as well. When prices rise, suppliers have an incentive to supply more and consumers to consume less. The reverse is true when prices fall. Optimal prices balance demand and supply, and consumers and suppliers adjust consumption and supply decisions accordingly.

3.3.3 Is Marginal Cost Pricing the Solution?

In order to maximize the benefits to society of producing and consuming a given type of good or service, users should be charged the cost of producing an extra unit of the good or service when they require it (that is, prices should equal marginal costs). Therefore, to the extent that location, quality, quantity, and time of day or year affect marginal cost, prices should vary accordingly.

Time of delivery, in particular, is an important factor in infrastructure sectors, where there is unused capacity most of the time. For example, while the marginal cost of supplying additional water at off-peak periods might be very low, in order to satisfy additional demand during peak periods, a water supplier might have to build costly extra capacity into treatment plants and water pipelines. The cost of doing so should be borne exclusively by those who require water during peak periods. Differentiating between peak and off-peak demand can be achieved, with varying degrees of success, through a number of schemes.

Note that, in general, compared with a pricing scheme, in which the cost of increasing capacity is spread across every consumer, marginal cost pricing is likely to depress demand that is the most expensive to satisfy. It thereby promotes the effi-

cient use of scarce resources and prevents unnecessary investments and operational costs.

Marginal cost pricing raises a number of issues, however. One issue, that is particularly relevant in the context of infrastructure is the fact that, in the presence of increasing returns to scale (that is, when the marginal cost of providing the service is lower than the average cost—a common situation in some infrastructure industries), marginal cost pricing will result in losses for the service provider. There are ways to compensate the service provider for the fixed costs that are not covered by marginal cost pricing: to keep the tariff structure unchanged and compensate the service provider through government payments or to allow the service provider to charge tariffs that cover the full cost.

Whether the first option is advisable or not depends to a large extent on the efficiency of the tax system and the credibility of government commitments. In many developing countries budget constraints are such that the state simply cannot be relied on to finance the fixed costs of infrastructure projects. Adopting the first approach in those conditions would result in low coverage and insufficient maintenance—as is actually the case in many parts of the world. Some argue, in addition, that it is easier to ensure that the service provider does not charge excessive prices when full costs have to

---

Box 3.2 Differentiating between Peak and Off-Peak Demand in the Supply of Infrastructure Services

Possible schemes aimed at differentiating between peak and off-peak demand include:

- *Charging different prices according to the time of service delivery.* This is widespread in the electricity and telecommunications sectors, for example, where prices often vary between night and day, between seasons, and so on.
- *Levying charges on certain types of appliances.* The use of air conditioning systems, lawn sprinklers, and other appliances giving rise to the peaks can be discouraged through taxation.
- *Proposing interruptible supply contracts.* In Washington, D.C., for example, the electricity

utility, PEPCO, offers rebates to those who agree to have their air conditioner cycled off for up to six hours on weekday afternoons during the summer.

- *Imposing emergency prices.* Such prices can be imposed in times of unforeseen capacity constraints on the system. For example, in Denver, during the drought of 1976, restrictions were placed on garden watering, limiting it to once every three days. But people could buy a US$15 permit to exceed the quotas. This scheme raised enough money to cover its own administrative costs and it kept water demand during the drought below full capacity (see OECD 1987).

Source: OECD (1987) and World Bank staff.

be included in the tariff charged to consumers, because consumers are usually better able than taxpayers to organize collectively to make sure that the service provider does not artificially inflate its costs. Finally, unless the activity at least breaks even, marginal cost pricing does not reveal whether it is worth it to society to incur the full cost of the service. Indeed, users might be ready to pay the marginal cost of supplying the service. They might, however, prefer to stop consuming it if they have to pay the full cost of production when that cost is higher than marginal cost.

The above arguments means that, for developing countries especially, the general prescription will often be to charge cost-covering tariffs. It is important, then, to select a way of doing so that minimizes the efficiency loss due to departing from marginal cost pricing (see Laffont and Tirole 1993: 19–35).

3.3.4 Cost-Covering Tariffs

Cost covering tariffs can be designed in several ways. Possibilities include the following.

3.3.4.1 Flat rate. Consumers are charged fixed prices regardless of the quantity consumed (figure 3.2). To the extent that the marginal cost is different from zero (and that the price elasticity of consumption is not zero), such a pricing scheme will

depart from economic efficiency. Departure from economic efficiency can be reduced somewhat if the rate is set higher for owners of appliances that contribute to peak demands.

Local telephone services, for example, are priced according to a flat rate system in the United States: there is a fixed monthly service charge and unlimited free local calling. Flat rates are also used in much of Latin America for unmetered water connections. Water charges are based on lot size and property value, regardless of the amount of water consumed. Under these conditions water demand may reach 500–600 liters per capita a day—about twice the norm for a metered system.

3.3.4.2 Fixed per-unit rate. While it provides a solution to the previous problem, this price regime—a per unit charge calculated so as to satisfy the break-even constraint—is also likely to be economically inefficient since differences in marginal costs are not taken into account and all consumers, at all times, are charged the same price (figure 3.3).

3.3.4.3 Value-of-service pricing. This pricing scheme takes demand and cost characteristics into account. It charges higher prices to users who are less price-sensitive. As a result, consumers change their demand patterns too little, compared with what they would do under marginal cost pricing.

Figure 3.2 Flat rate

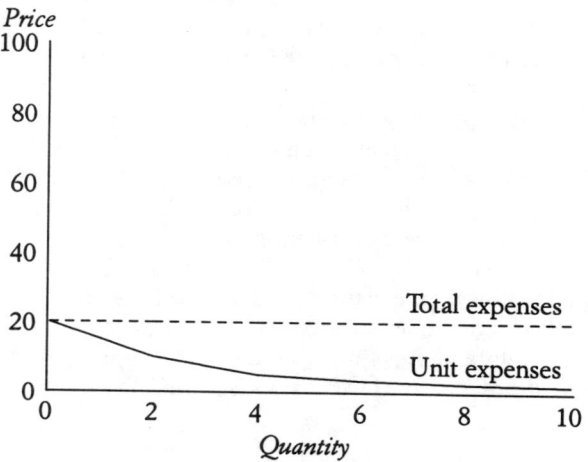

Source: Bauer (1996) and World Bank staff.

Figure 3.3 Fixed Per-Unit Rate

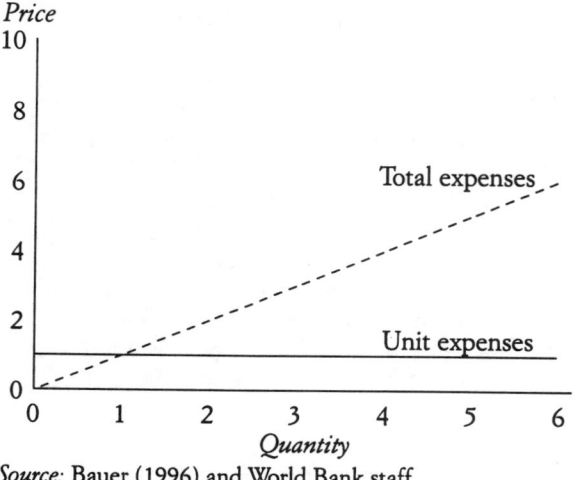

Source: Bauer (1996) and World Bank staff.

Economic distortion is therefore minimized.[9] While elegant in theory, this pricing scheme is extremely difficult to implement because of its heavy informational requirements (how demand varies with price, in particular, is very difficult to evaluate). Also, it may be socially unacceptable that those needing services most (and who will therefore accept high mark-ups without reducing consumption) should pay the highest price.

3.3.4.4 Two-part tariffs. Two-part tariffs comprise a fixed charge (which is usually paid to gain access to the service) and a per-unit charge. The per-unit charge can be set equal to marginal cost, while the fixed charge is used to make up for the revenue deficit (figure 3.4). As long as the fixed charge is not so high that users, who would otherwise have consumed some of the service prefer to be disconnected, consumption patterns will remain efficient, since the per-unit charge sends the right economic signals.

3.3.4.5 Declining block tariffs Declining block tariffs, of the kind presented in the box below, are usually advocated on the basis that larger consumers are cheaper to serve than smaller ones (figure 3.5). In telecommunications, for example, the unit labor cost of installing a telephone exchange with many lines is said to be lower than the cost of installing one with only a few lines. Declining per-

unit prices are justified as recognizing these cost differences. When costs do not decline with quantity, however, declining block tariffs depart from economic efficiency. Declining block tariffs will, in particular, not properly take into account the high investment costs that might be required to add capacity to the system and deliver larger quantities to some consumers. Some present another argument in favor of declining block tariffs: costs are recovered through the high per-unit price paid on the first units of consumption rather than through a fixed charge, thereby reducing the risk—mentioned above—that some users willing to pay marginal but not total costs will prefer to be disconnected. In such conditions declining block tariffs remain inefficient, however, as the price paid on the first few units of consumption is above marginal cost. A more efficient way of tackling the disconnection problem would be to maintain a two-part tariff but to subsidize those consumers who are unable to pay the fixed charge (see section 3.3.5).

3.3.4.6 Increasing block tariffs. In some cases value-of-service pricing, two-part tariffs, or declining block tariffs are seen as unfair because they penalize small users. When such a preoccupation looms large, one way of protecting small consumers is to implement increasing block tariffs. The Cancún and Cartagena water concessions, for

Figure 3.4 Two-Part Tariffs

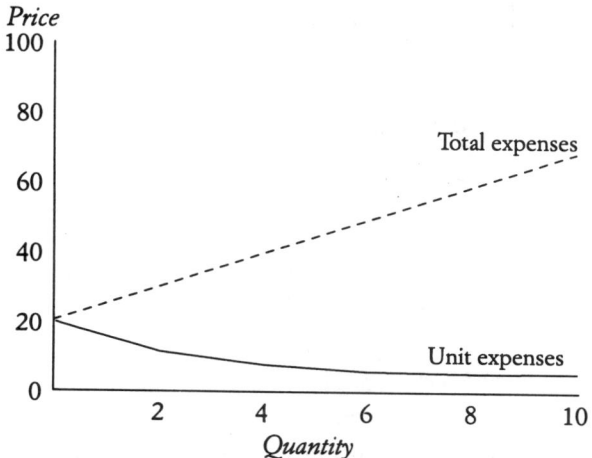

Source: Bauer (1996) and World Bank staff.

Figure 3.5 Declining Block Tariffs

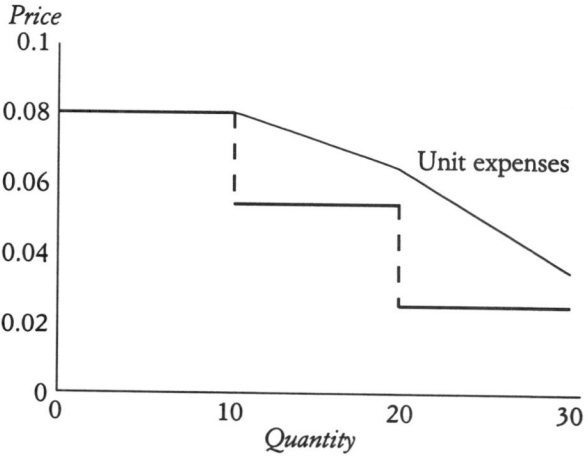

Source: Bauer (1996) and World Bank staff.

example, have, in addition to a fixed charge, per-unit charges that rise with consumption. If the overall tariff is to raise sufficient revenues in an activity characterized by increasing returns to scale, however, higher blocks will have to be priced above marginal costs, and the resulting distortions in consumption patterns could be severe. In addition, if small users pay less than marginal cost, the system generates cross-subsidies, which create additional problems (explained below). Finally, increasing block tariffs of the kind depicted in figure 3.6 do not discriminate between rich and poor as everyone benefits from the low price charged on the first units. Another type of increasing block tariff whereby large users pay a high price for all units of consumption, while small users pay a lower price could constitute an improvement in that respect.[10]

3.3.5 Dealing with Subsidies

As argued above, when budgets are tight and investment needs are large, the general policy prescription should be to charge cost-covering tariffs. Some argue that exceptions are justified when the consumption of services generates positive externalities (for example, improvement of health from installing proper sewerage systems). But pricing such services below costs to encourage their consumption will rarely make sense in poor countries,

where the first priority should be to ensure that sufficient financing is available to dramatically increase the number of people with access to infrastructure services.

Another argument in favor of pricing some services below cost is that the poor cannot pay cost-covering tariffs. In fact, international experience clearly demonstrates that in the developing world subsidizing infrastructure services cannot, normally, be defended on the basis that it truly helps the poor, since the poorest typically have no access to these services. Rather, price subsidization schemes often result in lack of revenue to finance the extensions required to link the poorest communities to infrastructure networks or lack of incentives on the part of service providers to extend coverage to those communities. In addition, poor members of society do generally pay very high prices to obtain services either through self provision or from the informal sector.[11]

When subsidies are nonetheless deemed absolutely necessary, they should be designed with six main interrelated objectives in mind. They should be affordable given the current budget; be precisely targeted to the most needy; minimize distortions in resource use; maintain incentives for productive efficiency; allow for the introduction of competition; and be implemented in a transparent manner so that the direction and magnitude of subsidies can be kept under close scrutiny.

Systems of cross-subsidies, whereby some users pay less than what it costs to provide the service to them, while others pay more to compensate, are common but have negative consequences. Consumption patterns will be distorted not only for those who benefit from the subsidies, but also for those who are net contributors to the scheme. Further, a monopolistic structure has to be maintained or new entrants have to be forced to contribute to the scheme. Otherwise, new entrants could offer lower prices to the customers paying higher prices, thereby eliminating the source of subsidies needed by the incumbent. Finally, cross-subsidy schemes are notoriously nontransparent since all transfers are made internally by the service provider.

Figure 3.6 Increasing Block Tariffs

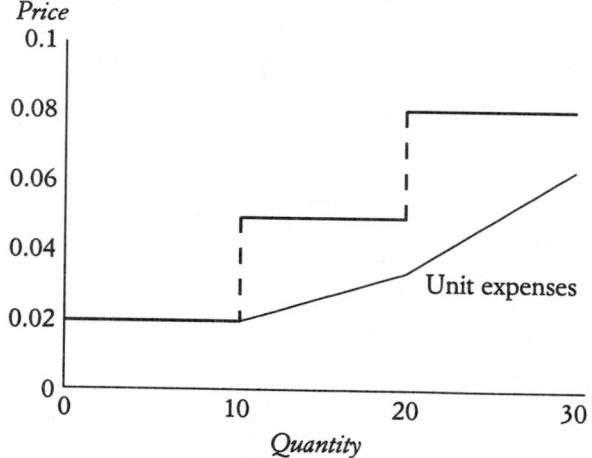

Source: Bauer (1996) and World Bank staff.

International experience illustrates a range of alternatives for dealing with this issue. One approach would be to finance carefully targeted subsidies through the budget and administer them as part of a cross-sectoral scheme. Subsidies thus become an integral part of the welfare system, rather than the responsibility of infrastructure providers, and are therefore more transparent. Distortions are minimized, and the system will allow the introduction of competition. In addition, to maintain incentives for the provider to be efficient, budget payments can be made only for each unit of service actually provided. Chile, for example, has replaced its cross-subsidy system with such a scheme in the water sector (box 3.3).

When the first-best approach is considered unfeasible, some countries adopt second-best strategies that still enable competition to be introduced. One approach is to finance carefully targeted subsidies through special funds, which are financed from explicit levies on all consumers, either directly or indirectly, by collecting the levy from service providers in proportion to their market share. The rural telephone funds established in the Unites States and Australia provide illustrations of this approach (see Irwin 1997).

3.4 Price Adjustment

3.4.1 Main Design Issues

Over the life of a 20- or 30-year concession much is likely to change—from the costs of major inputs, to specific service requirements, to the details of the wider legal environment in which the concessionaire operates. In practice, many of these changes cannot be predicted accurately. Accordingly, concession contracts must allow prices to be adjusted over time, without prior knowledge of what those adjustments should be or what will trigger them.

We can usually distinguish between three types of price adjustment rules: indexation rules, rules for periodic revisions of the basic tariff and of the

---

Box 3.3 Replacing Cross-Subsidies in the Water Sector—Chile's Approach

Chile recently replaced its cross-subsidy system with a comprehensive subsidy scheme for low-income households, aimed at assisting with the purchase of a variety of public services. Every two years the Ministry of Planning conducts a detailed national survey to determine household poverty. On the basis of that survey, the Ministry determines how many households require subsidies, as well as the monetary volume of subsidies required by the municipalities. The finance ministry reviews this assessment and requests the necessary budget provision from Congress. Implementation of the subsidy scheme is the direct responsibility of the municipalities.

In the case of water the subsidy covers 25–85 percent of the charges for the first 20 cubic meters of consumption. The municipalities pay it directly to the service provider—rather than the households—on the basis of services actually provided (that is, on the basis of the bills actually sent to consumers). The goal of the scheme is to ensure that water and sanitation services do not consume more than 5 percent of household income. Households failing to pay their share of the bill have their subsidy suspended. Initially, the onus of proving entitlement to the subsidies was laid on households. However, low take-up rates prompted water companies to collaborate in identifying needy customers by examining tariff payment records. It is now believed that all eligible households in urban areas (about 18 percent of the population) are covered by the scheme.

In addition, the water company provides loans to poor families to help pay for water connections, which can cost between US$200 and US$800 (the cost of connection to the system is often the greatest hurdle to expanding consumer access to infrastructure services in poor neighborhoods). A typical loan would require a 15 percent down payment, with monthly payments over five years at commercial interest rates.

While the Chilean model has numerous advantages and is being followed by other countries, such as Hungary, it relies on strong local administrative capacity coupled with high government commitment. It might therefore not be easily transferable in countries where such assets are lacking.

Source: Rivera (1996: 37).

indexation rules themselves, and rules for price adjustment in the face of unforeseen events. The first two types of rules are the topic of this section (examples of such rules can be found in table 3.1 and Article 2.2, paragraph 2, of the *Guide to Power Purchase Agreements* in annex 2). Price adjustments in the face of unforeseen events are discussed in section 3.9. The question of who should be designated to apply the price adjustment (and other) rules is addressed in chapter 5.

Multiple issues arise in the context of price adjustment provisions. Some of the most important ones include:

- How should indexation rules be designed? Should specific indexation parameters apply to particular components of the cost structure or should a general index be applied to the overall tariff?
- How frequently should prices be changed?
- What procedures should be followed to revise the basic tariff and indexation rules? How often should these rules be revised?
- Against which types of cost changes should the operator be protected?
- How can incentives for productive efficiency be preserved?
- How do price adjustment rules affect the commercial decisions of the operator?

3.4.2 Basic Principles of Price Adjustment

Some basic principles guide the design of price adjustment rules. Broadly, the objective of these rules is to ensure that the concessionaire will continue to face pressure to seek efficiencies, but will also be able to earn a reasonable rate of return. In order to arrive at a rule for attaining this objective, we must decide which factors affecting a concessionaire's costs and profitability should be taken into account in adjusting the price level. We also must determine when and how to adjust the price level. These decisions hinge importantly on two factors: the proper allocation of risk and management of the transaction costs of price adjustment.

3.4.2.1 Risk allocation. The question of which factors a price adjustment mechanism should incorporate is closely related to the question of which risks should be allocated to the concessionaire, which to the government, and which to some other party. As mentioned in section 3.1.3, prices and other terms should be adjusted when they reflect events outside the control of the company, but not otherwise. The protection granted to the operator against price changes should also be devised so as not to distort operating, investment, and finance decisions. Protection against exchange rate changes, for example, raises that issue (box 3.4).

Box 3.4 Protection Against Exchange-Rate Movements and Neutrality of Price Adjustments

Price indexation designed to protect against fluctuations of the exchange rate can bias an operator's decisions. For example, prices may be indexed in the following way: the component reflecting the cost of domestically purchased equipment is adjusted with inflation, and that of imported equipment with exchange-rate movements. If the company has a favorite supplier of equipment abroad, it will be tempted to use imported equipment because it is insured against exchange-rate adjustments, even though locally produced equipment may be cheaper. It would, therefore, be preferable to use a more neutral criterion to adjust prices.

For example, one might adjust the component of

water prices that reflects the cost of nontradable goods (goods not traded outside certain geographical regions, where prices reflect only demand and supply conditions in the relevant region) with inflation, and the component that reflects the cost of tradable goods (goods traded across borders, where prices reflect world market conditions) with the exchange rate—regardless of whether the goods have actually been imported or produced domestically. Because in open economies prices of all tradable goods would tend to adjust with exchange rate changes, the company would be protected against exogenous price changes but would have no special incentive to purchase either imported or domestic goods or services.

Source: Klein (1996a).

3.4.2.2 Transaction costs. The task of price adjustment rules is to convert observed changes in costs or profitability into allowable price changes. This process can be open to considerable dispute and can be very difficult and costly to implement. Price adjustment rules—and the processes by which they are applied—must try to economize on transaction costs. An important factor to achieving this objective is to strike an appropriate balance between rigidity and flexibility when designing price adjustment mechanisms. This balance, in turn, will depend in large part on the degree of unpredictability of the events requiring price adjustments.

The existence—if not the exact rate—of inflation is foreseeable and can be taken into account through relatively specific indexation formulas. The general consumer price index, for example, can be used, at prespecified intervals, to adjust prices (box 3.5).

Where available, indexes to measure cost inflation for specific cost factors can also be used (box 3.6).

Over longer periods several factors other than inflation are likely to affect costs and profitability. These might include, for example, major changes in the costs of raw inputs not picked up by the index, technological evolution that completely modifies the cost structure of the activity (that is, changes in the weights, α_i), or changes in demand resulting from shifts in population. Such changes and their likely impacts are more difficult to predict than "regular" inflation. It is therefore more difficult to devise in advance detailed rules that take such changes into account. Most concessions provide for a price review about every five years to reevaluate the adequacy of existing formulas and more generally accommodate the effects of those changes. In this area the emphasis is on establishing adequate procedural rules for the reviews rather than on devising specific price adjustment formulas.

3.4.3 Main Pricing Rules

The different pricing rules described below (rate of return regulation and price caps) are too often presented as being starkly different from one another. In reality, it is only the degree to which various pricing rules exhibit advantages or disadvantages that differs. Besides, as indicated below, multiple variants and hybrids are possible. As far as their incentive properties are concerned, pricing rules can be placed on a continuum. To determine those properties with precision and figure out how a particular rule compares with another, we must analyze the specifics of the formula.

3.4.3.1 Rate of return. Rate of return regulation ties the revenues of a utility to its costs, measured

---

Box 3.5 Price Cap Formula

$$P_t \leq P_{t-1}\left[1+\left(\frac{I_t - X_t}{100}\right)\right]$$

P_t: Price at period t
I_t: Measure of inflation between period t and $t-1$
X: Measure of expected efficiency gain

Source: World Bank staff.

Box 3.6 An Example of a Price Adjustment Formula

If the maximum permitted price at period t-1 is defined as:

$$P_{t-1} \leq \sum_i \alpha_i\, C_{i,t-1}$$

The maximum prices at period t will be adjusted in the following way:

$$P_t \leq \sum_i \alpha_i C_{i,t-1}\left[1+\left(\frac{I_{i,t} - X_{i,t}}{100}\right)\right]$$

$$where \sum_i \alpha_i = 1.$$

The maximum price in period t (P_t) equals the weighted sum of cost factors at time t-1 ($C_{i,t-1}$) adjusted for an index of cost inflation for cost factor i between period t and t-1 ($I_{i,t}$) and a factor reflecting expected efficiency gains between t and $t-1$ ($X_{i,t}$).

Source: Klein (1996a).

as expenses (operating expenses, depreciation, and taxes) plus the return on the capital committed to its operations (figure 3.7). The objective is to limit the utility's revenues so that it is able to recover its expenses and to earn a specified rate of return on its invested capital. The rate of return approach is used in, for example, Canada, Japan, the United States, and Hong Kong.

The first step is to identify the utility's overall revenue requirement, which involves determining the expenses of the utility, the investments undertaken to provide the services, and the allowed rate of return on these investments. The level of expenses can be obtained from the accounting costs for a test year, which is generally the most recent year for which audited information is available. The capital dedicated to producing the services (which is also called the rate base) can be valued according to a range of different methods (described later in box 3.15). Finally, the allowable rate of return is typically a weighted average of the cost of debt and the cost of equity.

In the Unites States the revenue requirement of the utility is then translated into consumer prices. Rate review can be initiated by the company, the regulator, or other intervenors when the revenue actually raised is higher or lower than the revenue requirement or when the revenue requirement must be changed (because expenses or the rate base have changed or because the rate of return is no longer adequate). In Hong Kong the

rate of return regulation for electricity has been linked to a development fund. Surplus profits flow to a fund, which can then be drawn on in years when profits fall below the agreed level (see Klein and Smith 1994: 39).

The rate of return system presents one main advantage:

- *Security to investors and therefore lower capital costs.* In the "pure" rate of return system described above, the company is assured that its expenses will be reimbursed and the specified rate of return on its investments achieved.

But, the system also exhibits some weaknesses:

- *Weak incentives for efficiency.* The company has very little incentive to minimize costs since it knows that these can be recouped through higher tariffs. In fact, however, in systems with regulatory lags (in which tariffs are not adjusted instantaneously or retroactively to reflect changes in cost conditions), the company does, in effect, have some incentives to control costs, as it might benefit for a time from lower than expected costs. This is not the case in a system such as that applied in Hong Kong, however, since any gains from cost cutting would eventually have to be transferred to the development fund.
- *Overinvestment.* To the extent that returns on the rate base are more attractive or secure than on investment alternatives, the utility will have incentives to overinvest in capital. This is commonly called the Averch-Johnson effect.

3.4.3.2 Price cap. Over the past decade or so some countries have started experimenting with a different approach to economic regulation, in an effort to overcome the weaknesses of the rate of return method. Instead of limiting the operator's revenues in the aim of allowing for a specified rate of return on its investment, the regulator fixes the price that can be charged for long periods of time according to a formula that takes into account future inflation and future efficiency gains expected from the utility (this is the RPI-X formula used in

Figure 3.7 Rate of Return Regulations

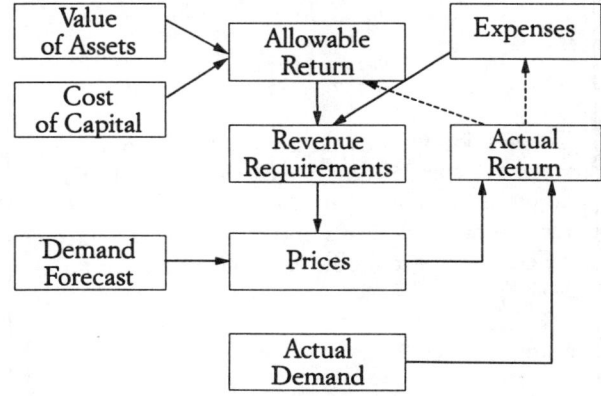

Source: Bauer (1996) and World Bank staff.

the United Kingdom). A stylized example of a price cap formula is provided in box 3.5. In some cases additional factors can be inserted into the formula to take expected variations of future costs into account. Such variations could result, for example, from a tightening of quality standards or from the implementation of a large expansion program.[12]

The purpose of consumer price indexation is to compensate the concessionaire for exogenous cost increases. Other indexes that more closely reflect the exogenous costs of the concessionaire's inputs may be used instead. These indexes may reduce the risks faced by the concessionaire without blunting incentives. To the extent that they track the operator's actual marginal cost more closely, they may also lead to prices that are allocatively more efficient (see section 3.3). Hungary, for example, includes a producer price index rather than a consumer price index in the price cap formula used in the telecommunications sector.

Price caps are becoming increasingly popular. In addition to the United Kingdom, Argentina, Malaysia, Mexico, New Zealand, Peru, Puerto Rico, Singapore, and the United States have adopted them in telecommunications. In addition, New Zealand uses them for postal services, and Argentina for gas and electricity.

Advantages of the price cap system include:

- *Stronger incentives for efficiency.* The provider has incentives to improve efficiency since it retains the benefits of lower-than-expected costs for the period during which prices are fixed (which is typically longer than under a rate of return system). Such incentives, however, depend on the proper exercise of regulatory powers: at the price review prices can be adjusted to reflect the new level of efficiency as well as future expected efficiency gains, but should not be readjusted so as to retroactively

---

Box 3.7 Successive Revisions of the Price Caps in the UK Telecommunications Sector

British Telecom was privatized in 1984. The initial general price cap covered slightly more than 50 percent of its sales and was set at the retail price index (RPI) minus 3 percent (X) for a period of five years. At each revision, not only was the value of X modified, but the basket of services covered by the general cap was altered. In some cases additional caps were imposed on services not included in the basket.

At the first price cap review in 1989, the range of services covered by the cap was extended slightly to include operator-assisted calls, the cap was tightened to RPI minus 4.5 percent, and the period before the next review was reduced to four years. Although the price caps were not scheduled for review until 1993, a number of key revisions were made in 1990-91 in the context of a review of the regulated duopoly. International services were added to the basket of regulated services, and the price cap was tightened again to RPI minus 6.25 percent. Other related changes included a more generous RPI plus 5 percent for most business rentals, low-user rebates, and the possibility of introducing volume discounts for bulk users, provided British Telecom adhered to RPI minus 0 for the median residential bill.

In the second (official) price cap review in 1993 the scope of price caps was extended to some 70 per-

cent of British Telecom turnover—the only services now not regulated by price controls are calls from telephone boxes and priority fault repair services. The price cap for the general basket of services (exchange lines rentals; local, national, and international call charges; connection charges; and operator-assisted calls) was made more stringent at RPI minus 7.5 percent. Rebalancing within the general basket is also restricted by an RPI minus 0 percent for all individual prices other than exchange line rentals, where there is an individual price cap of RPI plus 2 percent, and a maximum connection charge. These pricing arrangements are intended to remain fixed until the next scheduled review in 1997. A recent consultative document issued by the regulator proposes a cap ranging from 5 percent to 9 percent below RPI.

Despite the successive tightenings of the price cap on British Telecom and the other utilities in the United Kingdom, a windfall tax on the privatized companies has been proposed to compensate for the "excessive" profits they have made. Such a posteriori modification would of course undermine the rationale for establishing a price cap regime in the first place and would likely discourage future efforts to increase efficiency.

Source: Glynn (1992: 90-99).

eliminate the profits made during the previous period (box 3.7).

There are, however, several disadvantages, including:

- *Higher risks for investors and therefore higher costs of capital.* With prices fixed for long periods of time, the company benefits from higher than expected efficiency but suffers when costs turn out to be higher-than-expected. Those risks are particularly important when many of the costs are exogenous to the company. This is the case, for example, when most of a company's costs are fixed and when demand can swing independently of the behavior of the company.
- *Weaker incentives to maintain quality.* As the company benefits from cost reductions, it might be tempted to lower quality in order to keep costs under control, therefore efficient monitoring is required (see section 3.1.3). In some cases, however, such a temptation might not exist. A price-capped firm might in fact have incentives to raise quality, for example, if the higher costs that it incurs are more than compensated by increased demand for its products.
- *Difficulty of making correct predictions about the future.* Price cap regulation demands a great deal of information as it requires estimating a future real price, future efficiency increases, necessary investments and so on . When predictions turn out to be wrong, it is often impossible to resist pressure for change, which reduces incentives for efficiency (see box 3.7).

3.4.3.3 Revenue cap. Revenue caps are a variant of price caps, designed primarily to address the problems of utilities, most of whose costs are fixed (box 3.8). In addition, a revenue cap eliminates the incentives to maximize sales to consumers, which utilities have under a price cap.[13] Both arguments were mentioned when Northern Ireland Electricity was privatized in 1993 with a revenue cap rather than a price cap.

Several models are possible: maximum revenues can be determined without reference to cost elements, or they can be linked to factors driving fixed costs, such as the number of consumers.

3.4.3.4 Hybrids between rate of return and price cap systems. In practice, most regulatory systems are hybrids of pure rate of return and pure price cap regulation. If price reviews are frequent enough, price cap regulation closely resembles a rate of return regime. Further, as mentioned above, regulators might, in practice, be tempted not only to readjust prices for the future, but also to claw back some excessive profits made before the periodic review. Once again, this reduces incentives for efficiency and makes price caps similar to rate of return regulation.

In addition, some specific features can be introduced in the regulatory regime, with the explicit aim of striking a balance between rate of return and price cap systems. Essentially, the objective is to retain at least some of the incentives for efficiency that are present under a price cap regime, while reducing the risks borne by investors.

- *Review of investments undertaken under rate of return regulation.* This system is used in the United States, where investments will be included in the rate base only if they are considered "used and useful" and if they pass a "prudence test" (see Bauer 1996: 12). This system increases the incentives of the company to be prudent in its investment strategy. It of course also increases the risks that it has to bear and might give to long and costly judicial-like processes to determine whether specific investments should be included in the rate base.

Box 3.8 Revenue Cap Formula

$$R_t \le R_{t-1}\left[1+\left(\frac{I_t-X_t}{100}\right)\right]$$

R_t: Revenue at period t

I_t: Measure of inflation between period t and t-1

X: Measure of expected efficiency gain

Source: World Bank staff.

> **Box 3.9 Electricity Distribution Pricing in Chile**
>
> Chile's method of electricity pricing is distinctive, in particular because of the innovative approach it takes to rate of return regulation. The price system is made up of regulated rates for consumers with peak demand of less than 2 megawatts and freely negotiated rates for the rest. The final price to regulated consumers has two components: a node price at which distribution companies buy power from generators and from the transmission grid, and the value added of distribution.
>
> The value added of distribution is calculated every four years. The procedure involves determining the costs of an optimally operated firm and setting rates that provide a 10 percent real return over the replacement value of assets. These rates are then applied to the real companies in order to ensure that the average return falls between rates of return on assets of 6 percent and 14 percent. If the average actual return falls outside this range, the rates are adjusted to reach the upper or lower limit depending on whether they fall above or below.
>
> The operating costs of the benchmark "efficient firm" and the replacement value of assets are based on a weighted average of estimates made by the industry and the regulatory agency. Although each study is intended to be relatively objective and "technocratic", the residual discretion in the system is illustrated by discrepancies between the regulator's and the investor's calculations of distribution costs and asset values, which in some cases have diverged by more than 50 percent.
>
> *Source:* Bitran and Serra (1994).

- *Benchmark (yardstick) regulation.* This approach aims at evaluating the various cost components that determine the overall revenue requirement either by comparing the performance of different companies or by estimating the costs of a model efficient firm. The first approach is used in the water industry in the United Kingdom (10 companies provide both water and sewerage services; more than 20 others only provide water). The second model is used to regulate electricity distribution prices in Chile (box 3.9). Such a system is likely to greatly increase incentives for efficiency without some of the risks associated with forward-looking price caps. Designing an appropriate model firm might, however, be both difficult and contentious.
- *Price caps with cost pass-through.* The incentive properties of the price cap system are not undermined as long as the cost elements that can be directly passed on to consumers are truly exogenous to the utility. In practice, however, the distinction between exogenous and endogenous shocks will rarely be perfectly clear.
- *Sliding scale rules.* These rules provide for profit and loss sharing between the company and the government. An example is given by the concession for the El Melon Tunnel in Chile, which states that if the concessionaire's rate of return exceeds 15 percent, its profits above that level must be shared equally with the state. Another example is the system governing the New York Telephone Company, established in 1986 (table 3.3). Such systems reduce, to some extent, both incentives for efficiency and risks. Depending on the design of specific rules, such systems will tend to resemble a price cap or a rate of return regime.

3.4.3.5 A hybrid of a price cap and revenue cap. A hybrid price cap-revenue cap system has been introduced in the United Kingdom for the Regional Electricity Companies (box 3.10). Allowed changes in revenues, between periodic reviews of the over-

Table 3.3 An Example of Sliding Scale Regulation: The New York Telephone Company

Rate of return	Revenue adjustment
Over 15 percent	Revenues adjusted down by 0.5(return-15) percent
Between 13 and 15 percent	No adjustment
Under 13 percent	Revenues adjusted up by 0.5(13-return) percent

Source: Laffont and Tirole (1993: 16).

Box 3.10 Hybrid Price Cap/Revenue Cap Formula

$$R_t \leq [k(P_{t-1} D_t) + (1-k)R_{t-1}] \left[1 + \left(\frac{I_t - X_t}{100}\right)\right]$$

R_t: Revenue at period t
I_t: Measure of inflation between period t and t-1
X: Measure of expected efficiency gain
P_{t-1}: Price at period t-1
D_t: Number of units distributed at period t

Source: World Bank staff.

all formula, depend both on the application of an index to factor prices (as under a price cap regime) and on the application of the same index to total revenues (as under a revenue cap regime). The respective weights given to the two indexes depend on the balance between fixed and marginal costs (when marginal costs are high, the price index is given greater weight so that the price regime is closer to a price cap system, and vice versa).

3.4.3.6 Summary comparison of the different options. This section summarizes the main proper-ties of the different regulatory regimes studied above with respect to incentives for efficiency and risks.

- *Incentives for efficiency.* The variables covered by regulation and those that are not differ according to the type of regulatory regime. The variables not covered by regulation are those that the oper-ator has incentives to control in order to maxi-mize its profits. Both price caps and revenue caps provide large incentives to control costs. Unlike revenue caps, price caps also give the operator incentives to increase the quantity of service pro-vided when prices exceed costs. Rate of return in its pure form, on the other hand, does not pro-vide incentives to the operator to control costs or maximize quantity supplied.
- *Risks.* The level of risk associated with a given activity can be measured by the beta values (box 3.11).

As expected, price regimes, such as price caps, that give operators the highest incentives to control costs—that enable operators to keep the benefits of maintaining low costs but penalize them for high costs—are also those that carry the highest risk for

Box 3.11: Beta Values

When a stake is held in a particular security, two types of risks must be considered. Firm-specific risk can be eliminated by portfolio diversification, as changes in one share price will be offset by opposing movements in others. Market risk, on the other hand, derives from economywide factors that affect all securities simultaneously, albeit to varying degrees, and there-fore cannot be reduced by diversification. The most commonly used measure of the undiversifiable risk associated with a company is its equity beta value. This measures the extent to which the returns on the security move with the market as a whole. It is defined as follows:

$$\beta_{Ei} = \frac{\text{covariance } (r_i, r_m)}{\text{variance } (r_m)}$$

where β_{Ei} is the equity beta value for security i,
r_i is the return on security i, and

r_m is the return on the market portfolio.

The equity beta measures two types of risk: fun-damental business risk and financial risk. When mak-ing comparisons across countries; we should look at fundamental risk. This is measured through the asset beta, calculated as follows:

$$\beta_{Ai} = \beta_{Ei} (1 - G_i) + G_i \beta_{Di}$$

where β_{Ai} is the asset beta for security i,
β_{Ei} is the equity beta for security i,
G_i is the gearing ratio for security i, and
β_{Di} is the debt beta for security i.

A general assumption is that $\beta_{Di} = 0$, which simplifies the calculation to: $\beta_{Ai} = \beta_{Ei} (1 - G_i)$.

Source: Alexander, Mayer, and Weeds (1996).

the utilities. Rate of return regimes, which grant operators complete protection against cost increases, have the lowest risk. Hybrid options, in which risks and rewards are split between operators and other parties, are somewhere in the middle (table 3.4).

3.5 Specific Performance Targets

3.5.1 Main Design Issues

Concessions often contain specific performance targets imposed on the operator. Such specifications can relate, for example, to construction time, coverage ratios, minimum investments, output quality, output quantity, collection ratios, and safety and health standards.

Specific coverage ratios, for example, were included in the bidding documents for the Buenos Aires water concession as well as for the Cancun water concession.[14] The Senegal water contract requires that specific investments (a minimum number of new connections and minimum length of pipes to be renewed) be undertaken every year. Other contracts, for example, the freight rail concessions and the gas transmission and distribution concessions in Argentina, impose minimum yearly investments in dollar terms. The 26-year operation and maintenance contract for water in Cartagena, Colombia imposes higher quality standards, a reduction in unaccounted for water from 52 percent to 25 percent, and a rise in the collection rate from 62 percent to 100 percent in 10 years. The French water lease contract (table 3.1) included specific performance targets among the technical provisions related to operation (health provisions; quantity, quality, and pressure; and verification and reading of meters) and to works (quality standards). See also Article 2.1 of the *Guide to Power Purchase Agreements* in annex 2.

Important questions related to the design of performance targets include:

- How necessary are specific performance targets?
- What elements of the operator's performance are best suited to constitute appropriate targets?
- To what extent does the need for specific performance targets vary with the type of pricing rule?
- How does the level of monitoring and regulatory capacity affect the need for performance targets?

3.5.2 Rationales for Imposing Performance Targets

Often, the objective of imposing specific performance targets is to force operators to act differently than they would under the original or underlying incentive scheme put in place by the general price regime and the sharing of responsibilities between parties. One example is the imposition of quality standards, which operators would not maintain otherwise, for example, because they operate under a price cap and would be tempted to lower quality to lower costs (see section 3.4.3.2). Another example is the imposition of coverage ratios, which operators would not meet under the current price regime. The coverage ratios might, for instance, require that service be extended to rural communities at costs higher than can be recovered from the imposed tariff schedule.

When considering whether or not specific performance targets should be used to modify the behavior of operators, the fundamental question is whether it would be more appropriate to achieve the same objectives through other means, such as a modification of the basic allocation of responsibilities or a modification of the pricing rules. The answer will depend on two main factors.

Table 3.4 Average Asset Beta Values by Regulatory Regime and Sector

Regulation	Electricity	Gas	Water	Telecom
Price Cap	0.57	0.84	0.67	0.77
Rate of Return	0.35	0.20	0.29	0.47

Source: Alexander, Mayer, and Weeds (1996).

The first relates to the pros and cons of possible alternatives. For example, adopting a rate of return system might decrease operators' temptation to reduce quality (and could therefore alleviate, to a certain extent, the need to impose and monitor quality standards), but it might also lower their incentives to control costs. With respect to coverage ratios, another approach would be to replace uniform tariffs by a price regime that allows for tariff variations in order to reflect cost differences among users. As argued above, this option will often be recommended because it promotes allocative efficiency and economic resource use. In addition, in many cases it will eliminate or very much reduce the need to superimpose specific investment or coverage obligations, since the price regime itself gives the operator adequate incentives to expand coverage.

The second factor to take into account is the monitoring and enforcement capabilities of authorities. Specific performance targets will deliver the expected results only if the behavior of the operator can be adequately monitored and if the targets can be effectively enforced. Overwhelming evidence suggests that one should not underestimate the drawbacks of relying on specific performance targets—as opposed to relying on the original sharing of responsibilities and price regime—to reach the objectives pursued. Indeed, performance monitoring is often difficult, since authorities usually know less than the firm about the firm's operations. In fact, in developing countries monitoring and enforcement capabilities are often limited. Imposing specific performance targets should, in general, be seen as a solution of last resort.

Finally, some arrangements do not add much to the incentive scheme already in place through the original allocation of responsibilities and overall pricing rules. This is, for example, the (not unusual) case of investment requirements that operators would have met even if the requirements had not been specifically imposed on them (because it happens to make commercial sense to increase coverage, for instance). One possible reason for explicitly imposing such obligations is that it makes a private infrastructure project more politically palatable: promoters can point to the concrete promises (in terms of investments, for example) that have been obtained from the private party.

3.5.3 Lessons of Experience

Once it has been decided that specific performance targets should be imposed on the operator, the following lessons of experience should be taken into account.

3.5.3.1 Preserve the autonomy of the concessionaire. This should be done by specifying end results to be achieved rather than means to be used. Too often, authorities are tempted to impose some specific targets regarding the means to be used by the operator (such as the minimum amount of required investment) in an effort to prevent unrealistic bids and to ensure that service requirements will be met. To organize an adequate prequalification process and to require that candidates post sufficient bid and performance bonds would generally constitute a more appropriate way of eliminating unqualified bidders and unrealistic proposals (see chapter 4). In addition, to the extent that the type of service required can be precisely defined, it is generally much better to fully tap the private sector's creativity and know-how, and leave the operator free to decide how to organize the supply of the service. Even if the awarding authorities themselves do not overly restrict the autonomy of the operator, there is a risk that the regulator might do so. This risk is particularly important when the regulator is made up primarily of former employees of the old public company who used to be in charge of actually providing the service. In such cases the temptation for the regulator to micromanage the concessionaire might prove irresistible. Some observers argue that this problem arises in the Buenos Aires water concession, in which the regulator is staffed largely by former employees of the public company (box 3.12).

3.5.3.2 Maintain sufficient flexibility. In many cases the targets that are set prove ill-adapted and difficult to modify in new circumstances. The Argentine freight rail concessions, for example, exhibit this problem (see box 3.13). One possible

---

Box 3.12 Control of Means and Results in the Buenos Aires Water Concession—One View

"Whereas the concessionaire defends the character of the concession contract as one that specifies results rather than means of achieving them, the regulator believes that, as the representative of the owner of the system—the Argentine Government, it has the obligation to ensure that results are achieved with adequate procedures and high quality standards. Thus the agency emphasizes that the contract must be understood as a contract of means as well as results. The key issue is the degree of freedom that Aguas Argentinas should have to fulfill the contract's targets through "investment optimization strategies," in other words, to achieve a given objective with less capital investment and with higher profits. ETOSS, the regulatory agency, is concerned about the quality and the sustainability of investments. This problem will tend to become more acute during the later stages of the concession."

Source: Rivera (1996: 65).

---

answer is to identify more suitable targets initially (for example, maximum waiting time for connection rather than specific investment targets, which could prove to be inadequate if demand projections are incorrect). Another solution is to design the targets in a more flexible way. The investment requirements included in the Senegal water lease, for example, are expressed so as to leave a large degree of discretion to the operator with respect to the type of investments to be undertaken.[15] Investment obligations could also be regularly reviewed in line with new demand forecasts.[16] Finally, the parties could devise specific renegotiation mechanisms (see section 3.9.3).

3.5.3.3 Ensure that performance targets are realistic. Overly ambitious or otherwise unrealistic performance targets lose their incentive powers. A recent review of management contracts has shown that many of these contracts suffer from this defect. For example, the management contract for the Manila Light Rail Transit Authority had a success fee linked to profits. But, given the government's pricing policy, it was practically impossible for the contractor to make a profit and thus receive the success fee (see Shaikh and Minovi 1995).

3.6 Penalties and Bonuses

3.6.1 Main Design Issues

Concession contracts will generally contain promises of bonuses and threats of penalties to enhance operators' incentives to carry out their

---

Box 3.13 Unattainable Investment Obligations in Argentine Freight Rail Concessions

In 1993 Argentina's national freight rail network was partitioned and concessioned under 30-year contracts. As part of the concession agreements, winning bidders agreed to invest about $1.2 billion in the rail network over 15 years.

Despite substantial efficiency gains in service, however, traffic levels have fallen short of expectations, reaching only 60 to 70 percent of projected traffic. Actual revenues are estimated to be only about half of initial projections. Consequently, several of the concessionaires have failed to make promised investments, thus incurring penalties from the regulator. Operators are even abandoning some lines.

Given the lower-than-expected traffic levels, the investment amounts agreed in the contracts are likely to be unnecessary and uneconomic, even if the concessionaires could afford to finance them. With no flexible mechanism for contract renegotiation, the government faces the dilemma of enforcing the contracts to the detriment of the operating companies and the national rail system, or ignoring investment promises on the basis of which the concessions were awarded, thus undermining the credibility of the program.

Source: Carbajo and Estache (1996).

general responsibilities under the contract and to meet the imposed performance targets. Penalties and bonuses can take a variety of forms. For example, AES Corporation built the Lal Pir power plant in Pakistan under a BOT contract, with an incentive for speedy completion of the plant that allowed them to increase the tariff per kilowatt-hour, originally set under the power purchase agreement at US 6.5¢, by an additional 0.25¢ if the plant was finished on schedule. Argentina telephone concessionaires are rewarded by having their initial exclusivity period extended by an additional 3 years if they meet certain service and expansion targets. Articles 46 and 48 of the French model lease contract deal with financial penalties and the threat of termination (see table 3.1). See also Article 2.5 of the *Guide to Power Purchase Agreements* in annex 2.

Some of the main questions relating to the design of bonuses and penalties include:

- When are bonuses and penalties necessary?
- How can the level of monitoring and regulatory capacity be taken into account while designing bonuses or penalties?
- How can bonuses and penalties be designed to maximize economic efficiency?

3.6.2 *Lessons of Experience*

International experience demonstrates the importance of the following guidelines:

- *Minimize the regulatory burden.* As mentioned above with respect to performance targets, public authorities' monitoring and regulatory capacities are often severely limited. Like performance targets, specific bonuses and penalties should be imposed only when it has been clearly established that changes in the overall allocation of responsibilities and in the general price regime would not constitute a better way to bring about the expected results. Even then, a variety of means can be used to facilitate the monitoring activities of public authorities, such as requiring that penalties be paid directly to the users to induce the users to report breaches of contracts.

- *Provide for a range of penalties.* Relying on the threat of imposing only the most severe penalties, such as termination, would risk being unduly detrimental to the relationship between the parties and would, in any case, lack credibility (a contract will not be terminated for minor faults or shortcomings on the part of the operator). In order to be able to send appropriately calibrated signals, it is important to provide a menu of penalties, including, for example, different levels of financial penalties in addition to the ultimate sanction of contract termination. In Argentina's electricity transmission sector, for example, there is a detailed schedule of penalties to be paid by the transmission company in case of outages. These penalties vary according to the relative importance of the affected assets and the duration of the outages. Scheduled outages and those resulting from criminal acts of third parties are penalized at lower rates, and total monthly penalties are capped at 50 percent of monthly revenues. If the company accumulates excessive yearly penalties, the government has the option of terminating the concession.

- *Enhance economic efficiency.* Penalties and bonuses should ideally reflect the economic costs and benefits of the behaviors that they are trying to prevent or promote. In some cases, for example, instead of seeking to completely eliminate a given type of conduct, penalties could be related to the economic loss caused by that conduct (for example, penalties for pollution could be calibrated to cover society's loss incurred by pollution). Then, the operator would have proper incentives to adopt economically efficient behavior (that is, to break the rules when the resulting economic loss for society—covered by the penalty—is smaller than the benefit derived by the operator). Liquidated damages are often, in effect, calculated to cover the economic loss incurred by the beneficiary. For example, liquidated damages payable when a construction contractor fails to meet certain milestone dates normally cover additional interest costs arising from the delay and may compensate equity investors for lost income and fixed costs incurred.[17]

3.7 Public Parties' Security Rights

3.7.1 *Main Design Issues*

Public parties to concession agreements will generally insist on putting in place some additional mechanisms aimed at lowering the risk of noncompliance on the part of private operators (including the risk that operators might not pay the penalties imposed on them). Instruments that can be used include performance bonds or other similar tools, step-in rights to the benefit of public authorities (that is, authorities' right to take over from the private operator and directly carry out the functions that the operator is failing to perform), and insurance to be taken out by the private operator. Articles 45 and 47 of the French lease contract (table 3.1), for example, deal respectively with performance bonds and step-in rights. Performance bonds are also mentioned under Article IV of the *Guide to Power Purchase Agreements* in annex 2.

The design of each of these instruments raises certain questions, including:

- What is the exact purpose of the instrument?
- What risks does it cover (scope, amount, duration)?

- What are the procedural requirements for the use of such instruments?

3.7.2 *Performance Bonds and Similar Tools*

Performance bonds can be required from the private operator to guarantee its obligations under the contract, including, for example, the payment of any indemnities or other fees owed to the public authorities (box 3.14). The risk of losing the bond might also act as a powerful deterrent in preventing the operator from "walking away" from a given project if disputes arise. There is evidence, for example, that in the case of the Tucuman water project in Argentina, in which conflicts arose between the private concessionaire and the authorities on matters of water quality and pricing, the performance bond posted by the operator did have an impact in this respect. Figure 3.8 indicates the amount and duration of performance bonds and guarantees that would typically be required for International construction contracts.

- *Performance bonds.* The purpose of performance bonds is to provide additional funds in case the contractor fails to perform for any reason.
- *Advance payment guarantee.* Typically, the contractor will receive advance payment from the authorities to assist in purchasing and assembling

---

Box 3.14 Aguas Argentina's Performance Bond

Article 10.1 of the concession contract requires the establishment of a US$150 million performance bond to guarantee the concessionaire's obligations. These include, among others, liabilities of the concessionaire, social security payments owed by the concessionaire, and fines owed by the concessionaire for a variety of reasons, including delays in undertaking investments, termination of contract because of a fault committed by the concessionaire, costs incurred by public authorities to complete works that should have been done by the concessionaire, and so on.

Source: World Bank staff.

The performance bond must be deposited, either at the Banco de la Nación Argentina, or at another main bank, on an account accessible to the "Secretaria de Obras Publicas y Comunicaciones." In principle, the concessionaire's obligations are payable on request from the Ente Regulador. But, if the concessionaire fails to pay, payment can be obtained by order of the Secretaria de Obras Publicas y Comunicaciones, through a withdrawal from the performance bond. The concessionaire must then reconstitute the performance bond no more than days after it has been completely or partially used up.

Figure 3.8 International Construction Contract Performance Bonds and Guarantees

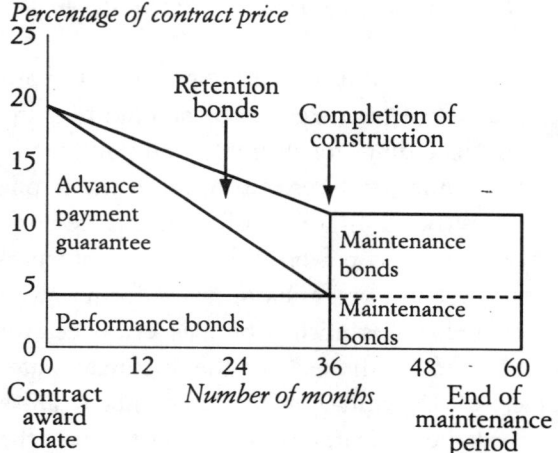

Percentage of contract price

Source: Nevitt (1989).

the materials, equipment, and personnel necessary to start construction. The contractor must then provide a guarantee to the authorities to back its obligations. As construction proceeds, the value of the guarantee can be reduced.

- *Retention bonds.* These bonds represent a portion of progress payment held back by the authorities in order to provide a fund to cover unforeseen expenses caused by a contractor mistake in construction.
- *Maintenance bonds.* These bonds provide a source of funds for correcting defects in the construction or performance of the project that are discovered after construction is completed. Typically, the performance bonds and the retention bonds are converted to maintenance bonds upon completion.

3.7.3 Step-In Rights

Step-in rights enable authorities to take over the operation when the concessionaire does not perform its functions adequately, so that service is interrupted or service quality is seriously deteriorating. The costs and risks associated with the measures adopted by the authorities under step-in right provisions are borne by the private operator. These provisions typically identify the breaches of contracts

that justify direct intervention by the authorities; they require that the authorities give notice to the private operator; they provide for a cure period, during which the concessionaire is allowed to take remedial actions; and they specify the maximum duration of the authorities' intervention, as well as the type of measures they can adopt. If, at the end of the intervention, the concessionaire is not in a position to resume its activities, the contract can be terminated with cause by the public party.

The Côte d'Ivoire–Burkina Faso rail concession, for example, provides a fairly standard example of step-in right provisions. It states that if the concessionaire does not maintain adequate safety standards for the maintenance of rail infrastructure, the state holding companies, after having organized a hearing for the concessionaire, can force the concessionaire to adopt necessary measures. If such measures are not adopted, notice must be given to the concessionaire. Fifteen days later, if the concessionaire has remained inactive, the state holding companies can complete the necessary works with risks and expenses borne by the concessionaire.

3.7.4 Insurance

Public parties to a concession agreement will often require the private operator to take out private insurance in order to reduce the risk of bankruptcy and, consequently, of service interruption.[18] A project will generally be covered by different types of insurance, including:

- Construction all-risk insurance (protection against property damages due to Acts of God occurring at any time between procurement and the completion of performance testing).
- Advance loss-of-profits insurance (protection against income losses due to delays resulting from the same risks as those covered under construction all-risk insurance).
- Adjunct liability coverage (insures against the obligation to pay compensation for bodily injury or property damage to third parties resulting from project work).

- Property insurance covering business interruption from property damage due to Acts of Gods during the operational phase.
- Third-party general liability (which might include coverage for workers' compensation, automobile accidents, and pollution cleanup).

3.8 Duration, Termination, and Compensation

3.8.1 Main Design Issues

Concession contracts almost always specify that the concession will end at some date in the future and that, in certain circumstances, it can be terminated before that date. In the French water lease (table 3.1), for example, the duration is specified in chapter 1, the "General Economics of Contract," while early termination and what happens at the end of the lease are discussed in chapter 9, "Guarantees, Sanctions, and Disputes," and chapter 10, "End of Lease." The *Guide to Power Purchase Agreements* in annex 2 refers to these issues in Article 5, "Term and Termination."

This section focuses on the following questions of concession design:

- Should the concession have a scheduled end date, and, if so, what should the length of the concession be?
- Under what conditions should the parties be able to terminate the concession before its scheduled end date?
- Should the concessionaire be compensated at the end of the concession for the remaining value of investments made during the concession, and, if so, how should the compensation be calculated?

3.8.2 Duration and Termination: What Happens in Practice

3.8.2.1 Scheduled termination. Concession contracts come with widely varying terms. Management contracts usually have a duration of 3 to 10 years. Leases tend to last longer, often between 10 and 15 years. BOTs and concessions *stricto sensu* frequently have terms of 15 to 30 years. Some last even longer. The city of Casablanca, for example, gets bulk water from a private company under a 50-year concession (Guislain 1997: 205), while the town of Loiret in France signed a BOT water contract with the Compagnie Générale des Eaux, in 1931, that has a term of 99 years. Sometimes, as in the case of the Chilean power sector, there are concessions with no end date at all (Guislain 1997: 243).

Occasionally, the concession's duration is determined by bidding. In the Talca–Chillán stretch of route 5 in Chile, for example, it was one of the criteria by which bidders' proposals were judged. The regulator set a minimum toll and, if two or more firms offered this toll, the winning firm would be the one that offered the shorter franchise-term (Engel, Fischer, and Galetovic 1996a).

3.8.2.2 Early termination. Concession contracts can often be terminated before their scheduled end if:

- Both parties agree.
- The concessionaire has failed to meet its obligations and has not remedied the problem after notification by the government.
- The concessionaire becomes bankrupt.
- The service provided under the concession becomes inherently unprofitable, because, for example, of the introduction of a new service provided with better technology.

French law also permits the conceding authority to terminate concession contracts in the "general interest." The government can do this even if the concessionaire is fulfilling its obligations, but it must compensate the concessionaire for lost profits. Typically, the conceding authority must give the concessionaire notice of its intention to terminate the contract some time before termination occurs. The notice period in France is usually about 2 years. British water licenses also provide for termination without fault on the part of the licensee but, by contrast, require the government to give 10 years' notice.[19]

3.8.3 Scheduled and Unscheduled Termination: Rationale and Drawbacks

Concessions need not have an end date. Nor must they provide for early termination. In the United States, for example, utility companies have what are effectively, if not in name, unlimited-duration concessions. Although it is conceivable that the firms will lose their licenses and be replaced in the future, the strong expectation is that the authorities will permit them to remain in business indefinitely.

3.8.3.1 The Rationale for Termination. What, then, is the reason for specifying an end date and providing for the possibility of early termination? Both scheduled and early termination help the government to regulate, by permitting competition for the market to take place not just at the initial award of the concession but afterward as well. The scheduled termination allows the government to stage another competition for the market, even when the concessionaire has done nothing that is demonstrably wrong. As section 1.3 argued, such a competition encourages firms to keep their costs as low as possible and forces them to reveal to the government the lowest profitable price at which the service can be provided. The possibility of early termination, on the other hand, allows the government to replace a concessionaire before the scheduled re-award in case of clearly unsatisfactory performance—further strengthening the concessionaire's incentives to perform well.

The U.S. style of regulation makes no use of this form of competition for the market. Instead, the regulator must examine the performance of the firms it regulates and estimate itself the lowest price that permits the firms to turn a profit.

3.8.3.2 The cost of termination provisions. The advantages of continuing competition for the market, however, come at a cost. Because the concessionaire risks losing the concession in the future, it may be less willing to make investments in assets that it will benefit from only if it keeps the concession.

The effect is most evident in the period just before a concession ends—whether the end is early or according to schedule. A water concessionaire, for example, would be reluctant to undertake a large-scale expansion of its piped network in the last year of its concession. Similarly, it would have an incentive in the last year to skimp on maintenance.

But termination provisions can affect the concessionaire's incentives even at the beginning of the concession. The risk of early termination is always present to some degree and, if significant, will reduce the benefits to the concessionaire of any investment with long-term benefits. Further, infrastructure investments with very long lives may generate some benefits in the years after the concession's scheduled end, even if they are made right at its outset. Since the concessionaire is uncertain whether it will reap those benefits, it will discount them more heavily than would be desirable from the country's perspective.

This problem doesn't afflict investments in all assets, however. If its concession is terminated, the concessionaire could sell, to take one example, any cars it owns for their market value. It would not have taken an enormous risk by purchasing them. Similarly, a company with a concession for a bus route can afford to buy buses even if it may lose the route in the near future, because it can easily sell the buses or use them to serve another route. The problem arises with investments that have little value outside the concession for which they are undertaken—that is, investments that are largely sunk. Roads, bridges, and tunnels, for example, are for all practical purpose immovable, while water and gas pipes are movable but only at an unreasonable cost.

3.8.3.3 The trade-off. In writing the termination provisions of a concession, then, the government has two aims:

- Obtaining the benefits of competition for the market.
- Allowing concessionaires to recoup investment costs.

The question is how to write the contract so as to get the best trade-off between these two goals.

3.8.4 *Options*

3.8.4.1 *Handling simple cases.* In certain simple cases the government can achieve good results just by setting an appropriate duration.

First, when concessionaires do not need to make long-term sunk investments, the concession contract should be short, since short concessions then permit frequent competitions for the market without jeopardizing investors' returns on socially desirable investments. Concessions for trash collection and bus routes are examples, and the evidence suggests that they work well when they are bid every couple of years (Kwoka 1996).

Second, if the concession involves a large one-off sunk investment and subsequent investment and maintenance requirements that are relatively unimportant, the government should set the duration of the contract equal to an estimate of the economic life of the initial investment.

3.8.4.2 *Handling Difficult Cases.* Many concessions are not so simple. Often they involve large sunk costs and continuing significant investment and maintenance throughout the concession. Below, we consider the following options for dealing with these cases:

- Combining shorter concessions with higher prices.
- Allowing the concession's length to be determined endogenously.
- Biasing the rebidding in favor of the incumbent.
- Financially compensating losing incumbents for their investments.

3.8.4.3 *Combining shorter concessions with higher prices.* One option for allowing concessionaires to recover the costs of desirable long-term investments, while maintaining the advantages of frequent competitions for the market, is to allow concessionaires to charge high prices during the term of a short contract. Consider, for example, a bridge that will have a life of 25 years before major repairs are needed. If the tolls were set high enough, the costs of building

it might be recouped during a 10-year concession. At the end of the 10 years the competition for the next concession would cause prices to fall to levels not much above the costs of operating and maintaining the bridge. Short concessions for long-lived assets would thus lead to periods of high prices followed by periods of low prices.

One problem with this option is that the initial toll might have to be very high, unnecessarily discouraging the use of the bridge during the first concession. The second is that, because high tolls reduce traffic volume, the costs of an economically desirable bridge might not be recoverable at any toll over a 10-year period. Some worthwhile bridges—whose cost would be recovered over 25 years—would thus remain unbuilt.

3.8.4.4 *Allowing the concession's length to be determined endogenously.* A second option worth considering is to let the length of the concession be determined by events rather than being fixed in advance. In particular, the concession can end when the concessionaire has earned a given level of revenue. The concession for the Queen Elizabeth II Bridge in Dartford, the United Kingdom, for example, will end when the concessionaire's cumulative revenue has reached the level of outstanding debt or after 20 years, whichever comes first (HM Treasury 1996). In Chile it has been proposed that toll roads be awarded to the bidder seeking the lowest net present value of revenues, calculated according to a discount rate set in advance by the government (Engel, Fischer, and Galetovic 1996b). An advantage of this approach is that it reduces the likelihood that the concessionaire will not benefit from worthwhile investments when those benefits take longer than expected to materialize.

3.8.4.5 *Biasing rebidding in favor of the incumbent.* A third option for encouraging investments whose value will outlive the current concession is to give the incumbent an advantage in the rebidding. Even when the bidding rules do not distinguish among firms, the incumbent has one advantage over other firms. During the concession it will have developed special knowledge of the demands of

local customers, the condition of the assets, and so on. It therefore knows better than other bidders what the concession is worth. It has been argued, however, that the government should actually favor the incumbent in the bidding, giving the concession to a new firm only if the latter's bid beats the incumbent's by more than a specified margin. The advantage of the proposal is that it encourages the incumbent to make worthwhile investments, since it has a greater chance of retaining the concession and therefore appropriating the long-term benefits of those investments. At the same time, however, the bias in favor of the incumbent reduces the extent to which other firms put competitive pressure on the incumbent (for more on the theory, see Laffont and Tirole 1993, chapter 8).

3.8.4.6 Financially compensating losing incumbents for their investments. A final option for reconciling competition for the market with investment incentives is to give financial compensation to incumbent concessionaires who lose their concession when it is rebid. The winning bidder or the conceding authority can, for example, be required to pay the losing incumbent a sum of money equal to the undepreciated value of the investment. Suppose a bridge cost $25 million to build and was expected to depreciate in value by $1 million each year until, in 25 years, it was fully depreciated. If the incumbent lost the concession after 10 years, it would receive $15 million in compensation. The pro-forma French water lease (table 3.1) provides for compensation in this way:

> The infrastructure that is financed by the lessor and forms an integral part of the lease will be returned to the local government in return for, if the assets are not fully amortized, an indemnity calculated, either by mutual agreement or according to the opinion of an expert, taking into account, in particular, the amortization conditions of the assets.

The problem here is to design a compensation rule (that is, an asset-valuation rule) that gives the concessionaire incentives to undertake all desirable investments without also giving it incentives to overinvest. Paying too little compensation discourages good investments, while paying too much encourages investments undertaken solely to get compensation. In theory, paying compensation can resolve the problem at hand, permitting repeated competition for the market while preserving desirable investment incentives. In practice, it can be difficult to devise a compensation scheme that gets the incentives right.

3.8.5 Compensation Rules

3.8.5.1 Who should pay the compensation? Frequently, concession contracts state that the government will take over the business at the end of the concession and will pay any compensation that is due. When the government does not intend to reaward the concession in a second round of bidding, only the government can be expected to pay compensation. But when the government plans to put the concession out to bid again, there is no reason why the compensation should not come from the new bidder. In either case the concessionaire will want to be satisfied that someone will pay. If the government is to pay, what guarantee is there that it will honor its obligations? If the new entrant is to pay, what happens if the government decides not to rebid the concession? What happens if nobody bids?

3.8.5.2 Determining the compensation by bidding or administrative rule. It is possible to have firms bid on the amount of compensation they are willing to pay the incumbent to take over the business. In the Argentine electricity distribution industry, for example, the concession goes to the bidder offering to pay the most compensation to the incumbent. The incumbent can bid, too. If it wins, it keeps the concession and no money changes hands (one can think of the incumbent paying its bid to itself). Although the incumbent can afford to bid any amount of money, it has no reason to bid more than it thinks the concession is worth.

This arrangement goes some way toward protecting the concessionaire's incentives to make long-term investments. It should result in the concessionaire's either keeping the concession or receiving payment, not from the state whose commitment to compensate the concessionaire might lack credibility when budgets are tight, but from a private bidder. However, the compensation value that a firm bids depends on its estimate of the price it will be permitted to charge for the service. Therefore, the amount of compensation offered will reflect the market value of previous investments only to the extent that the government does not drastically modify the price regime before the rebidding. In addition, the rebidding no longer helps the government set the price for the service, and the government therefore has to resort to traditional price regulation. As a result, the rebidding does not help translate efficiency gains into lower prices for consumers. In its effects, the Argentine system resembles divestiture with the periodic possibility of a takeover. That possibility of a takeover—or change of concession operator in the Argentine case—does something to encourage efficiency, but it does not directly help consumers.

Governments that want to use repeated competitions for the market to help set prices must therefore consider administrative rules for determining compensation. Box 3.15 describes some possibilities.

3.9 Force Majeure and Other Unforeseen Changes

3.9.1 Main Design Issues

As mentioned above, concession contracts are often concluded for long periods of time during

---

Box 3.15 Measures for Determining Compensation at the Termination of a Concession

The following are five asset-valuation methods, presented in order of increasing sophistication, that could be used to determine the amount of compensation to be paid to the concessionaire for sunk investments at the termination of the concession.

- *Historical cost.* This is the traditional accounting method of valuation for the purposes of financial reporting. It takes the cost of the asset when it was purchased and depreciates it over a certain period of time. As a measure of current value, it can be misleading because it ignores inflation and thus tends to undervalue assets.
- *Inflation-adjusted historical cost.* Historical cost can be adjusted to take inflation into account by increasing book value according to either a measure of the general inflation rate, such as the CPI, or a measure more closely related to the assets involved.
- *Depreciated replacement cost.* An alternative is to consider what it would cost to buy the equivalent asset now—or, since similarly degraded second-hand assets may not be readily available, what it would cost to replicate the investment now, less an estimate of the asset's depreciation in value since investment. A problem with the historical cost and depreciated replacement cost is that they do not consider changes in the value of assets brought about by changes in technology.
- *Optimized depreciated replacement cost (ODRC)—or modern-equivalent-asset (MEA) value.* This is a refinement of depreciated replacement cost. It is the cost of replacing the asset with the cheapest asset that does the same job (the optimal asset). For example, if a new pipe-making material has been put on the market since the pipes in a water concession were laid, the optimized replacement cost is the cost of replacing the pipes using the new, cheaper material. As before, the cost of the new pipe must be depreciated to account for its deterioration. ODRC solves the problem of changing technology, but, like its predecessors, has the effect of compensating concessionaires according to some measure of the cost of investment. Concessionaires could thus be compensated even for making investments that were economically undesirable—that is, investments with benefits that fall short of their costs, even when the costs are as low as possible.
- *Optimized deprival value (ODV)—or market value.* The method of optimized deprival value attempts to take into account value as well as cost: the ODV is the minimum of the ODRC and economic value, where economic value is the maximum of the net present value (NPV) of future earnings and disposal value, and disposal value is the amount the asset could be sold for. All together, this implies that:

ODV = min [ODRC, max (NPV of future earnings, disposal value)]

(box continues on next page)

Box 3.15 Measures for Determining Compensation at the Termination of a Concession (continued)

To avoid incentive problems, the estimate of future earnings must be based on an estimated future tariff that is independent of the bids made when the concession is re-awarded. In principle, ODV accounting may generate compensation payments that give concessionaires the right incentives. But determining the ODV of the concessionaire's assets is difficult, requiring assessments of technology, the concession-

aire's expected cash flows, and its cost of capital. The choice of accounting rule must of course take into account the practicality, as well as the theoretical advantages of the options. In addition, it should be noted that ODRC and ODV subject the concessionaire to certain risks that do not arise with the simpler measures of value. As a result, they may raise the cost of the concessionaire's capital.

Source: World Bank staff.

---

which unforeseen changes are bound to occur. In section 3.4 we discussed changes caused, for example, by inflation or technical evolution, which can be taken into account through price indexation formulas or through price revisions at regular intervals. Here, we examine events that are too unpredictable and whose effects are often too dramatic to be dealt with in that manner. These events are primarily changes imposed by public authorities and Acts of God. Most concessions will include specific provisions to take the possible occurrence of such events into account. Some French contracts (such as that in table 3.1) do not, however, deal explicitly with this issue because the French Conseil d'Etat has developed a sophisticated body of case law on this topic, which is an implicit part of any concession arrangement (see box 3.16). On the other hand, the *Guide to Power Purchase Agreements*, in annex 2, contains a whole section (Article XI) devoted to a discussion of force majeure.

Questions related to the treatment of unforeseen changes include:

- Which categories of events must be dealt with?
- What mechanisms can be used to adapt contractual arrangements in the face of unforeseen changes?
- What are the pros and cons of such mechanisms?
- How does one reconcile the need to take such changes into account with the need to ensure sufficient stability of the terms agreed on at the time the contract was concluded?
- Who should bear the risk in each case?

3.9.2 Categories of Unforeseen Changes

Force majeure and other unforeseen changes include various categories of events:

- Acts of God—natural disasters, wars, civil wars, major economic crises, and so on, which make execution of the contract more difficult, more expensive, or impossible.
- General policy decisions of the authorities, regarding, for example, the tax regime, environmental standards, customs regulations, and conditions to convert and transfer local currency, which affect a whole range of operators, including the concessionaire.
- Decisions of the authorities that specifically modify the obligations of the concessionaire or the conditions under which the concessionaire operates. Such decisions can, for example, take the form of authorities modifying the obligations of the concessionaire "in the interest of the service" (authorities could require, for instance, that the perimeter of the concession be extended and that service be provided to a new neighborhood). Some laws or regulations that affect the concessionaire specifically can be modified. Or, the structure of the market in which the concessionaire operates can be fundamentally altered (for example, opening a previously monopolized market to competition).
- Decisions of the authorities that reveal the will to terminate the agreement—breach or cancellation of contract or regulatory agreements, expropriation, creeping expropriation, failure to grant or renew necessary approvals, and so on.

Box 3.16 Unforeseen Circumstances in French Administrative Law

In France an extensive body of case law developed by the Conseil d'Etat has progressively distinguished three types of unforeseen circumstances likely to affect private infrastructure contracts. This case law, which spells out precise consequences if these circumstances arise, constitutes an integral part of any concession arrangement.

Force majeure theory applies to events that: are completely independent of the will of the parties, are unforeseen and unforeseeable, and make the execution of the contract completely impossible. Some Acts of God, such as wars or natural disasters, fall into this category. The occurrence of force majeure events enables the private operator to ask the judge to terminate the contract and prevents the public party from imposing penalties for nonexecution.

Fait du Prince theory applies to measures adopted by the contracting public party that directly affect the situation of the private operator. The most typical case is when authorities unilaterally modify the obligations of the concessionaire (the French Conseil d'Etat rec-

ognizes the right of public authorities to unilaterally modify administrative contracts "in the interest of the public service"). Public authorities must then compensate the private operator for its entire financial loss (that is, the operational deficit, if any, as well as foregone profit). The legal basis for the compensation is the right of the private party to maintain the "financial equilibrium" of the contract.

Imprévision theory applies to events that are abnormal and unforeseeable, are completely independent of the will of the private party, and lead to a substantial deterioration of the financial situation of the private party. Economic crisis, for example, might qualify, as might general measures affecting a whole range of operators, such as a change in the tax regime or a currency devaluation. Public authorities must compensate the concessionaire. The amount of the compensation has been debated for a long time but recently the Conseil d'Etat has applied the same rule as that under the Fait du Prince Theory (compensation of the operational deficit plus foregone profit).

Source: De Laubadère, Vénézia, and Gaudemet (1995: 731–39).

In some countries the notion of force majeure will encompass only a very limited subset of the above categories (for example, only Acts of God that make execution of the contract impossible). Some countries might maintain a broader definition (including, for example, some general policy decisions of the authorities affecting entire categories of operators). The definition of force majeure matters to the extent that the occurrence of events that qualify as force majeure will generally excuse nonperformance on the part of the private party (box 3.17).

3.9.3 Mechanisms to Deal with Unforeseen Changes

At least four main types of schemes can be devised beforehand to deal with unforeseen changes:

- Include in the agreement specific provisions governing possible renegotiation processes between the parties. Such provisions might, for example, specify that the contract must be

renegotiated "in good faith," at regular intervals, or if certain types of events occur, possibly with the support of a predesignated facilitator (see Myers 1996: 110–11).

- Confer the power to modify the agreement to a third party. In essence, this is the solution adopted by countries that have set up independent regulators. Provided they are granted sufficient discretion, regulators can compensate operators in case of unfavorable developments, and sometimes also impose clawbacks in favorable situations. In the UK water industry, for example, the regulator sought and obtained, in both 1992–93 and 1993–94, price increases that were lower than those allowed by the original 1989 formula, because the recession in Britain had driven construction prices to a level 15 percent below that assumed in 1989 (see Armstrong, Cowan, and Vickers 1994: 347).

- In some countries public authorities reserve the right to unilaterally modify agreements in

---

Box 3.17 Defining Force Majeure

Force majeure is a doctrine of contract law that is invoked to excuse nonperformance of the operator because of unforeseen circumstances. In many legal regimes a great deal of uncertainty surrounds the definition of force majeure.

In France the Conseil d'Etat has, over a long period, progressively specified the criteria that deem an occurrence as force majeure. Even though some ambiguity remains (see Antonmattei 1996: 3, 907), it is clear that the concept has received a rather narrow definition, generally excluding, for example, actions by the government (see box 3.16). Elsewhere, force majeure has to be defined in the transaction documents, often by listing the specific events that qualify. Commonly listed occurrences might include: war or military activity; strikes, lockouts, and other labor disturbances; riots or public disorder; changes in laws, rules, or regulations; severe storms and natural disas-

ters; and epidemics and quarantines. Contracts will usually also add an additional category of loosely defined, unforseeable, and unpreventable events that cause material interruption, damage, or destruction; delay the performance of any obligation under the contract; or interfere with its performance and are beyond the control of the parties.

In some cases the range of force majeure events can be quite broad. Given the consequences attached to the qualification of an event as force majeure (that is, the fact that it excuses nonperformance on the part of the private operator), attempts should be made to limit the number of qualifying events to those that pose a physical or legal impediment to construction or operation of the project and not merely those that make it more expensive or inconvenient. It is also advisable to specifically exclude certain events that the parties agree should not excuse nonperformance.

Source: World Bank staff.

---

response to unforeseen changes, but commit to safeguard the financial interests of the concessionaire. This is the case in France, under the "Fait du Prince" theory developed by the French Conseil d'Etat (see box 3.16).

- A variety of insurance schemes will cover the risks associated with the occurrence of unforeseen events. Private insurance schemes that cover losses due to Acts of God were discussed in section 3.7.4. Coverage of risks arising from government actions are discussed in box 6.2.

Some of these mechanisms, however, may be of limited practical use in the face of truly unpredictable and unforeseen events that have a great impact on the parties' agreement. The decision to introduce competition into previously protected markets provides a good example of such events. Only a general commitment on the part of the government to preserve the financial interests of the monopolist is likely to provide effective protection in such a case. In the absence of such commitment contracts will have to be renegotiated and disputes settled through arbitration or by the courts, if no agreement is reached (box 3.18).

In the absence of provisions to deal with unforeseen circumstances, the bargaining power of the parties becomes crucial at the time of renegotiation. In some cases a monopolistic operator might be able to "take the authorities hostage" after concluding the contract, for example, because it is the only party with the capacity to operate the project. In other cases, when project technology is relatively basic (toll roads, for example), when there are other operators ready to take over, or when the sunk costs incurred by the operator are particularly high, it is the monopolist who might be in the weaker position.[20]

3.9.4 Who Should Bear the Risks?

Acts of God are part of the unavoidable risks of doing business. They should normally be borne by the operator, who can obtain some protection by taking out insurance. The argument that such risks should be borne by the government because taxpayers have a lower cost of risk bearing than investors is not really convincing (see discussion of that issue in section 6.2.3). Risk allocation regarding unforeseen events generated by the government is discussed in section 6.2.1.

Box 3.18 Introducing Competition in Previously Protected Markets: Three Examples

SingTel is the sole provider of domestic, international, and mobile telephone services in Singapore. Competition in the mobile market was set to begin in May 1997. The monopoly on basic services was set to extend until 2007. The telecommunications ministry, however, decided to end it seven years ahead of schedule in order to promote more rapid innovation and competition in the sector. Currently, around 1.3 million Singaporeans, one-third of the population, own shares in SingTel. In order to compensate shareholders for the loss of the exclusive right, the government will pay a lump sum of 1.5 billion Singapore dollars to the company.

A comparable situation arises for power utilities locked into expensive power purchase agreements with independent power producers, when changing technology or evolving competition create lower generation prices in the market. New York state, for example, plans to introduce energy competition by 1998 and has asked utilities to submit proposals on how they could implement competition. Consequently, the Niagara Mohawk Power Corporation (NiMo) is seeking to buy out its contracts with 44 independent power producers. NiMo pays out $1 billion on some 150 independent power producers contracts every year and pays $0.06 per kilowatt, which is substantially higher than market rates. NiMo has gone to court and lobbied the state to challenge the independent power producers contracts, claiming that it is on the brink of insolvency. In fact, it is in the interest of the independent power producers to renegotiate rather than watch NiMo go bankrupt. They are likely to settle for partial compensation of the value of the contracts.

The State of Victoria in Australia has recently had to manage the transition to competition in power generation. The first major private entry into the sector involved a 33-year take-or-pay power purchase agreement, with the state electricity utility assuming all construction risk during completion. Subsequently, Victoria introduced full competition in generation and complementary reforms in transmission and distribution. It chose, however, to grandfather the power purchase agreement in order to avoid adverse effects on the overall business environment, despite potential efficiency losses.

Sources: Mandelker (1996); Oxford Analytica (1996); and Kholi, Mody, and Walton (1996).

3.10 Dispute Settlement

3.10.1 Main Design Issues

Very few concessions will operate in the long run without disagreements arising at some point between parties to the agreement or with other players. Thus the parties will want to think in advance about dispute settlement. Concession agreements can include a number of techniques to help resolve conflicts, including judicial, quasi-judicial, administrative, arbitral, and nonbinding alternative dispute resolution techniques. The French model lease contract (table 3.1) includes a provision for conciliation and dispute resolution by the administrative tribunal in Article 50. Article XIV of the *Guide to Power Purchase Agreements* in annex 2 recommends including dispute settlement provisions comprising negotiations, international arbitration, and possible referral to an expert for resolution.

Some of the main issues related to dispute settlement include:

- What makes a concession different from other contracts in terms of dispute resolution?
- What dispute resolution techniques are available?
- What makes the different techniques more or less appropriate for concessions?
- What does one need to know about arbitration? Does the host country permit arbitration? What should the arbitration clause in the contract include? What rules and institutions can one rely on and refer to in the contract?

3.10.2 Basic Challenges of Dispute Settlement

Concessions often have five characteristics that pose challenges for dispute resolution.

- *Many occasions for conflicts.* Concessions typically involve many players whose interactions can give rise to conflicts. For example, disputes can arise between the concessionaire and the government (conceding authority); a competitor, when one controls the network and the other has a right to use it; the regulator, for example regarding tariff increases; a state-owned enterprise; its suppliers or workers; its customers; consortium members; and lenders, shareholders, or insurers.

What does this mean for dispute settlement? Because of the sheer number of disputes that can arise from concessions, and the potentially high costs associated with them, and because these disputes can involve public and private parties, as well as domestic and foreign parties, the concessionaire will want to ensure that it has access to reliable, neutral, and noncorrupt forums for dispute resolution.

- *Long-term nature of the concession relationship.* Most concessions last a long time and, in the long run, disputes are bound to arise. Notwithstanding current or past disputes, however, the parties will need to maintain a working relationship over many years, maybe decades. The dispute resolution mechanism should therefore help the parties stay on good terms.

- *Public nature of concession services.* Another characteristic that sets most concessions apart from other types of contracts is the public nature of many concession services. Often there is a need to avoid interruptions in the provision of public services. If disputes arise regarding disconnection rules (for example, in the case of nonpayment), or in general if a dispute leads to interruption of service, a decision must be made quickly. Also, if concessionaires provide the service directly to private customers, many parties may be interested and involved in the dispute and will want a voice in the process. These factors require the adoption of dispute resolution techniques that are able to offer a resolution quickly and are open and inclusive.

The public nature of the service is not as strong when concessionaires do not provide services directly to private customers. For example,

with power purchase agreements concluded between producers and state utilities, the requirement for openness and inclusiveness in dispute resolution is not as important.

- *Large investments in immobile assets.* Most concessions involve large investments in immobile assets (that is, they involve substantial sunk costs). This type of investment leaves investors vulnerable to political pressures since they are not able to pick up and go. Therefore, investors must be able to enforce the remedies and compensation provided for in the contract.

- *Complexity and sophistication of projects.* Concessions generally consist of intricate webs of legal arrangements for the construction, financing, and operation of infrastructure. In terms of dispute resolution, this implies a need for expertise in dealing with complex commercial, legal, and technical issues.

3.10.3 Dispute Settlement Mechanisms

There are several techniques to resolving disputes, including judicial, quasi-judicial or administrative, arbitral, and nonbinding dispute resolution. As a general rule disputes relating to an agreement are subject to the jurisdiction of the courts. The courts involved will usually be those of the jurisdiction in which the subject matter of the dispute is located. In the case of a concession agreement, this will generally be the jurisdiction in which the infrastructure is located.

When private parties from different countries enter into an agreement, they will often choose the country or state whose courts will have jurisdiction.[21] For example, in Latin America project financing agreements often provide that parties submit their disputes to the jurisdiction of New York state and federal courts.[22] When a government is party to an international agreement with foreigners, however, as a matter of sovereignty, it will typically not consent to grant jurisdiction to the courts of another country (Skadden, Arps, Slate, Meagher, and Flom 1996: 64).

A number of countries have recourse to quasi-judicial or administrative bodies, such as independent regulatory agencies, to resolve some of the disputes arising from concessions. In Peru, for example, the Electrical Concessions Law (DL 25844) holds that the Board of Directors of the Electricity Tariffs Commission has the responsibility to "[R]esolve as the last administrative resort all matters submitted by interested parties relating to the setting of rates" (article 15). The public law of the host country will usually specify mechanisms for appealing decisions of the regulator (see section 5.6.3 on the appeal process for regulatory decisions).

Arbitration is a technique for dispute resolution under which the parties agree to submit some or all of their disputes to an arbitral tribunal that is empowered to render decisions (called "awards") that are binding on the parties. Arbitration tribunals often comprise one, three, or five members. The parties typically choose members based on their expertise on a particular subject matter. The assistance of local courts is also needed in order to enforce arbitral awards. Arbitrations can be domestic (that is, they can take place in the host country of the investment) or international (that is, they can take place in a country other than the host country of the investment).

Nonbinding alternative dispute resolution (ADR) includes a wide range of techniques for dispute resolution that are nonbinding on the parties (that is, they are designed to be purely advisory).[23] ADR procedures can be independent of any formal procedure, whether judicial, arbitral, or other, or, alternatively, it can be used in combination with such procedures. Some examples of ADR schemes include:

- *Informal dispute resolution mechanisms.* There are many informal mechanisms to resolve disputes, ranging from regularly scheduled consultation meetings between the parties (where disagreements are brought forward early on so that they can be amicably resolved) to the use of technical advisers with powers to recommend a settlement.[24]
- *Conciliation and mediation.* Both conciliation and mediation involve a third party trying to help resolve a dispute. Traditionally, only the mediator recommends to the parties how they

can settle their disagreements. Conciliators do not make such recommendations (Folsom and Minan 1991: 1,060).

In most cases arbitration institutions facilitate conciliation or mediation procedures before formal arbitration in the hope of avoiding the latter procedure. Also, most courts in the United States, for example, have court-annexed mediation programs that aim at reaching a similar goal, which is to avoid litigation (Myers 1996: 104).

3.10.3.1 Judicial. Parties to concession agreements often think that courts are inappropriate for resolving their disputes. Some of the concerns that arise are that:

- The court system may be too cumbersome, slow, and expensive.
- The adversarial nature of the proceedings may damage the long-term relationship of the parties.
- The courts may lack sufficient technical expertise for the type of dispute in question.
- The courts may not be completely neutral arbiters of disputes involving private and public parties or domestic and foreign parties.
- The courts may be corrupt.

Litigation in well-developed court systems can offer some advantages if many parties are involved in a dispute and if the discovery of evidence is important. This is mainly because traditional courts are equipped with well-developed rules on "joinder of parties" (that is, rules that would be used to join contractors, for example, to a dispute arising from a concession contract—to which they are not a party—when they share part of the responsibility for the breach) and on the production of documents and witnesses (see McConnaughay 1995; Nelson 1989).

Because concessions operate in many countries where judicial systems are underdeveloped and because of the concerns listed above, parties will often want to agree on a dispute resolution mechanism in their concession agreement that will permit them to avoid the jurisdiction of the courts as much as possible. In some cases, however, the parties cannot totally avoid domestic courts. Legal disputes arising from contracts with local employees, banks, suppliers, and customers generally fall within the exclusive jurisdiction of local courts.

3.10.3.2 Quasi-judicial or administrative. Recourse to quasi-judicial or administrative bodies is often seen as appropriate if disputes:

- Have a strong public policy component. For example, this would be the case for disputes arising from regulatory decisions that required that broad discretion be applied in the public interest. We typically see this with the application of anti-trust rules.
- Require timely resolution and are likely to be recurrent. For example, an independent regulator may be best placed to resolve disputes regarding access conditions to a network.
- Require technical expertise for their resolution. Infrastructure regulators are often appointed on the basis of their expertise in areas relevant to their functions.
- Involve many players. An independent regulator can often provide an open and inclusive forum in which customers, providers, and governmental actors, for example, can interact to resolve disputes.

Quasi-judicial or administrative bodies can also promote the sustainability of the parties' relationship by offering a less confrontational approach to dispute resolution. The disadvantages of this method of dispute resolution are often linked to the independence and accountability of the quasi-judicial or administrative bodies themselves (discussed in chapter 5).

3.10.3.3 Arbitral. The advantages usually claimed in favor of arbitration are:

- *Confidentiality:* for example, as it relates to commercial secrets.
- *Expertise:* parties can choose arbitrators on the basis of their technical expertise.

- *Neutrality:* arbitrators can be chosen from among individuals unrelated to the parties in dispute.
- *Integrity:* arbitrators can be chosen from among individuals of high moral repute.

Speed is also usually considered one of the main benefits of arbitration. But if the dispute is technically complex, arbitration is not always quick. Further, increased formality in recent years has also engendered important delays and costs. Arbitration, therefore, has lost some of its appeal in that respect. In countries with inefficient court systems, however, the costs and delays of arbitration can still be minimal compared to the judicial alternative.

Foreign investors often see international arbitration, as opposed to domestic arbitration, as the only mechanism able to provide them with some assurance of repair and compensation if relations with the government sour. International arbitration may also be the most reliable mechanism for obtaining enforceable awards. This is the main reason why most large infrastructure projects involving foreigners include an international arbitration clause (see section 3.10.5 for details).

Domestic arbitration may be important, if permitted by law, when the transaction does not have an international dimension allowing the use of international arbitration conventions or when the government refuses to submit itself to international arbitration.

Some of the disadvantages of international arbitration in dealing with concessions are its:

- Inability to resolve conflicts that require urgent attention or timely resolution.
- Impracticality for the resolution of recurrent issues.
- Difficulty in accommodating the participation of interests other than the disputing parties.
- Inability to resolve disputes arising from regulatory decisions that required broad discretion to be applied in the public interest.
- Adversarial nature.

There may also be constitutional and policy impediments to arbitration (see section 3.10.5.1).

3.10.3.4 Nonbinding Alternative Dispute Resolution.

ADR mechanisms typically have the following benefits (Myers 1996: 105):

- *Control:* the parties control the negotiations and can decide to discontinue them at any time if they are unproductive.
- *Flexibility:* the third party assists in exploring alternative and creative solutions in order to meet the needs of the parties.
- *Speed:* a session can be scheduled quickly and requires relatively little preparation time.
- *Economy:* some cases can be resolved within a few hours.

For certain technical matters, it will often be quicker and more productive for the parties to submit their disputes to an expert. In the case of a BOT for a power generation plant, for example, these disputes could include those relating to the satisfaction of completion tests and billing (White and Case 1995).

The greatest weakness of ADR is a direct consequence of its strengths. Because the parties are able to withdraw at any time from the process, and because the recommendations, if any, are nonbinding, the parties are never assured of a resolution (for details, see Paulsson 1996: 210).

3.10.4 Summary

Table 3.5 looks at four techniques and identifies the cases for which they are appropriate to resolve concession disputes. A number of techniques found in some countries have not been included, for example, the use of specialist courts or domestic arbitration.

The analysis thus far leads us to two broad conclusions. First, a number of dispute settlement techniques can, and often should, be included in a concession agreement. This need stems largely from the particular characteristics of concession agreements and the inability of any one method to meet all of the parties' goals. Issues will arise as to the interactions of certain techniques, and the parties will need to give serious thought to how to avoid inconsistencies.

Second, in order to determine the availability and appropriateness of any particular dispute settlement mechanism, a close analysis of the relevant laws and the contract in question is usually necessary. In this context seeking the advice of well-qualified advisers, particularly lawyers, will be important before pursuing any particular options.

Table 3.5 Some Dispute Settlement Techniques and their Appropriateness for Concessions

Characteristics of concessions	Goals in dispute settlement	Courts	Independent regulator	Nonbinding ADR	International arbitration
Many occasions for conflicts	Access to reliable, neutral, and noncorrupt forums	=	=	+	+
Long-term nature of relationship	Sustainability of the parties' relationship	–	+	+	–
Public nature of services	Prompt resolution, open and inclusive process	–	+	+	–
Large investment in immobile assets	Enforceability	=	–	–	+
Complexity and sophistication of projects	Expertise	–	+	+	+

+ Usually appropriate.
– Usually inappropriate or presents difficulties.
= Appropriateness highly dependent on the independence and accountability of the decisionmaking body.
Source: World Bank staff.

3.10.5 Focus on International Arbitration

In most large infrastructure projects involving foreign investors and operators, the legal arrangements contain a clause that provides for binding international arbitration. There are two main forms of international arbitration: institutional and ad-hoc arbitration. Institutional arbitration implies the existence of a permanent institution that administers arbitration procedures, for example, by supporting the nomination of arbitrators and administering the proceedings (Paulsson 1996: 214, 217). Ad hoc arbitrations, on the other hand, are intended to be self-executing (Paulsson 1996: 213), that is, the arbitration clause or agreement itself is intended to provide all the rules for the arbitration.[25]

This section introduces three important issues related to international arbitration:[26]

- Impediments to international arbitration.
- Submission to international arbitration.
- Arbitration rules and institutions.

3.10.5.1 Impediments to international arbitration.
Some countries have constitutional and policy impediments to international arbitration. For example, the constitution may state that the Supreme Court has exclusive jurisdiction over certain disputes involving the executive branch. In addition, there may be explicit constitutional or other legal provisions restricting the state from submitting to international arbitration. In Turkey the Constitutional Court determined in March 1996 that concessions were administrative law contracts and, as such, were subject to dispute resolution before Turkish administrative courts exclusively (Wilson, Solsky, and Sarad 1997: 36; Cakmak 1996: 8–17).

Other obstacles may arise from legal traditions that do not favor international arbitration. In Latin America the Calvo doctrine, for example, required that foreigners be treated the same as nationals and, as a result, required their submission to local jurisdiction. The Calvo doctrine, however, has been largely superseded following liberalization of Latin American economies and the widespread acceptance by Latin American states of international arbitration as a means of settling investment disputes.[27]

3.10.5.2 Submission to international arbitration.
Actual submission to international arbitration requires the consent of the parties concerned. There are different ways of giving this consent. The most common is through an arbitration clause—in a concession contract, for example. These clauses give consent to arbitration before a dispute occurs.

In order to be workable, an arbitration clause should include, at a minimum, a clear choice of the arbitration mechanism that will apply and a clear definition of the scope of the disputes to be arbitrated (Paulsson 1996: 222–23). The parties may also wish to include in the clause a choice of: the law to be applied to the merits of the dispute (that is, the law that applies to the interpretation and application of the contract itself); the place of arbitration; the number of arbitrators and other requirements regarding nationalities and qualifications of arbitrators; and mandatory prior recourse to conciliation or mediation (Paulsson 1996: 222–23).

As an illustration, the following is the model clause used by the International Centre for Settlement of Investment Disputes (ICSID) for submitting future disputes to arbitration:

> The [Government]/[name of constituent subdivision or agency] of name of Contracting State (hereinafter the "Host State") and name of investor (hereinafter the "Investor") hereby consent to submit to the International Centre for Settlement of Investment Disputes (hereinafter the "Centre") any dispute arising out of or relating to this agreement for settlement by [conciliation]/[arbitration]/[conciliation followed, if the dispute remains unresolved within time limit of the communication of the report of the Conciliation Commission to the parties, by arbitration] pursuant to the Convention on the Settlement of Investment Disputes

between States and Nationals of Other States (hereinafter the "Convention").

Increasingly, though, governments are giving consent another way. They are giving their consent, in advance, to arbitration for certain types of disputes in bilateral and multilateral investment treaties and in an increasing number of national investment laws. This is how it works. The provision for arbitration in the law or treaty constitutes an offer by the government to submit disputes to arbitration. This offer must be accepted by investors to make it effective. Investors can generally give their matching consent at any time—that is, consent may be given simultaneously with the submission of a request for arbitration or conciliation, or even by means of such a request (Parra 1996).

In general, however, investors may not want to rely exclusively on such provisions and may wish to include an arbitration clause in the contract, for two reasons. First, a dispute emerging from the operation of the concession may not be covered by the investment treaty. In other words, in order to be covered, a dispute would have to constitute a breach of specific commitments made by the government under the treaty. Second, in the case of investment laws there is always the risk that the law may be changed or repealed, and the offer of arbitration may, as a consequence, be withdrawn before it is accepted by investors. In any case the parties may want to be more specific than the law or treaty in providing for arbitration (for example, they may want to specify the number and nationality of the arbitrators). Therefore, the parties can still benefit from including an arbitration clause in the concession contract.

Finally, if the contract, regulatory framework, or other laws and treaties do not specify a particular arbitration procedure, the disputing parties are free at any time to agree to submit their dispute to binding international arbitration. Parties should be cautious about relying on this alternative, however, as an agreement on such matters is usually more difficult to achieve once a dispute has erupted.

3.10.5.3 Arbitration rules and institutions. Table 3.6 presents the main instruments contain-

Table 3.6 Main Instruments and Institutions Related to International Arbitration

Instruments	Procedural rules	Enforcement rules	Institutional support
International Centre for Settlement of Investment Disputes Convention and Center[a]	✔	✔	✔
Panama Convention and Inter-American Commercial Arbitration Commission[b]	✔	✔	✔
International Chamber of Commerce rules and International Court of Arbitration[c]	✔		✔
New York Convention[d]		✔	
United Nations Commission on International Trade Law Arbitration rules (for ad-hoc arbitrations)	✔		
Domestic law based on United Nations Commission on International Trade Law model law on international commercial arbitration	✔	✔	

Notes: See Annex C for a list of member countries of the Organization of American States that indicates which countries are parties to the ICSID, New York, and Panama Conventions.

a. ICSID is a public international organization established by the 1965 Convention on the Settlement of Investment Disputes between States and Nationals of Other States (the ICSID Convention). ICSID is part of the World Bank Group.

b. The Panama Convention is the 1975 Inter-American Convention on international commercial arbitration. Arbitrations are held under the auspices of IACAC.

c. Arbitrations are held under the auspices of the International Court of Arbitration of the ICC.

d. The New York Convention is the New York Convention on the Recognition and Enforcement of Foreign Arbitral Awards, 1958.

Source: World Bank staff.

ing rules for international arbitration and a sample of international arbitration institutions. Procedural rules govern the conduct of arbitrations, including the composition of the arbitral tribunal, the conduct of the proceedings, and the award. Institutional support refers to the institutions that administer arbitrations by, for example, helping with the constitution of arbitral tribunals. Enforcement rules set the conditions for recognizing and enforcing arbitral awards made in the territory of a state other than the state in which the recognition and enforcement are sought.

The New York Convention is the main international treaty dealing with the recognition and enforcement of arbitral awards. According to the Convention, countries can make certain reservations to its application (see Article 1). A reservation that most member countries have made stipulates that a member—once it has made the reservation as to reciprocity—will only recognize and enforce awards under the Convention that have been made in the territory of another contracting state. The Convention also names a number of grounds that would permit a court to refuse the recognition and enforcement of an award, including incapacity, denial of a fair hearing, and public policy.[28] The Panama Convention and UNCITRAL's model law include enforcement rules that are based on the New York Convention.

The ICSID Convention breaks rank with the New York Convention and other conventions based on the same rules as it limits the role of national courts in enforcing arbitral awards. In fact, the parties to an arbitration cannot challenge ICSID's award before national courts. Only a committee appointed by ICSID for this purpose can review ICSID awards (see Article 54 of the ICSID Convention).

There are many other institutions that administer arbitrations, including many regional arbitration centers. To name a few: the American Arbitration Association (AAA); the Stockholm Chamber of Commerce, and the Kuala Lumpur Regional Center for Arbitration. The procedural rules they use are often those of, or similar to those of, UNCITRAL and ICC. The parties will need to decide which forum is best suited to their particular needs. One factor that may influence this choice is the forum's private or public nature. Some commentators see private institutions like the ICC or the AAA as more appropriate for purely commercial disputes. In cases that have an important public policy component, a forum such as ICSID, which is an intergovernmental organization, may be more appropriate. In fact, the argument goes, ICSID was

---

Box 3.19 International Centre for Settlement of Investment Disputes

Arbitration under the ICSID Convention is limited to legal disputes arising directly from an investment between an ICSID contracting state (or one of its designated agencies or political subdivisions) on the one hand, and a national of another contracting state on the other. The concept of investment, not defined by the Convention, is sufficiently broad to cover infrastructure projects. Membership in ICSID now stands at 126 of the World Bank's 180 member countries.

When either the state party to the dispute or the state of the other party (but not both such states) is not an ICSID contracting state, the dispute may be submitted to arbitration under the Centre's Additional Facility Rules. Also among the functions performed by ICSID on a voluntary basis is the appointment of arbitrators in ad-hoc arbitration proceedings. ICSID's secretary-general has done this for an infrastructure dispute in South America.

In early 1997 two concession cases were submitted to ICSID and are awaiting the constitution of a tribunal. One case concerns a water and sewer service concession in Argentina [Compañia de Aguas del Aconquija S.A. and Compagnie Générale des Eaux (CGE) v. Argentine Republic (ARB/97/3)] and the other a waste disposal BOO in Mexico [Metalclad Corporation v. United Mexican States (ARB(AF)/97/1)]. The Mexican case has been submitted to ICSID under the provisions of the North American Free Trade Agreement (NAFTA).

Source: Escobar (1997) and ICSID (1996).

created for the specific purpose of making determinations in disputes involving public and private parties (box 3.19).

On the other hand, a dominant factor in the choice of a forum is familiarity and experience. In practice, the ICC is by far the most commonly used forum for the arbitration of international disputes and receives more than 300 requests every year.

Notes

1. République Française (1980). The model contract is intended to serve as a possible reference to municipalities and private water suppliers.

2. A distinction can be drawn between sponsor companies (which are not necessarily parties to the contract) and project companies (that is, operating companies, with legal personality, which are normally subsidiaries of the sponsors and are established specifically for the needs of the project).

3. See World Bank (1997) for more detailed checklists of issues to be dealt with while designing concession agreements.

4. HM Treasury (1995) Paragraph 3.20 discusses how the risk that the law will be changed should be allocated. It states that "The key issue is whether the change in the law is discriminatory in respect of the particular project or service. Risk in respect of changes in law and regulations of general application should lie with the private sector. However, where the regulatory change is specific to the service provided by the supplier (...), it may amount to a change in the purchaser's requirement."

5. See, for example, the discussion of the incentives of a price cap regime with respect to quality, in Section 3.4.3.2.

6. We return to this topic in section 6.3.3.

7. For more on risk sharing and allocation of risks, see Milgrom and Roberts (1992: 206–47) and McAfee and McMillan (1988: 24–45).

8. On the sharing of responsibilities between the public authority and a private operator regarding, in particular, maintenance, renewals, and investments, see also chapter 1.

9. In fact, in order to minimize the distortion in consumers' demand patterns, the mark up that each consumer pays above marginal cost should be inversely proportional to that consumer's price elasticity of demand. In economic theory, this is known as Ramsey pricing.

10. For a detailed analysis of different tariff structures, see Brown and Sibley (1986: 26–97).

11. For instance, according to 1990 estimates, in Guayaquil, Ecuador's largest city, only 45% of urban dwellings have access to indoor drinking water, while 36% have no access at all to piped water. In slum neighborhoods consumers must buy from private vendors. Private vendors buy water at subsidized prices and then sell it at a high mark-up. Studies showed that water bought at 70 sucres per cubic meter was resold at between 4,000 and 6,000 sucres per cubic meter, a mark up of 5,700–8,500%. In slum neighborhoods consumers spend up to a quarter of family income on water, often of poor quality (Oxford Analytica 1996). A study of five Latin American countries found that water and sewerage subsidies to better-off consumers were 1.3 to 2.8 times those to poor customers. Similar results were reported for Algeria and Hungary, where the subsidies for services such as electricity, household gas, and urban transport to the better-off were 2.5 to 3.8 times as high as subsides to the poor (Petrei 1987).

12. It should be noted that if such additional factors reflected the future costs of the operator perfectly, there would be no need for the X factor (indeed, the cost factors would capture all efficiency gains). In practice, however, it is impossible to devise a formula that would perfectly capture all future changes in the magnitude and structure of costs of a well-managed company. An efficiency factor remains useful, therefore, to capture some of the unpredictable ways in which a good manager will lower costs.

13. Reducing incentives to maximize sales might be an advantage only to the extent that some market failures exist (negative externalities, such as pollution) and that the service is consequently priced lower than required to maximize overall welfare.

14. In Buenos Aires the share of the population with home water connections was to rise from 70 percent to 90 percent by year 10, and then to 100 percent by year 30. Similarly, the share of the population with sewerage was to rise from 51 percent to 73 percent by year 10, and then to 90 percent by year 30. The 30-year water concession in Cancún, Mexico requires that water coverage be increased from 61 percent to 95 percent and sewerage coverage from 34 percent to 95 percent within two years.

15. Article 50.2.1 of the contract states that every year the lessee must renew 17 kilometers of pipes of a certain type (wherever it is most needed) or "an equivalent distance of pipes of a different type," according to a schedule annexed to the contract (that is longer distances for smaller or cheaper pipes and shorter distances for larger or more expensive pipes).

16. As a result, however, the operator could be exempted from its investment obligations even if the lower demand forecasts were due to its own bad per-

formance (such a scheme could therefore give rise to some moral hazard problems).

17. Contractor liability under liquidated damages is almost always capped, however, at some percentage of the construction contract price. Liquidated damages are often 10 to 15 percent of the contract price for gas pipelines, for example, while for longer-gestation and more technically complicated coal-fired power generation projects they may be as high as 35 to 40 percent.

18. For more detail on risk coverage available from private sources, see American International Underwriters (1997).

19. See the website of the Office of the Water Services (OFWAT) at http://www.open.gov.uk:80/ofwat.

20. For examples of self protection mechanisms through which a private party might try to enhance its bargaining position vis-à-vis the government see Kerf and Smith (1996: 52–56).

21. The issue of choice of judicial forum in a contract (and its enforcement) raises a number of issues that are beyond the scope of this paper. National law or case law on the subject should be surveyed as approaches differ between countries.

22. Credit agreements are also generally governed by New York law. See St.-John-Needham (1994).

23. The term alternative dispute resolution (ADR) usually includes arbitration as another alternative to litigation. For our purposes, we separate arbitration from other ADR mechanisms on the basis of the binding nature of the arbitration award.

24. The parties in Hong Kong's Chek Lap Kok Airport Project adopted a multitiered dispute resolution mechanism, which is described in McConnaughay (1995: 249–50).

25. Because this is usually very difficult to do, organizations like the United Nations Commission on International Trade Law (UNCITRAL) elaborated rules for use in ad-hoc arbitration procedures in order to facilitate matters for the parties. Still missing, though, is a back-up organization that is able to step in and rule on a challenge to arbitrators, for example. For details see Paulsson (1996: 212–14). See also Table 3.6.

26. For a more detailed treatment of international arbitration see: Redfern and Hunter (1991) and Fouchard, Gaillard, and Goldman (1996).

27. Escobar (1997). For a discussion of the Calvo doctrine and its consequences, see Amador (1992: 521–22). See also Peters and Schrijver (1992: 355–83).

28. For details on reservations and grounds for refusals under the New York Convention, see Redfern and Hunter (1991: 457–65).

CHAPTER 4

Concession Award

The success of a concession depends not only on getting the provisions of the contract right, but also on designing an appropriate method for awarding the concession. The issues include:

- Whether to use competitive bidding (or some other method) to award the concession.
- Whether to have a prequalification process for interested bidders.
- How to structure and evaluate bids.
- Whether to have sealed or voice bids.
- Whether to have single or multiple bidding rounds.

The design of the bidding and award procedures can have a significant impact on the economic efficiency and transparency of the concession. This chapter describes options for approaching these issues and summarizes recent lessons from international experience.

It is important to note that the options described below do not necessarily conform to procurement guidelines required by some multilateral institutions for projects they finance. Rather, the discussion attempts to address a wide range of options and their merits and limitations without pointing out how these practices might deviate from multilateral procurement guidelines. But, it is important for governments to bear these guidelines in mind when designing a concession award procedure if they are to preserve the possibility of donor financing for that project.

4.1 Choosing the Method of Award

There are a wide variety of concession bidding and award procedures and a range of options for the detailed design and implementation of these processes. Essentially, however, the methods can be broadly grouped into three categories: competitive bidding, direct negotiations, and competitive negotiations. In practice, these methods constitute a continuum, and any award process is likely to incorporate elements of competition and negotiation at various stages. The techniques for selecting a private partner or project may be contrasted more generally with a system of free entry, in which there are no formal selection procedures (see chapter 1).

4.1.1 Competitive Bidding

Under a competitive bidding process, tendering generally involves the following elements:

- Public notification of the government's intent to privatize an existing infrastructure service or award a concession for a new private infrastructure project or service, generally including a request for expressions of interest.
- Distribution of information memoranda, bidding documents, and related draft contracts to potential bidders.
- A formal process for prequalifying potential bidders.
- A formal public process for presenting proposals, evaluating proposals, and selecting the winner.

Within this broad framework there may be important design differences on, for example, whether and how to prequalify bidders, how bids will be structured and evaluated, and how offers will be presented and awarded. These issues will be described in detail later in the chapter.

Most countries favor competitive bidding. Governments generally cite three reasons for using competitive bidding: it ensures transparency in the contract award, it provides a market mechanism for selecting the best proposal and typically results in lower costs, and it stimulates interest among a broader range of potential investors. Competitive bidding is easiest to design and implement when the product or service required is fairly standard, the technical parameters can be defined with reasonable certainty in the bidding documents, and there is limited scope for innovation and creativity on the part of an operator.

Virtually all governments use competitive bidding for privatizing and concessioning existing infrastructure services for these reasons and because most countries have public procurement rules in place that mandate public bidding for the sale or concession of all government assets. In the case of new infrastructure projects involving some form of monopoly franchise, most governments favor competitive bidding (if a formal process is in place), though some have the flexibility to use other methods (such as competitive negotiations or direct negotiations) if the project circumstances warrant a different approach (see section 4.1.2).

As mentioned above, donors may require particular procurement practices and will typically mandate competitive bidding in the projects they support. The World Bank, for example, has developed procurement guidelines dealing specifically with concession contracts (box 4.1).

4.1.2 Direct Negotiations and Unsolicited Proposals

Under direct negotiations, the project idea generally originates with a private sector sponsor, rather than with the government. A developer or operator seeks to negotiate directly with a government or government-owned utility on the terms and conditions for an infrastructure project, whether it be a management contract, concession *stricto sensu*, BOT, BOO, or privatization. There may, in fact, be circumstances in which a full-blown competitive bidding process may not yield the best result for consumers. Such instances could include:

- Projects in smaller municipalities, where it may be too costly to arrange a competitive bidding process or where it may be difficult to attract developers and operators.

Box 4.1 Guidelines for Selecting Concessionaires and Procurement under World Bank Loans

In January 1995 the World Bank adopted new rules dealing specifically with private infrastructure or concession contracts that it finances. The new guidelines link the way the private developer or operator is selected to the way it will have to procure Bank-financed goods, works, and services.

The main principle is that competitive bidding should be used at one of two stages. If the private concessionaire is selected competitively under international competitive bidding or limited international bidding, as defined in the *Bank Guidelines on Procurement*, the concessionaire is free to use its own procedures to procure contracts financed by the World Bank (as long as these come from eligible countries, that is, World Bank-member countries). When it is not selected competitively, the concessionaire will be expected to procure goods, works, and services on an international competitive or limited international bidding basis, in accordance with standard Bank procurement rules.

The World Bank determines whether a specific selection process meets the criteria set forth in its guidelines. It is therefore prudent to involve Bank staff from the beginning of the process if the government or concessionaire wants to hold onto the option of letting a competitively selected concessionaire procure goods and services using its own procedures.

Source: World Bank (1996).

- Emergencies and natural disasters, in which major projects or repairs must be completed rapidly.
- Projects involving proprietary or innovative technology.

In countries without a track record or a proven legal and regulatory framework for private concessions, governments may choose to enter direct negotiations for some initial projects on a pilot basis in order to gain experience and build a record with investors. This approach provides the necessary time and experience to properly design the framework for infrastructure concessioning before launching a broad competitive bidding process for other infrastructure projects.

There are several examples of direct negotiations for private infrastructure projects. Direct negotiations were used for the early independent power producers (IPPs) in Indonesia and the Philippines, although both countries have subsequently adopted competitive bidding. Twelve states in the United States with competitive bidding procedures in place for procuring power also allow direct negotiations under certain conditions and subject to specific rules. In addition, a number of states require no bidding, and utilities continue to negotiate directly and sign contracts with independent power producers.

The United Kingdom and the Australian State of Victoria are recent examples of governments that allow some degree of flexibility in public tendering of private infrastructure projects. In 1994 the U.K. government issued guidelines for ministries concerning the tendering of privately financed projects (HM Treasury 1994). The guidelines emerged from a lengthy public consultative process in which the government sought views from developers, financiers, and the public. The guidelines set out the framework for competition, competitive negotiation, and direct negotiation. They recognized that, "Competition must keep its central place in public procurement. Its form, however, will vary according to the value and complexity of individual cases.... In the context of the private finance initiative the advantages in terms of

stimulating innovation may in exceptional cases justify alternatives to competitive tendering."

The U.K. Guidelines further stipulate that direct negotiation with a single promoter is possible if:

- A private sector promoter identifies an entirely new project.
- A private sector promoter comes forward with a project in response to an invitation from a public sector body, based on the delivery of outputs that are not specifically defined but that fall within broad functions, policies, or initiatives.
- A private sector promoter proposes to proceed with a project already identified by the public sector in a way that is genuinely innovative.

Similarly, in 1994 the Australian State of Victoria issued guidelines pertaining to the tendering of private infrastructure projects (Department of the Treasury 1994). The guidelines encourage private investment in infrastructure and allow developers to propose new initiatives. The government's policy is to proceed with open competitive bidding for awarding the projects, but the guidelines permit direct negotiation in circumstances "where the private sector proponent has offered the Government a proposal which embodies a unique and proprietary concept as an essential component of the proposal and where the proposal is cost effective when measured against the Government's benchmarks."

In general, in cases where governments do not use competitive bidding, they should introduce some degree of competition into the processs, or otherwise replicate competitive forces, in order to ensure both transparency and economically efficient outcomes. Several possible mechanisms could be used. For example, if innovative designs or technology are being proposed, it may be possible to contract the design phase directly and then hold competitive bidding for implementation. If it is not possible to separate design and implementation, and the government proceeds without using competitive bidding, safeguards could be built in to ensure transparency and efficiency. These could include:

- Using external advisers and consultants to assist the government in assessing proposals.
- Benchmarking against the cost of similar projects.
- Announcing the proposed project terms and conditions, and allowing other developers an opportunity to better the terms within a specified period—this feature is incorporated in the Philippines BOT Law (box *4.2*).
- Establishing an independent advisory panel to review the proposed transaction.

Periodic rebidding of the concession would also help ensure longer-term economic efficiency in cases where the initial concession was directly negotiated.

4.1.3 Competitive Negotiations

It may also be possible to combine elements of competitive bidding with direct negotiation to promote transparency, while preserving the innovative or proprietary aspects of developers' proposals. For example, governments could initially use a competitive process to solicit proposals in response to broad output specifications and then negotiate directly with one or more developers. In this manner competition would be used to narrow the number of potential developers, and negotiations would be used to work out detailed terms and conditions of the contract. The government would have fallback bidders if negotiations with the preferred bidder failed.

Alternatively, the government could negotiate simultaneously with several developers to further enhance the competitive aspects of negotiated transactions. This is often referred to as competitive negotiations. Under this method governments (or government-owned utilities) specify their objectives and solicit proposals from private operators through a request for proposals (RFP). The government (or utility) then reviews the proposals, selects those that are deemed technically responsive to the RFP, and negotiates the contract terms with the selected bidders. The process may involve simultaneous negotiations with several bidders with the objective of awarding a single contract. Alternatively, it may result in the award of several contracts.

This competitive negotiation approach is well-suited to projects in which:

- There is scope for innovation and different approaches by developers, and authorities hope to elicit imaginative proposals for projects.

Box 4.2 Philippines Build-Operate-Transfer Bidding—The "Swiss Challenge"

Under the Philippines BOT Law, national or local authorities may accept unsolicited proposals for BOT projects on a negotiated basis if :

- The project involves a new concept or technology and is not already listed on the roster of priority projects identified by the government.
- No direct government guarantee, subsidy, or equity is required.
- The project is submitted to a price test or "Swiss challenge" from competitors.

The price test works as follows: the agency awarding the project must invite comparative proposals to any unsolicited proposal it has received. The invitation to tender must be published in a newspaper of general circulation for at least three weeks. The published invitation must inform potential bidders where to obtain tender documents, however, proprietary information contained in the original proposal is confidential and may not be disclosed in the tender documents. Competitors have 60 days to submit competitive proposals. If a lower-priced proposal is received, the original proponent has 30 days to match it and win the contract. Otherwise, the award goes to the lower bidder.

This challenge has been used, for example, in the case of a New Zealand developer who submitted a proposal to the National Power Corporation to rehabilitate and maintain a 350 mega-watt hydro plant, challenging an unsolicited proposal by an Argentine company.

Source: Republic of the Philippines (1994).

• It would be difficult to secure financing on the basis of standardized contract documents.

In these circumstances simultaneous negotiations with several prequalified bidders may be the preferred approach for awarding one or several projects.

Many states and utilities in the United States use this approach for procuring new power generation. A 1991 survey of procurement methods undertaken by the National Independent Energy Producers (an association of independent power producers) demonstrated strong support for this method, citing three advantages. First, since the terms are not fixed, it permits developers to be more creative and tailor projects to the particular needs of the utility in terms of timing, siting, fuel supply, design, performance, security, and contract-termination provisions, once they reach the negotiation stage. Second, it removes the potential incentives that arise under price-based competitive bidding for some bidders to offer unrealistic projects that will do well when evaluated against price criteria, but may never get built. Third, it offers a more rational way to screen qualified potential suppliers.

Another example of the use of competitive negotiations is the Hong Kong East Harbour Tunnel, involving the construction and operation of a tunnel between Hong Kong and Kowloon. The government advertised in the *Government Gazette* for bids for the construction and operation of the proposed

---

Box 4.3 The United Kingdom Private Finance Initiative—Bidding and Award Procedures

Although the guidelines for the United Kingdom Private Finance Initiative (PFI) include a presumption in favor of competitive tendering, they do not require it. In fact, the use of a negotiated procedure involving several bidders at once is "strongly recommended where the conditions for using it are met." In some cases public bodies may also proceed with a single tender procurement procedure.

The reason given for this latitude in methods of project bidding and award is to encourage private sector companies to come forward with innovative ideas. By allowing for considerable flexibility in the design and procurement of projects, the private sector is given the greatest scope for influencing project development, while a more restricted procedure might dampen innovation and provide inadequate scope for negotiation with bidders.

If competition is used, the first step is the publication of a notice of the proposed project in the *Official Journal of the European Community*. The project is generally loosely defined in this initial notice in order to allow for varied and attractive solutions from bidders. Companies expressing interest must then prequalify by providing basic information about their financial standing, commercial and technical capabilities, and relevant experience. This information is used to assess the capacity of bidders to undertake the project, and thus to compile an initial shortlist.

In order to minimize bidding costs, normally no more than three or four bidders are invited to provide a full tender. However, authorities have considerable flexibility in determining the number of bidders. Bidders may submit an outline or indicative proposal to serve as the basis for discussions with the tendering authority. Detailed negotiations will then be pursued with the final bidders. The target timetable from publication of the initial notice to contract award is 12 to 15 months.

Project requirements generally specify a particular output in terms of capacity and availability of service. Final bidders are then given an opportunity to comment on requirement specifications before they are finalized and to suggest alternative solutions for inclusion in their tenders. Intellectual property rights are to be protected, and ideas emanating from different bidders may not be combined in the project design. If an idea submitted by an unsuccessful bidder is used in the project, appropriate compensation must be paid.

Bid appraisal criteria are chosen and communicated to bidders as part of an invitation to tender. But the weights given to various elements of cost, quality, and deliverability of tenders need not be given to bidders. Because the appraisal involves weighing a number of subjective conditions of comparative bids, a "reasoned, judgmental approach" to evaluating unquantifiable factors is advocated. The outcome of the appraisal may be either the immediate award of a contract or the identification of a preferred bidder with which to carry on final negotiations.

Source: HM Treasury (1996). See also HM Treasury (1995).

tunnel. Bidders were given a very preliminary engineering design and traffic estimates prepared by the government. Interested bidders were required to submit technical and financial proposals. The technical proposal had to specify project details, including whether the bidder would also build a parallel tunnel for the metro (bidders had the option of including this in their proposal). The financial proposal had to include the proposed toll to be charged to users during the 30-year life of the concession.

Of the nine proposals received, eight passed to the next stage; one was rejected on the grounds that the consortium did not have sufficient financial capacity or technical and operational experience. The government, with the assistance of an external advisor, reviewed the eight proposals for three months and, based on this review, shortlisted three bidders. The government asked them to provide additional information on their proposals. Upon receiving this information, the government entered into parallel negotiations with all three. Following competitive negotiations, bidders were asked to resubmit their toll proposals. A winner was selected, and a letter of understanding signed. The agreement was then ratified by the Legislature.

Regardless of the method of award chosen, the solicitation and evaluation of bids and the negotiation of contracts involve complex legal, financial, and technical issues. It is necessary to stress the importance of qualified, professional advisers to the success of concession design and implementation. The issues involved in such projects typically lie outside the scope of traditional civil service work, and the use of specialized external advisers to the government is advocated, especially given that private investors will generally employ their own teams of experienced advisers on such projects. For more on the hiring of advisers see box 2.3.

4.2 Prequalification and Shortlisting

When awarding concessions for the provision of a monopolistic infrastructure service, governments usually want to ensure that the winning consortium has the technical and financial capacity to operate the concession successfully. They do not want to

award it to an operator that offers the best deal on paper but later fails to deliver what was promised.

One way to reduce this problem is to design the concession contract so that it is attractive only to operators who are confident that they can operate the business successfully. This can be done by writing a contract that imposes stiff penalties for poor future performance and requiring firms to post a bond sufficient to pay the penalties. If poor performance can be objectively observed, and the bidding parties believe that they will indeed forfeit their bond in case they fail to meet the contract's performance standards, this system should deter those who lack the requisite technical and financial capacity from bidding for the concession.

In practice, however, it may be difficult to enforce penalties specified under the contract, and the performance bond may not prevent bidding by overconfident operators. As a result governments will often go through a process of prequalifying prospective bidders to further weed out unsuitable firms. Prequalification may also be used to reduce the number of bidders, thus stimulating qualified firms to prepare good proposals.

In addition, governments typically limit the total number of prequalified bidders to a shortlist of three or four, because the costs associated with more bidders often exceed the benefits of additional competition. For bidders there are high costs associated with preparing bids and negotiating the transaction. A large number of bidders reduces the chances each has of winning the bid and hence discourages investment in the preparation of proposals. More bidders also raise costs to governments since officials and their advisers will usually face more requests for clarification or additional information, and more bids will have to be evaluated.

There are several issues that must be considered in conducting a prequalification of bidders, including:

- The type and minimum degree of experience and capacity required of potential operators.
- The criteria to be used for prequalification and the quantitative or qualitative method for evaluating potential bidders against these criteria.

- The form and extent of involvement by the lead operator in the bidding consortium (for example, minimum equity position, technical assistance contract, and so on).
- The stage in the bidding process at which prequalification should take place (for example, before bidding documents are distributed or at the time of bidding).

4.2.1 The Operator's Experience

Generally, governments seek bidders with a proven track record in the service being concessioned or privatized. But the degree of experience and capacity required of bidders will depend in part on the size and attractiveness of the market to be served, the sector and service being concessioned, and the number of established firms currently operating in the world market in this sector. There is a good argument for "right-sizing" prequalification to fit the concession and expected investor interest—that is, smaller concessions may set less rigorous prequalification criteria in order to ensure a sufficient number of bidders and, hence, real competition in the award process.

4.2.2 Prequalification Criteria

In a formal prequalification process governments often use quantitative criteria related to technical and financial capacity (table 4.1). These criteria generally refer to such aspects as:

- Operations by the bidder in one or more comparably sized markets (generally expressed in terms of the customer base in those markets).
- Financial strength of the bidder.
- Minimum operating revenues from a comparable service run by the bidder.
- Minimum required equity of companies in the consortium.
- Quality of service provision in comparable operations.

While many of these criteria reflect the size of operations, governments often include performance criteria to ensure that potential bidders demonstrate a minimum level of efficiency in their relevant operations elsewhere. These may refer to such items as labor productivity (volume of output or service per employee) and cost efficiency (operating costs per unit of service). The challenge is to identify the right parameters by which to judge quality. Performance criteria should be used judiciously, namely in sectors and services where cross-country comparisons are meaningful (not subject to wide variations in underlying conditions) and where performance data are reliable and verifiable by a third party (such as the home-country regulator).

Prior to setting the prequalification criteria, governments (with the assistance of their advisers) often undertake a preliminary "road show" to promote the transaction and assess the degree of investor interest. By doing this, they can set the criteria to ensure that there will be a sufficient number of bidders, based on their prior knowledge of investor interest and the technical and financial characteristics of potential bidders. While this procedure is by no means essential, it may avoid the unpleasant surprise of announcing criteria and finding that there are no interested bidders who qualify.

Alternatively, some governments have opted for a less rigid evaluation process without quantitative criteria. Bidders submit information on their experience and qualifications, and these submissions are reviewed by the government to ensure that firms' financial and technical capacity is satisfactory, but without using explicit quantitative criteria. This process gives the government more flexibility, but it is subject to complaints about lack of transparency from bidders who do not pass the screening.

In assessing a firm's prior experience with similar operations in other countries, it may be useful to review the company's performance data, regulators' reports, and customer surveys or opinion polls showing the level of public satisfaction with the service provided.

4.2.3 The Operator's Participation

Once the government has determined that it wishes to have a prequalification process, it may also spec-

Table 4.1 Examples of Prequalification Criteria in Private Infrastructure Transactions

Sector	Country	Transaction	Prequalification procedure	Technical criteria	Financial criteria
Electricity	Peru	Lima electricity distribution privatization	Qualification at time of bidding; bidders must exceed a score of 80 percent against six weighted quantitative technical and financial criteria	Customers and energy sales per worker, total customers, and energy sales	Minimum total value of assets and net worth
	Argentina	Electricity distribution concessions	A guarantee to carry out the bidding process was required of bidders at the time of prequalification	Consortia to include qualified operator with minimum experience and ownership in consortium	Minimum asset value of bidding companies; proven increase of at least 10 percent in asset value in three years prior to bidding
Transport	Mexico	Concessioning of rail freight lines	Registration through written statement of interest; authorization of registered parties by the Ministry of Communications and Transportation based on uniform criteria	Demonstrated legal, technical, and administrative capacity	Demonstrated financial capacity
	Hungary	BOT for toll road	Invitations for prequalification based on approved preliminary design plans evaluated by expert assessment committee	Capacity of bidders to design, build, maintain, and operate toll road	Capacity of bidders to finance road without state aid
Water	Argentina	Buenos Aires concession	$30,000 fee for prequalification documents	Minimum population of largest city and aggregate population served by bidder	Minimum requirements for total annual billing and net share capital; consortium shareholding distribution regime
	Bolivia	La Paz concession	Qualification process to take place at same time as economic bids presented	Consortia must include water operator with minimum experience and extent of service	Minimum net worth and maximum debt-to-equity ratio of operator
Natural gas	Mexico	Concessioning of distribution	Registration of interested bidders and meetings between regulator and prospective bidders to clarify information prior to technical bids; small registration fee	Documentation of technical and administrative capacity	Documentation of financial capacity

Source: World Bank staff.

ify the form that the operator's participation should take in the bidding consortium. Governments often want an experienced operator to have a long-term stake in the success of the concession and will insist that the operator have a majority (or at least a significant) equity stake in the bidding consortium. If the operator is a large multinational company, this would also enhance the bidding consortium's ability to raise financing. On the other hand many operators may find this requirement too onerous, particularly for smaller concessions. Rather than requiring an equity stake in the consortium, an alternative is to require that the bidding consortium have an operating or technical-assistance contract with a qualified operator, that is, the operator would manage the company (or at least provide specified technical assistance) but not hold any equity.

4.2.4 The Timing of Prequalification

The timing of prequalification is also important. Some governments have opted to hold prequalification early in the bidding process, that is, prior to the distribution of any draft bidding documents. Early prequalification formalizes discussions with potential bidders, since only prequalified bidders receive the draft bidding documents for comment, undertake due diligence, and participate in the bidding. This formalization enhances the transparency of the process. One drawback of early prequalification is that it forces potential investors to form consortia early in the process and reduces their flexibility to change consortium partners during the preparatory phase. This problem can be mitigated to some extent by allowing the reorganization or merging of consortia prior to the actual bidding. However, governments may want to limit the merging of competing consortia in order to avoid collusion between bidders and to maintain a sufficient number of bidders.

Another option is to defer qualification until the actual bidding. With this approach bidders must prove that they meet qualification criteria established by the government at the time of bid submission. If they do not meet these criteria, they will be disqualified from the bidding. While deferring prequalification provides bidders with extra time and flexibility to form consortia, it also creates greater uncertainty among bidders concerning how many groups are likely to submit bids. The expectation of a large number of bidders may deter some investors from incurring the costs involved in preparing a bid.

4.2.5 Transfer of the Concession

While prequalification helps to ensure that bidders have the required technical and financial capacity to undertake a project, it does not ensure satisfactory future performance. As discussed in chapter 3, the concession contract should include incentives for efficient management and sanctions for poor performance. It is also important that regulatory institutions be in place to supervise and enforce contract compliance.

Often governments design concessions to preclude operators from transferring their shares (or operational management responsibility) in the concession company during the life of the concession. This restriction is designed to ensure that there will always be an experienced operator managing the concession. But it may make financing difficult to obtain, because lenders generally seek transferability rights in the event that operators default on their loans. The possibility of a takeover by another operator also gives the government a means of exerting pressure on an inefficient operator. A possible solution is to allow transferability to another operator, with the approval of the government, and provided that the new operator satisfies the original prequalification criteria.

4.3 Bid Structure and Evaluation

Given the complexity of many infrastructure privatizations and new investment projects, it is often difficult for governments to evaluate and compare proposals from different bidders. In designing the bid evaluation process, governments must decide:

- Whether to have a two-stage process involving the sequential evaluation of technical and financial proposals.

- Which specifications to include for the technical and financial proposals.
- How to assess whether a technical proposal is fully responsive to the specified requirements.
- How offers should be evaluated and compared.

4.3.1 Technical Proposals

Many governments have adopted a two-stage process (either in the place of or in addition to a prequalification round) whereby bidders present separate technical proposals containing business and investment plans. These proposals are evaluated before proceeding to the financial offers. Often the evaluation is conducted on a pass/no-pass basis—that is, only those bidders that pass the technical evaluation proceed to the financial evaluation. The winning bidder is then selected on the basis of the best financial proposal from among those who passed the technical evaluation.

This approach was used in the Buenos Aires water privatization. Four prequalified bidders submitted technical proposals setting out their business plan, including investments, financing, and so on. These plans were then evaluated by the government to assess their adequacy with respect to the service requirements in the concession contract. The committee concluded that three of the four plans were technically responsive; the fourth was deemed nonresponsive, principally because it included an innovative proposal for a sewage treatment plant that was considered by the committee to be nonviable. After the technical evaluation, the three bidders that passed proceeded to the financial proposal stage. The concession was awarded to the bidder with the best financial proposal (in this case the lowest average tariff to consumers).

An alternative is to weight the technical and financial evaluations. This method was used to select the new private concessionaires for the Argentine freight rail privatization. Bidders submitted detailed business plans with technical and financial information. The proposals were evaluated on the basis of the following weighted criteria: proposed investment plan (30 points), promised additional investments (5), organizational plan

(25), maintenance plan (8), concession fee to be paid (12), payment required by the passenger trains for trackage rights (5), and number of personnel to be retained from the public company (15).

A process involving a technical evaluation of proposed business plans has important drawbacks, however. It often involves considerable discretion and judgment on the part of the evaluation committee, which reduces the overall transparency and automaticity of the award process. Experience has also shown that changing market conditions after contract award often require operators to make significant (and justifiable) modifications in their business plans and investment programs. These changes reduce the meaningfulness of the evaluation process to the extent that it relied heavily on the assessment of the proposed business plans.

Given these drawbacks, many governments have opted for a process whereby all bidders bid on the same technical specifications or service requirements, and the evaluation is based solely on financial proposals. To ensure that the technical specifications and service requirements are viable, governments will generally issue a preliminary version to bidders for comment and discussion prior to finalizing project plans. After consultation and receiving bidders' written comments, the government finalizes the bidding package, and all bidders bid on the same technical specifications and requirements.

Although the technical specifications are standardized for all bidders, there may still be a two-stage procedure. In this case the technical proposal may simply involve providing legal documentation to meet standard bidding requirements. Alternatively, it may be used to qualify bidders (if a prequalification process was not used earlier) or reduce the number of prequalified bidders that advance to the financial evaluation. In this case the technical proposal would contain information on the bidder's technical and financial capacity and experience in order to assess these against certain specified thresholds. This procedure is, however, quite different from a two-stage bidding process whereby bidders submit proposed business and investment plans for evaluation.

4.3.2 Financial Proposals

There are many different options for structuring financial proposals (table 4.2). Some of the more common options include bidding on:

- The highest price, in cash or debt retirement, to be paid for the assets or shares of the enterprise being privatized or highest concession fee (one-time or annual) paid to the government.
- The lowest cost to the government for constructing or operating facilities or services.
- The largest amount of new investment to be undertaken by the operator.
- The lowest tariff to be charged to consumers.
- The lowest net present value of the future revenue stream to the developer from the service or project.
- The lowest subsidy that the government must provide to the winning bidder to operate a loss-making service.

In addition, there are other criteria on which projects may be bid, such as the maximum extent of new service coverage promised or the minimum length of the concession period. While not strictly "financial" criteria, these bear directly on the level of investment to be undertaken or on the consumer tariffs required by the developer.

The choice of which method to use will depend on several factors, such as: whether the transaction involves an existing service or a new project, the amount of risk and ownership to be transferred to the private operator, and the government's objectives for the transaction. If the transaction involves privatizing existing assets or shares, a common practice is to have bidders bid the amount of cash (or debt retirement) they would pay the government for the assets or shares being privatized (assuming that the pricing regime is specified in the concession contract).[1] In this case the winner is simply the highest bidder. This method is used by most governments to divest existing enterprises.

Peru, for example, privatized its electricity distribution assets in Lima and received $389 million in cash payments for 60 percent of the shares. However, basing awards on the highest fee can encourage concession designs that limit competition in the sector in order to attract a higher price for the concession. While conferring exclusivity rights on the concessionaire may indeed raise more revenue for the government, it results in higher prices to consumers for infrastructure services.

In some privatizations governments may decide that short-term revenue needs are less important than private investment in the company being privatized. In such cases they may structure the privatization to include the issuance of new shares, rather than (or in addition to) the sale of existing shares. Where new shares are issued, the proceeds will remain with the privatized company (for future investment), whereas proceeds from the sale of existing shares will go to the government. For example, Peru's telecommunications

Table 4.2 Examples of Financial Proposals

Infrastructure transaction	Structure of financial proposal
Peru: Lima electricity distribution privatization	Highest dollar value offered for assets
Argentina: Buenos Aires water concession	Maximum discount to existing tariffs
Philippines: power-generation BOTs	Lowest price (cents per kilowatt-hour) of power to be supplied
Chile: south access to Concepción toll road	Minimum toll and minimum one-time subsidy
Turkey: electricity distribution concession for Istanbul	Minimum margin on distribution required by the operator
Venezuela: cellular concession	Highest concession fee paid to government

Source: World Bank staff.

privatization combined the sale of existing shares (with the proceeds going to the government) and the issuance of new shares (with the proceeds remaining in the privatized company). Similarly, in Bolivia's capitalization program bidders bid on the value of new shares issued by the capitalized enterprises; proceeds remain with the company to finance future investment, while the winning bidder acquires a 50 percent stake in and management control of the company.

Where privatization of infrastructure involves a full concession but no sale of assets, governments frequently base the bidding on the highest proposed concession fee to be paid by the concessionaire. This fee may take the form of a one-time upfront payment or an annual payment for the life of the concession. If the fee is to be spread over the life of the concession, the bidding procedures generally specify the discount rate for translating bids from future to present value.

When a government's objective is to increase investment in the privatized company, it may choose to hold the bidding on the basis of new investment commitments. This method of bidding is commonly used when a government is concerned that the market value of a company being privatized is much lower than the book value (reflecting the government's historical investment) and that it will therefore be accused of giving away public assets. In such cases governments will often base the bidding on proposed investment commitments to demonstrate to the public that the new owners will invest in the privatized company.

Bidding on the basis of investment commitments has three important drawbacks. First, by locking in future investment levels, it prevents the operator from adjusting investments and operations to reflect changing market circumstances. Second, it has often proven difficult to enforce these commitments, thereby undermining the basis for the original bidding and contract award. Third, it may encourage excessive, economically unjustifiable investment.

Another bidding option, which is commonly used for either new infrastructure projects or concessioning of an existing service (where assets are not being

sold), involves bidding on the basis of the tariff to be charged to consumers. This was the method used for concessioning the water and sanitation services in Buenos Aires and Manila, where concessions were awarded to the bidder proposing the largest discount from the existing tariff structure. This method has also been used for awarding new toll road concessions and power generation plants.

Some innovative bidding schemes have been developed in the past three years for private infrastructure projects that involve considerable market risk. In the case of new toll roads, for example, experience has shown that it is very difficult to forecast traffic flows, thus generating high risk for the operator (or the government in the event that it has provided traffic or revenue guarantees). To address this problem, Chile is now considering bidding on the basis of the net present value of the future revenue stream from the collection of tolls, with the concession awarded to the operator who bids the lowest net present value. Under this bidding method the concession would not be fixed in length. It would terminate when the revenue stream (in net present value terms) reaches the original bid. Thus the concession length would automatically adjust to fluctuations in demand, thereby reducing market risk for the operator and eliminating the need for traffic or revenue guarantees from the government. This method is somewhat similar to that used in the private construction and operation of the QEII Bridge (Dartford-Thurrock River Crossing) in the United Kingdom, where the concession period is set at a maximum of 20 years or until the company has accumulated revenue equal to the project debt. For more on variable-length concessions, see also section 3.8.4.4.

In summary, there are many ways to structure the financial bid, and the choice can have important effects on the award and operation of the project and, ultimately, on consumers. In designing the financial bid, governments should seek to follow some basic principles, such as:

- Structuring the financial bid as simply and transparently as possible so that the bid award is automatic (that is, avoid complex formulas requiring subjective judgments or qualitative evaluations on the part of the government).

- Structuring the financial bid to promote economic efficiency, in terms of efficient consumption by users and efficient operation and investment by the concessionaire. For example, bidding on investment commitments may not promote efficiency if it leads to overinvestment or the uneconomic allocation of resources.

Similarly, bidding on tariff levels will not promote efficiency if the tariff structure is itself distorted or if it precludes improvements in the structure or level of tariffs during concession implementation.

4.3.3 Negotiations

Once the contract has been awarded, several steps typically remain in finalizing the project. There is often a negotiation stage between the winning bidder and the government to clarify some issues that arise as a result of gaps or lack of clarity in the draft contract documents. Additional issues may arise as the winning bidder seeks to negotiate and sign contracts with other project participants in order to bring the project to financial closure.

These postbid procedures can be lengthy and may sometimes lead to changes in contract conditions, which can have important implications for the bidding process. Extensive opportunities for postbid negotiations can cast doubt on the transparency of the process, as bidders may submit overly optimistic proposals to win the bidding if they are confident that they can secure changes in their commitments during subsequent contract negotiations. This concern is especially grave in cases where ex post negotiations result in changes in the very criteria on which the bid itself was awarded. For example, if the winner of the competitive bidding for a concession awarded on the basis of the lowest tariff is able to revise the tariff in subsequent negotiations, the validity and transparency of the bidding process itself is put into question.

While negotiations on matters such as the proposed tariff, concession period, and risk allocation are not uncommon in many concession awards, they are clearly contrary to the spirit of transparent competitive bidding and are barred by many internationally recognized procurement rules and guidelines. For example, Article 31 of the UNCITRAL Model Law on Procurement states that "no negotiation shall take place between the procuring entity and a supplier or contractor with respect to a tender submitted by the supplier or contractor." As much as possible, technical discussions and negotiations should be addressed in the technical proposal stage of the bidding. Postbid negotiation of nonsubstantial terms of the contract should be limited in order to avoid delay in the procurement process.

Measures aimed at reducing these risks include:

- Requiring detailed, firm evidence at the bidding stage that financial closure can be reached within a specified period. Investors' concerns should be taken into account early on to avoid delaying the process after bidding.
- Preparing draft contracts to minimize the scope for change as a result of postbid negotiations (this requires clarity and consistency in drafting). Bidders should be given the opportunity to comment on draft documents at an early stage.
- Keeping the runner-up in the wings as a fallback option during postbid negotiations. This option, however, should not be used by governments to try to squeeze a more favorable offer out of the winning bidder with the threat of re-opening the bidding.

4.4 Bidding Rules and Procedures

Apart from the structure of the bid, bidding rules and procedures should also be designed to ensure transparency and economically efficient outcomes. There are a number of important design issues, including:

- Whether to use a reserve price and whether to announce it.

- Whether and when to use sealed bids rather than open bids.
- Whether to have a single round or multiple rounds of bidding.
- Whether to have simultaneous or sequential bidding (in cases where several concessions with interdependent values are being awarded).
- Whether to require bid bonds and activity rules.
- Whether bidders should be remunerated for a portion of their bid costs.

4.4.1 Use of a Reserve Price

An important design issue is whether to use (and announce) a reserve price, whereby bids are rejected if they fall below a specified level (or above a specified tariff if bidding is based on lowest average tariff). While a well-designed competitive bidding process will yield the true market value without the need for a reserve price, governments may still feel that a reserve price is necessary as a safeguard against collusion (and hence, below-market bids) and also for public credibility.

The concept of a reserve price is often misunderstood by the public. Frequently, when the actual bid far exceeds the announced base price, there is criticism that the reserve price was set too low. But the reserve price should not be the government's best estimate of the market value (that is, the government should not be trying to guess the winning bid). Rather, it should be set at the minimal justifiable level in order to spur as many bids as possible—and hence a market outcome. Experience demonstrates that the more bidders there are, the higher the sales price and the more advantageous the outcome is likely to be for the government.

Announcing a reserve price tends to enhance both the transparency of the process and the information available to all bidders. But, in deciding whether to announce the reserve price, governments should also assess whether there is likely be only a single bidder for the project; if so, it may be preferable to keep the reserve price confidential.

4.4.2 Sealed Versus Open Bids

Another important design issue is whether to have sealed or open (voice auction) financial bids. Most governments use a sealed bid procedure, whereby bidders present single sealed bids that are opened in a public forum. Often, there is a significant spread between bids, which has led governments to conclude that sealed bids will produce the best results in terms of highest revenue or lowest tariff.[2]

Many game theorists, on the other hand, argue that open auctions—whereby bids escalate until all but the winner have dropped out—induce more aggressive bidding and yield higher prices under most circumstances (see McMillan 1992: 133–49, 1994: 145–62). While open auctions are fairly rare in infrastructure concessions, they have been used in the award of radio spectrum for mobile telephony in the United States. Proponents of auctions argue that, under sealed bids, bidders have less information on other bidders' estimates of project value. Thus there is greater likelihood under sealed bidding that the "winner's curse" will occur—that the winning bidder is the unfortunate one who, out of ignorance, overestimates the value of what is being auctioned. In order to avoid paying too much, experienced bidders will adjust their actual sealed bids downward to compensate in advance for the winner's curse. As a result of this compensation, sealed bids may actually yield a lower price than a voice auction (assuming bidders are experienced).

Despite these arguments, there may be good reasons to opt for a sealed-bid procedure. First, collusion between bidders is generally considered to be less likely with sealed bids than voice auctions; under a sealed-bid procedure, bidders' defections from collusive agreements (that is, the submission of bids above the colluded price) are harder for others to prevent than under voice auctions. Second, if bidders are inexperienced, they may be less likely to correct for the winner's curse under a sealed-bid with the result that the sealed-bid procedure may actually yield a higher price under these circumstances.

In summary, the issue of whether to have sealed or open bidding is an important design consideration that could significantly affect the behavior of bidders and, hence, the bidding outcome. In deciding which method to use, governments should assess such factors as the expected number of bidders, the possibility of collusion among bidders, and bidders' experience with similar projects.

4.4.3 *Simultaneous, Sequential, and Multiple-Round Bidding*

If a series of similar concessions is being auctioned (for example, rail lines and electricity distribution franchises), governments must decide whether to auction these simultaneously or sequentially. If the government is placing restrictions on the degree of concentration (such as preventing an operator from winning more than one concession), the bidding rules must specify how the winner will be determined in a simultaneous auction should the same company have the highest bid for more than one concession.

For example, in privatizing electricity distribution in Lima, the Peruvian government split the service area into two separate concessions to facilitate benchmark regulation.[3] The two concessions were roughly equal in size and customer base. They were awarded simultaneously in a single-round sealed bid procedure. Prequalified firms were allowed to submit separate bids for each concession, with the restriction that the same firm could not be awarded both concessions. The bidding rules specified that if the same firm had made the highest bids for both concessions, the government would select the winners on the basis of the bid combination that provided it with the highest revenue.

Mexico, in concessioning its rail lines, considered whether to have simultaneous or sequential bidding for the three main lines. The government stipulated that no firm could be awarded more than one concession in order to ensure competition among rail lines. In this case the government opted for sequential single-round bidding (commencing with the Northeast line), rather than simultaneous bidding of all three concessions. The

rationale was that the concessions were not of equal market value and, hence, it would be better to bid the most attractive first in order to reduce bidders' uncertainty.

It is also possible to run simultaneous auctions over multiple rounds. This bidding process was used for the auctioning of radio spectrum licenses by the U.S. Federal Communications Commission (FCC) and has since been replicated by Mexico in its spectrum auctions. In the FCC auctions bidders submitted computerized bids for spectrum licenses being offered in any number of markets. Their bids were then posted for all bidders to see, and rebidding took place over several rounds. Bidding continued until no new bids were received (though the FCC had the discretion to keep the bidding open or to close it after a specified number of rounds).

A simultaneous multiple-round auction allows bidders to continuously reassess their strategy and preferences in light of their competitors' bids. For example, a firm can assess how it is doing with respect to its competitors in several markets at once (for example, Chicago versus New York) and adjust its bidding strategy for the subsequent round. Simultaneous multiple-round auctions may be particularly useful when awarding several similar concessions with interdependent values.

In its spectrum auctions the FCC employed activity rules and penalties to ensure that the auctions closed within a reasonable period of time and that bids were serious. In each round the FCC established minimum bids (or bid increments from the previous round). To discourage bidders from waiting until the end of the auction to participate, the FCC imposed activity rules specifying the frequency of bids required to maintain eligibility. Bidders were granted five activity waivers that could be used during the course of the auction. They were also required to pay upfront fees related to the size of the markets they wished to bid on. Penalties were imposed for defaulting on payments after the bidding concluded.

The choice of bidding mechanism and the design of bidding rules are crucial. Governments should assess carefully the circumstances—the cost of bidding and expected strategic behavior of bidders—before deciding on the mechanism. It may be, for example, that in smaller transactions the cost to bidders and the government of a multiple-round auction will outweigh the expected benefits.

4.4.4 Bid Bonds

Governments frequently use bid bonds to ensure that bids are serious and remain valid until contract award and signature. Bid bonds can be significant for large privatizations or concessions. For example, the bid bond was $10 million for Lima's electricity distribution concession, a transaction valued at roughly $200 million.[4] In Manila's recent water and sanitation concession, the bid bond was $5 million. Not all governments, however, require bid bonds. The U.K. Private Finance Initiative discourages the use of bid bonds, arguing that "bid bonds are expensive and should not be sought other than in exceptional circumstances."

4.4.5 Cost Sharing

Preparing bids and proposals for infrastructure concessions can be costly for developers and operators. The transaction costs of preparing bids may easily amount to 5 to 10 percent of the project's total costs. Investors may thus be reluctant to prepare and submit proposals if the costs of doing so are high and their chances of winning are slim. This may be particularly true for entrants that are less

established. Prequalification and shortlisting of potential bidders may encourage firms to participate by limiting the number of bidders and, hence, increasing the chances of winning. But these will not lower the costs of preparing a bid.

Some governments have adopted cost-sharing mechanisms to defray bidders' costs in preparing and submitting bids. The U.K. Private Finance Initiative may offer such arrangements in projects where high bidding costs might otherwise limit the number of potential bidders. The decision to do this is left to the authorities carrying out the bidding and award process.[5] Reimbursement of all or part of the bidding costs may be considered particularly if a project is withdrawn after an invitation to negotiate has already been issued.

Notes

1. While the assets are sold, the operator is generally granted a concession to provide a specified service for a fixed period of time.

2. For example, the spread between the winning and second bids in Peru's telecom privatization exceeded $1.1 billion ($2.0 billion versus $850 million).

3. Each concession would exclusively serve one-half of Lima. In setting retail prices, the regulator would be able to compare the performance of the two operators.

4. The Lima electricity distribution concession was split into two concessions. The bid bond was $10 million for each concession. The winning bids were $212 million and $176 million.

5. For example, bidding costs were refunded in the competition for the Channel Tunnel Rail Link.

CHAPTER 5

Regulatory Institutions

5.1 Introduction

As discussed in previous chapters, concession contracts with detailed regulatory rules reduce the need for regulatory discretion. Even with very specific rules, however, multiple regulatory tasks still must be performed: competing bids must be evaluated; pricing rules must be applied (the impact of inflation on prices must be calculated in accordance with indexation formulas, for example); firms' behavior must be monitored to ensure compliance with pricing, quality, and other obligations; and decisions must be made on the application of sanctions for noncompliance. Furthermore, rigid rules have costs and, in some cases, some flexibility will be desirable. The application of rules governing access to bottleneck facilities or anticompetitive behavior, for example, will often call for judgments. Also, over long periods, pricing rules will eventually have to be reviewed.

The character of the entity or entities in charge of performing these tasks will have an important impact on both the technical quality of the work done and the confidence in the integrity of the regulatory system as a whole. These factors, in turn, will determine whether private operators will be willing to provide infrastructure services and under which conditions.

Whatever the nature of the regulatory entity, two important issues arise. First, the regulator must be able to balance the interests of the operator, the users, and the government without succumbing to pressures by one or more of these

parties. Second, some regulatory functions call for particularly sophisticated technical skills, and it is therefore especially important to endow the regulator with such capabilities. This chapter addresses the following questions:

- What can be done to help the regulator resist undue pressures?
- How can protection against undue pressures be combined with adequate accountability of the regulator?
- How can the regulator acquire necessary technical capabilities?
- Which functions should be performed by the regulator?
- How should the regulatory entity be structured, which procedures should it follow, and when should it start to operate?
- When the recommended solutions are politically unacceptable, what alternative strategies could be considered?

5.2 Establishing Independent Regulators

It is widely accepted that the regulator should maintain an arm's length relationship with regulated firms, consumers, and other private interests. The idea that the regulator should also maintain an arm's length relationship with political authorities, on the other hand, still remains an object of debate.

The rationale for giving the regulator independence in this second sense is strong, however. It stems from three related considerations. First, because consumers constitute a large proportion of voters and utility services are often perceived to be essential, governments face pressures to use regulation to advance short-term political objectives. There are numerous examples of justified price increases being withheld at the expense of investors, economic efficiency, and the longer-term interests of consumers.

Second, investors are aware of these pressures and of the vulnerability of their usually large, long-term, and immobile investments. Unless a government has made a credible commitment to rules that enable reasonable returns, private investment will not flow. Weaknesses in the credibility of that commitment will be reflected in higher costs of capital and, hence, higher tariffs.

Third, credible commitments are difficult to make because of the long-term nature of most investments. Highly specific rules can increase the comfort level of investors in some cases, but, as mentioned above, such rules might not be sustainable and are not appropriate in all cases.

In these conditions entrusting regulatory authority to government ministers presents serious drawbacks, as short-term political considerations are likely to weigh heavily on regulatory decision-making. The situation is worsened when the state remains the owner of utility enterprises, as there is then no arm's length relationship between the regulator and the firms.

In order to provide a satisfactory solution to this problem, a number of countries have established independent regulators with real autonomy from political authorities. Although generally a part of government, the regulator can be established so as to enjoy some protection against political pressures. Some of the concrete measures that can be adopted in that respect are:

- *Mandate.* An independent regulator will typically have its mandate clearly defined by law and will not be subject to direction by political authorities.
- *Appointments.* While the executive branch is usually responsible for making appointments, its discretion might be constrained by legisla-

tive provisions specifying particular qualifications (and disqualifications) for appointment, and sometimes also requiring the legislature to participate in the appointment process.
- *Terms of appointment.* Regulators are usually appointed for a fixed period, which may be subject to renewal. When a regulatory board or commission is made up of several individuals, their terms may be staggered to reduce the influence of any one government over the overall composition of the entity.
- *Security of tenure.* Appointees can be removed only in restrictively defined cases. Protection from arbitrary removal is essential for resistance to improper political pressures.
- *Agency funding.* Regulators can be given access to independent sources of funds, such as user fees or levies on the regulated industry. In order to prevent levies from growing too burdensome, the law establishing the agency often sets a cap on levies, usually defined by reference to industry turnover.[1] The cap sets the maximum levy, and actual levies are set annually to cover a budget approved by the legislature. When an agency is responsible for more than one industry, levies usually differ among industries, so that each industry covers the costs of its own regulation and contributes to costs shared across industries (see Smith and Shin 1995b).

Independent regulators have a long history in the United States and are being adopted by several OECD countries, including Australia, Canada, and the United Kingdom. The trend toward infrastructure privatization and reform has seen this model emulated in a growing number of developing and emerging economies. Recent examples include Argentina, Bolivia, Hungary, Jamaica, Malaysia, Mexico, Peru, the Philippines, Russia, and Venezuela. Even countries without independent infrastructure regulators have often adopted this model for other regulators with technically demanding and politically sensitive roles, such as antitrust regulators.

Proposals to establish such agencies, however, often remain controversial. In particular, there is often skepticism of independent regulation in countries with a long legacy of strong executive dominance and pervasive corruption. There are several possible answers to this concern. First, independence is not achieved overnight in any society. With time, as the regulator builds a constituency among consumers and investors, it can be expected to develop greater resistance to political pressures. Second, independence is a relative, not an absolute, concept, and progress must be measured at the margin. Any departure from direct political control can be expected to somewhat reduce the concerns of investors and, therefore, the costs of capital.

5.3 Reconciling Independence with Accountability

Independence must be reconciled with measures to ensure that the regulator is accountable for its actions. Checks and balances are required to ensure that the regulator does not stray from its mandate, engage in corrupt practices, or become grossly inefficient. Striking the proper balance between independence and accountability is notoriously difficult. A number of measures can be adopted to help achieve these objectives:

- *Mandate and review.* Decisions of the regulator should be subjected to an appeal process (this topic is further discussed in section 5.6.3).
- *Removal for misbehavior.* While security of tenure is an essential safeguard of independence, that protection should not extend to cases in which there is evidence of incompetence or misbehavior. To reduce concerns over removal provisions being misused for political purposes, causes for removal will have to be carefully defined. In addition, the legislature could be involved in the decision, with supervision by the courts.
- *Transparent decisionmaking.* This will typically include mechanisms for interested parties to make submissions on matters under consideration and for the regulator to publish decisions and the reasons for those decisions.

- *Review of budgets.* Agency budgets should be subject to scrutiny by the legislature and executive as part of the budget process.
- *Annual report.* The regulator is typically required to publish an annual report on its activities.
- *Other scrutiny arrangements.* The regulator's actions may be subject to scrutiny by other arms of government, including legislative committees and specialized audit or oversight institutions. In some countries, for example, an independent audit office or controller-general may have jurisdiction to review the conduct and performance of regulatory agencies.

5.4 Dealing with Constrained Regulatory Capacity

In order to ensure that the regulator has the requisite capacity to carry out its tasks, measures might be adopted to facilitate the recruitment of qualified personnel. Regulators should, for example, meet strict professional qualification requirements. Making sure that the regulatory entity has access to sufficient financial resources is also important if the entity is to attract qualified personnel. Such positions should, in addition, be exempted from civil service salary rules if such rules make it difficult to recruit and retain highly trained and experienced professionals.

Training regulators is also crucial. Training usually must cover relevant concepts from traditional disciplines in economics, law, and finance, but should also include broader training in negotiation analysis, media relations, and so on. No less important, newly appointed regulators can benefit considerably from contacts and exchanges with more experienced regulators from other countries. In some cases this is done through bilateral "twinning" arrangements between the nascent regulator and a more experienced foreign regulator. These arrangements may provide a basis for exchanging staff and materials or for providing other forms of support and advice. There has also been a recent trend toward the creation of networks among regulators. Recent examples include the Hemispheric

Energy Regulators Conference being developed in the Americas and the International Forum for Utility Regulation supported by the World Bank.

Finally, when in-house capacity is in short supply, one option is to contract out some regulatory responsibilities to an independent group or consulting firm. This might prove to be a very efficient way to overcome capacity constraints. For example, Chile contracts out the technical monitoring of water standards. Another task that could be undertaken by outside experts is the auditing of regulated firms' financial accounts.

There may be some limits to this approach, however. First, contracting out regulatory functions must be seen as legitimate; contracting out an entire system (including decisionmaking responsibilities) will usually be politically unacceptable. Specific regulatory tasks or functions may be more amenable to contracting out (examples were mentioned in the previous paragraph). Independent consultants can be given responsibility for conducting bidding processes, and dispute settlement is regularly handled by external arbitral bodies. Providing for the transfer of know-how from outside experts to in-house staff might also minimize resistance to the idea of contracting out some regulatory functions.

Second, to the extent that outside experts are entrusted with regulatory responsibility, it is essential to make sure that they are protected from undue pressures. Third, such outside experts must be kept accountable for their work. This means, for example, that it might be difficult, if profits or prices are controlled by reference to a very complex model (such as in the Chilean electricity sector), to contract out analytical work while retaining a sufficient base of information in-house to allow the consultants' findings to be checked on an informed basis.

One should note, in addition, that enhancing the expertise of the regulatory entity is not only a way of resolving technical capacity constraints but also of fostering the independence of the regulator. Highly qualified and well paid staff may be less likely to give in to political pressures or succumb to bribes or other inducements from industry (in Argentina, for example, regulators are more highly paid than the president).

5.5 Determining the Functions of Utility Regulators

5.5.1 Main Principles

There is a wide range of regulatory tasks that can be assigned to utility regulators. These include:

- Award of licenses or concessions.
- Administration of rules included in licenses or concessions (for example on tariff matters).
- Settlement of disputes between government and operators, between consumers and operators, and between different operators (on access matters, for example).
- Monitoring of firms' compliance with regulatory norms.
- Prosecution of firms for noncompliance, including the imposition of penalties.

Several factors will determine whether, and to what extent, any of the above tasks should be conferred on a utility regulator:

- Whether the activities in question are considered to be political or technical matters. Judgments of this kind vary among systems and over time. For example, political control over tariffs was once considered the norm. But there is now growing recognition that once the general policy principles are determined, society's interests will be better served by delegating responsibility for tariff administration to an independent agency. Tax and other distributional issues, in contrast, are still widely regarded as the exclusive province of elected bodies.
- Whether locating particular functions within a single agency has the potential to create significant conflicts of interest or dilute the agency's focus. For instance, giving a regulatory agency responsibility for actively promoting investment in a sector will often conflict with its role as an impartial arbitrator of investor and consumer interests.
- Whether, by contrast, locating particular functions within one agency has the potential to fos-

ter the development of expertise, coherent policies, and economies of scale. Especially in countries where there is a shortage of appropriate skills, there are benefits to limiting the number of different agencies and assigning related tasks to the same body.

- Whether the regulator enjoys the confidence of users and political authorities. New agencies may have their role limited initially and be given greater responsibility once they have proved their competence and reliability.

5.5.2 Utility Regulators' Roles with Respect to Ministers

There is a general consensus that ministers should retain responsibility for broad sector policy, including public investment, privatization, sector restructuring, taxation, subsidies, intergovernmental relations, and maintenance of the legislative framework. Even in these areas, however, agencies may be given formal or informal advisory roles. And gray areas remain. For example, many agencies are responsible for defining tariff structures, including those that include some degree of cross-subsidization between different classes of users. When subsidies are made more explicit, however, judgments on these questions will usually be seen as more appropriately made by elected bodies.

On the other hand, most independent regulators will be responsible for administering rules, settling disputes, and monitoring firms, although in some cases regulators might have only advisory functions with respect to the administration of certain rules.

There is less agreement over responsibility for granting licenses or concessions. In the United States regulators grant Certificates of Public Convenience and Necessity, which are functionally equivalent to licenses or concessions. In the United Kingdom the power to grant licenses is formally vested with the relevant minister, who can, however, delegate this task to regulators. In Jamaica the regulator must make recommendations on the award of licenses, but the minister makes the final decision. And in Argentina and Peru concessions are granted by ministers without involvement by the regulators. There is no general answer as to which approach is best. While ministerial control might expose the process to short-term political influences, some countries are concerned about delegating this sensitive task to a regulator. The Jamaican approach might represent a reasonable compromise in that respect. In any case the identity of the decisionmaker will matter less when detailed criteria for the award of a license or concession are specified and the decision is subject to effective review.

The agency's role in imposing sanctions on utilities for noncompliance with norms also varies among systems. In some legal systems the power to impose sanctions is reserved for the courts. In Colombia enforcement powers in the energy sector are not conferred on the regulator but on a separate Public Services Commission. In most cases, however, the regulator has the power to impose sanctions, although major sanctions—such as the cancellation of licenses or concessions—may require ministerial decisions.

5.5.3 Utility Regulators' Roles with Respect to Other Regulators

Utility regulators' main focus is on the control of firms with monopoly power. But utilities, like other firms, are subject to regulation on a variety of matters, including environmental and safety standards and restrictions on anticompetitive practices. In some cases existing agencies may exercise regulatory responsibilities of this kind. In the United Kingdom, for example, responsibility for regulating the water sector is divided between the Director General of Water Supply (economic regulation, including prices) and the Department of Environment (pollution and, hence, quality standards). Then, the issue of coordinating the actions of the utility regulator and the other involved agencies becomes crucial.

Quality standards have a direct impact on utilities' costs and, hence, on prices and the affordability of services. They should therefore be coordinated with economic regulation. If the utility regulator is not responsible for regulating quality parameters, it can, for example, advise the agency responsible for setting standards. Tariff rules can be designed in such a way as to permit certain cost increases to be passed on automatically, or to allow tariffs to be reviewed if there are significant changes in quality standards.

In many countries a specialist agency with economywide jurisdiction is responsible for antitrust regulation. Once again, it is important to clearly distinguish between the responsibilities and roles of the antitrust agency and utility regulators. Antitrust regulation and utility regulation may overlap in several areas. For instance, industry-specific regimes governing access to networks may overlap with general rules governing the misuse of market power, and some arrangements endorsed by the utility regulator may involve at least prima facie contravention of antitrust rules. It will usually be appropriate to give priority to industry-specific rules. In the United States and Canada the question of jurisdiction was left largely for the courts to resolve, leading to many decades of uncertainty and much costly litigation. The preferable approach is to establish clear rules governing the interaction of the two regimes from the outset.

On the other hand, both antitrust agencies and agencies in charge of regulating infrastructure services can usually contribute expertise to utility regulation—and this complementarity should expand as competition comes to play a greater role in utility industries. For this reason both agencies may be involved in reviewing proposed mergers, restrictive agreements, or anticompetitive conduct within utility industries. In some cases a member of the antitrust agency is made a member of the utility agency (as in Australia), or one agency makes formal submissions to proceedings conducted by the other. Antitrust agencies may also be given special roles in utility regulation, such as determining whether the conditions of effective competition are sufficiently absent to warrant price regulation (as in Mexico) or acting as an appeal body from the utility regulator (as in the United Kingdom).

5.5.4 The Breadth of Regulators' Authority

The pros and cons of organizing governmental entities on a sector-specific or cross-sectoral basis and in a centralized or decentralized manner have already been discussed in chapter 2. This section will therefore highlight only a few points that are of particular relevance in the regulatory context.

5.5.4.1 Sectoral coverage. There are three basic models around the world. Regulatory institutions can be:

- Industry-specific: separate agencies are established for electricity, gas, telecommunications, and so on (such as in Argentina and the United Kingdom).
- Sector-specific: separate agencies are established for energy, transport, and communications (such as energy regulators in Colombia and Hungary).
- Multisectoral: a single agency is established for all or most utilities (such as state-level agencies in the United States, Canada, and Australia, and national agencies in Jamaica, Costa Rica, and Panama).

Multisectoral agencies present some particularly important advantages. They generally report to a central ministry or directly to the head of state, which tends to enhance their independence with respect to specific sectoral ministries. They also foster the development of technical capacity by concentrating available resources in one agency and by enabling staff to learn across sectors. Finally, they make it easier for the regulator to deal with blurring industry boundaries, a particularly important point in the utility sector, where technological evolution drastically changes how some services are provided (witness the new telecommunications law enacted in February 1996 in the United States, which removes the regulatory barriers that separated the telephone, cable, and broadcasting industries).

On the other hand, political resistance often has to be overcome in order to set up an independent regulatory agency. Such resistance might be more virulent when the agency is to be entrusted with cross-sectoral competencies, as several line ministries might jointly protest against a decision perceived as depriving them of some of their responsibilities. Another concern is that a cross-sectoral agency might be unable to develop sufficient sector-specific expertise. Usually, though, this issue can be adequately dealt with through the creation of sector-specific departments within the institution (figure 5.1).

5.5.4.2 Degree of centralization. Some countries have established countrywide regulators (for example, the United Kingdom). Others have set up regulatory entities at the state, provincial, or municipal level. In France and Canada, for example, primary responsibility for regulating water utilities falls to municipal authorities. Other countries have adopted a multi-tier structure. In Germany, for example, the granting of concessions in the electricity sector is the responsibility of the municipalities, while the Länder (or states) determine rates. In the United States some national agencies are responsible for interstate regulatory issues, while commissions established at the state level deal with other regulatory matters.

A centralized approach, like a cross-sectoral one, may be an appropriate response to shortages of technical capacity, since such shortages tend to be more acute at lower levels of government. In addition, some infrastructure activities exhibit significant scale economies. Decentralized regulatory institutions might therefore have jurisdictions that are smaller than the minimum efficient size for particular activities. In such cases several regulatory entities may need to collaborate in elaborating and administering a common regulatory framework, which may increase costs and weaken the credibility and effectiveness of the regulatory regime.[2]

On the other hand, decentralization can reduce the information asymmetry between regulators and firms by bringing the regulatory authority closer to the regulated enterprise. In addition, it can foster experimentation with innovative approaches to regulatory problems. According to some commentators, such regulatory competition creates incentives for governments to improve the quality of their regulation and to emulate the most successful approaches (see, for example, Siebert and Koop 1993: 15–30).

5.6 Decisionmaking Structure, Procedural Considerations, and Implementation

Some countries entrust decisionmaking authority to a single individual (for example, the United Kingdom and Malaysia), while others use a commission or board (such as Argentina, Chile, the Philippines, and the United States). A commission will often be preferable, especially when there are concerns about improper influences on the regulator from industry or government (table 5.1).

5.6.1 Individual Decisionmaker or Commission

If a commission is chosen, decisionmaking will be facilitated by establishing an odd number of members and by limiting the total number of members.

Figure 5.1 Possible Structure of a Regulatory Commission

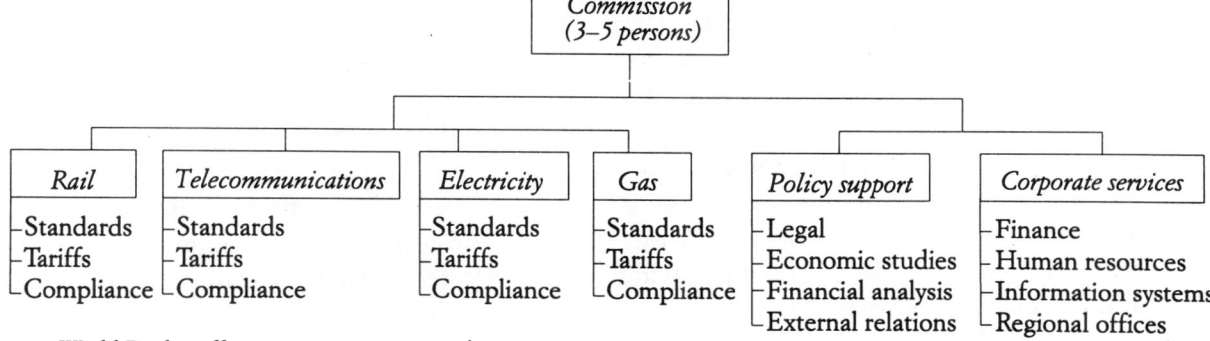

Source: World Bank staff.

Table 5.1 Individual Regulators Versus a Commission

Criteria	Individual	Commission
Speed of decisionmaking	+	−
Accountability for decisions	+	−
Vulnerability to individual preoccupations	−	+
Vulnerability to improper influences by industry	−	+
Potential to stagger the terms of commission members in order to weaken links with particular government	−	+
Potential to reflect multiple perspectives	−	+

Source: World Bank staff.

As a rule, the more commissioners there are, the slower the decisionmaking process and the weaker the direct accountability of individual members. Commissions with three members are found in Italy and the Indian state of Orissa; Argentina and Mexico have established commissions with five members; in the United States, regulatory commissions are typically made up of three or five individuals.

5.6.2 Opportunities for Participation by Regulated Firms, Users, and Other Interest Groups

For the regulatory agency to make well-informed decisions and for its decisions to be accepted as fair and legitimate, it is important that affected interests have the opportunity to present their views. It is sometimes suggested that such interests should be represented on the regulatory commission itself. This approach may offer a number of benefits. For example, it might improve the credibility of the government's arm's length relationship with investors, reduce the risk of capture by any one interest, and ensure that decisions reflect multiple perspectives.

Such an approach is not without risks, however. Great care is required in designing the body to ensure that representation is balanced and thus minimize the risk that decisionmaking will be captured by a particular interest group. Wide representation might also mean large numbers, thereby reducing individual accountability for decisions and often leading to longer delays in regulatory decisionmaking. Compromise decisions in a body with shifting alliances may make regulatory decisionmaking more difficult to predict, increasing

uncertainty for investors. Compromise decisions may also lack vigor and clarity, to the detriment of the community's long-term interests.

For these reasons it is generally preferable to adopt alternative participation models. At a minimum individuals or groups with a significant interest in a regulatory decision should be permitted to present their views to the agency before a decision is made. In the United States, the process for doing so usually involves formal hearings, which are often criticized for their legalistic nature, costs, and delays. Regulators in the United Kingdom initially adopted much more informal processes, although there is a trend toward greater formality. Some countries, including Argentina and Bolivia, are experimenting with ways of developing regulatory processes that more closely reflect local administrative traditions and resource constraints. In addition, representative bodies can be given advisory, rather than decisionmaking, responsibilities. Such bodies may be created at the initiative of the interests themselves or with the encouragement and support of the regulatory agency or government. The creation of special consumer councils may be especially important in countries that lack economywide consumer rights organizations.

5.6.3 The Review Process

Irrespective of whether the primary decisionmaker is a government minister or an independent regulator, effective review procedures are necessary to ensure that decisions are made in accordance with the regulatory commitments expressed in the law.

To be credible, the review must be undertaken by an entity that stands at arm's length from the original decisionmaker, the political authorities, and the regulated firms. As with the whole of the regulatory process, a high degree of transparency is essential.

In most countries appeals from the regulatory agency go straight to the courts. If the courts have a reputation for independence, they can play a critical role in supporting the credibility of regulatory commitment. But, if there are concerns over the independence of the judiciary, delays in the judicial system, or the capacity of the courts to make judgments on complex economic issues, it may be more appropriate for review functions to be given to another forum, at least as an intermediate step. In the United Kingdom, for example, the Monopolies and Mergers Commission acts as an appellate body with respect to license amendments. In Chile certain appeals are heard by an ad hoc tribunal led by a supreme court judge and comprising a law school dean and the dean of an economics faculty. In Bolivia appeals from sectoral regulators go to a superintendent general, whose mandate includes promoting consistency across sectors.

Grounds for appeal are usually limited to alleged errors of fact or of law, including failure to follow a required process. Appellate bodies are generally not permitted to reconsider the merits of the decision and substitute their own judgment. Some limited exceptions may be appropriate for appeals to specialist appellate bodies.

5.6.4 The Timing of Implementation

Infrastructure privatization in countries such as Chile and the United Kingdom involved establishing detailed regulatory arrangements prior to privatization. This mandate permits the regulator to supervise restructuring and pricing reform and offers consumers assurance that their interests will be protected, thus reducing possible resistance to privatization. It also allows investors an opportunity to develop a better sense of how the regulatory framework operates.

Argentina adopted an alternative approach. There, sales took place first, driven by the acute economic, financial, and political constraints the country was facing. In telecommunications, for example, privatization occurred in 1990, but the final structure of the telecommunications regulator has not yet been approved, and funding is lacking to enable the regulatory body to perform its duties. In this environment there has been some instability in the basic regulatory framework and concern that monitoring and enforcement are inadequate.

While Argentina's experience supports the view that creating a working regulatory framework and related institutions is not absolutely essential for privatization to proceed, there are clearly risks in this approach that may translate into higher costs of capital and a greater risk of consumer backlash. Other things being equal, there are persuasive grounds for establishing effective regulatory arrangements before or, at the latest, as part of the privatization process.

When the objective is to establish cross-sectoral institutions, an additional sequencing issue arises: should the regulatory institutions exhibit cross-sectoral features from the outset or should they first be organized on an industry or sector-specific basis? There are three broad options. First, a multisectoral entity can be established at the outset, with each industry brought within the regime at the time of or before privatization. This will often be the preferred approach. It has been adopted in Bolivia, for example. Second, when only some industries or sectors are being reformed, an agency could be set up with regulatory responsibility for only those industries or sectors. The competencies of the agency can then be expanded as new industries or sectors undergo reform. This approach is currently being considered in Uganda. Also, if an industry or sector-specific regulator already exists, new industries or sectors may be brought within its jurisdiction, thereby avoiding the creation of additional entities. Some states in the United States proceeded in that way. In general, the feasibility of progressively expanding the competencies of a regulatory agency will depend on how easily the structure and operation of the initial institution can be modified to meet a broader mandate.

Third, regulators can be established initially on an industry-specific basis, but consolidated over time through mergers. This also happened in some U.S. states, and this solution is being envisaged for the United Kingdom (see Helm 1994: 17–39) and Chile (see Bitran and Serra 1994). This strategy has a number of weaknesses, however, including the likelihood that existing entities will resist merger and that the benefits of cross-sectoral regulation will not be available during the critical early phases of a new regulatory system.

5.7 Finding Alternative Strategies

As already mentioned, some of the measures proposed above are likely to meet substantial political resistance. Delegating regulatory responsibility to a fully independent agency, in particular, might prove very controversial, and some political authorities may refuse to take that step. Such refusal is likely to translate into higher costs of capital. It might also lead to the adoption of overly rigid, specific pricing and other rules in an attempt to reduce concerns that the regulatory process will be captured by some interests. There are nevertheless some solutions that may partly compensate for the lack of an independent regulator and that may constitute steps toward the ultimate adoption of such a model.

- *Independent agency with an advisory role.* This solution was adopted in the United States during the early phases of the development of its regulatory framework (U.S. regulators with advisory powers date from 1839 in Rhode Island, but it was not until the early 1870s that commissions with mandatory rate-setting and other powers were established in Illinois, Iowa, Minnesota, and Wisconsin). A more recent example is that of Hungary's Energy Office. Where such agencies are established, their authority can be enhanced by requiring that their recommendations be published and that the final decisionmaker give reasons for deviating from the recommendations.

- *State holding companies with regulatory powers.* Some countries have conferred regulatory authority on commercial companies set up to manage the sector's assets. Such companies have usually been established in the context of lease arrangements. They are given responsibility for ownership, planning, and sometimes financing of infrastructure assets, as well as for regulating the lessee. Guinea and Senegal, for example, decided to establish such companies when lease contracts were concluded in the water sector. Although often fully owned by the state, those companies can be granted a certain degree of autonomy with respect to the responsible line ministry, and they can be exempted from civil service salary rules. They are not without drawbacks, however. For example, they tend to be staffed with ex-employees of the old public monopoly, who often have good operational skills but no expertise in regulatory matters, and who might be tempted to micromanage the private operator. State holding companies also tend to be organized on a sector-specific basis.

- *Dedicated unit within ministries.* While decisionmaking remains with the minister, bringing staff together in a dedicated unit may facilitate the development of expertise and may contribute to the development of professional norms that could strengthen resistance to ministerial direction. If civil service salary rules make it difficult to attract highly qualified professionals, it is essential to provide adequate funding for the outside consultants.

- *Use of courts.* If a country has an independent judiciary, it may be possible to expand its role in regulatory decisionmaking. Limitations to this approach include the low level of technical expertise of most courts, the delays and expense usually associated with litigation, and limitations in the remedies that courts can order and effectively supervise.

- *Use of arbitration.* As mentioned in section 3.10, arbitration can be used to deal with a certain number of regulatory issues, but it has some limitations: it may be a slow process, supervision for the implementation of decisions is limited, and it might raise issues of legitimacy when broad discretion has to be exercised or when multiple interests should be given the opportunity to intervene.

Notes

1. Examples include 0.5 percent for telecommunications regulators in Argentina, Peru, and Venezuela, 1.0 percent for the energy regulator in Colombia, and 2.0 percent for the water regulator in Peru.

2. On sectoral coverage and degree of centralization of regulatory institutions, see Smith and Shin (1995a).

CHAPTER 6

Government Support

6.1 Types of Government Support

Government support to infrastructure projects can take a variety of forms. Key provisions can be divided into two categories. First, the government can provide direct or indirect financial support to the project. This form of support is discussed in this chapter (see box 6.1 for examples of common financial support mechanisms). Second, government support might be needed with respect to the securities and remedies required by lenders. Lenders might, for example, require that the government give them the right to step in and cure any alleged breaches before the concession is terminated or substitute a new company to take over the concession, provided the substitute has the required technical and financial capacity to complete or operate the project. Such support is often critical to make projects bankable and therefore feasible. Lenders' security rights are discussed further in annex 4.

6.2 Rationale and Design Issues

Government financial support can be provided through three basic types of instruments: subsidies, financial investment (debt or equity), or guarantees.[1] This section aims to identify the different cases in which government support is justified and, in each case, which of those three instruments is most appropriate.

Three distinct justifications are commonly presented in favor of government support:

Box 6.1 Key Provisions for Government Support of Infrastructure Projects

The main provisions for government support commonly sought by project sponsors include:

- Direct financial contributions, such as grants, loans, equity participations, and asset transfers.
- Exemption from, or reduction of, taxes, royalties and other levies and duties.
- Complementary investments.
- A period of exclusivity.
- The adoption of necessary legislation and the issuance of appropriate approvals and consents for the implementation and operation of the project.
- Guarantees of supply or off-take agreements.

- Exemptions from restrictions on the import and export of all necessary plants and equipment.
- A guarantee of convertibility and transferability of local currency earnings.
- The right to keep foreign currency sale proceeds offshore.
- Compensation if new planning or environmental laws detrimental to the profitability of the project are adopted.
- A guarantee that the project development and operation plan will not be changed without prior consent of the sponsors, except in some narrowly specified circumstances (for example, on the grounds of national security).

Source: Freshfields (1995).

- The existence of uninsurable political risks.
- The assertion that some services should be provided below cost.
- The assertion that the government has a lower cost of risk bearing than private investors.

6.2.1 First Assertion: The Existence of Uninsurable Political Risks

6.2.1.1 Rationale. Traditional political risks include: the risk of expropriation (nationalization without "just compensation," either by a single act or by a series of measures that amount to "creeping expropriation"); the risk of political violence (war, civil war, terrorism, sabotage, and so on); convertibility and transfer risk (the conversion of local currency into foreign exchange may be impossible because of exchange controls; transfer of foreign currency out of the country may be blocked by the central bank). Such risks—when they are relatively severe—will not be accepted by private investors and are not easily insured in private markets (box 6.2). It is generally accepted that such risks should be borne by the government that directly causes them and is in a better position to control them.

The definition of political risks can, however, extend beyond the traditional political risks described in the paragraph above. Modifications of

---

Box 6.2 Political Risk Insurance

Investment insurance for political risk is available from a number of national public agencies, multilateral institutions, and the private sector. The first public plan offering inconvertibility coverage to companies investing abroad was established in the United States in 1948. In 1971 the function of providing political risk insurance in the United States was taken over by the Overseas Private Investment Corporation (OPIC). Other national programs include EID/MITI in Japan and Treuarbeit in Germany. The Multilateral Investment Guarantee Agency (MIGA), a member of the World Bank Group, began offering political risk insurance in 1988, and other multilateral institutions, including the International Bank for Reconstruction and Development and the Inter-American Development Bank, now offer political risk guarantees with a government counter-guarantee.

MIGA and most national systems cover risks arising from expropriation, war, civil strife, and currency inconvertibility and nontransferability. In order to be eligible for coverage by a national agency, investors must generally be citizens of that country or a corporation established under that nation's laws. Rules on what types of investments can be covered and the countries for which coverage will be extended vary among agencies. OPIC currently offers coverage in about 140 countries that are judged to observe human rights and workers' rights and have a low per capita income. EID/MITI and Treuarbeit have no restrictions on eligible countries, although Treuarbeit does require the availability of adequate legal protection, such as a bilateral investment treaty with Germany. MIGA coverage is available in the 128 countries that are MIGA members. The maximum term offered by the national agencies and MIGA is about 15–20 years. Exposure limits vary as well: OPIC offers maximum coverage of $200 million per project, while MIGA's limit is $50 million per project. These two public insurers make up the bulk of the market. Investment cover by members of the Berne Union, an association of national credit and investment insurers (which includes the agencies mentioned above and about 40 others representing 34 countries), totaled more than $15 billion in 1996, with an outstanding portfolio of $44 billion.

In recent years the private market for political risk coverage has grown rapidly. The major players in the industry include the American Insurance Group (AIG) and Lloyds of London. While these insurers can offer a broad range of coverage for different risks, including expropriation and, to a more limited extent, inconvertibility and political violence, the terms and exposures available are usually more limited, and fees can be substantially higher than those of public agencies. Most private insurance coverage is only for one to three years, although AIG now offers a facility with a coverage of ten years.

Note: For more details on the forms of political risk coverage available from American, German, and Japanese public insurers and MIGA see annex 5.
Source: Berne Union and World Bank staff.

the legal framework, unfavorable regulatory decisions, and failure by publicly owned enterprises to uphold their obligations to the project can, at least in some cases, also be classified as political risks. The extent to which the government should protect private investors against those risks is, however, a rather difficult issue to settle.

6.2.1.2 Modifications of the legal framework.

Whether the government should compensate operators for changes in legislation that adversely affect their activities is a question that has been examined above. As mentioned in section 3.1.3, much will depend either on whether these changes specifically affect the operator or on whether a wide range of businesses are affected in the same general way.

6.2.1.3 Regulatory risk.

As far as regulatory risk is concerned, an important issue is the degree of discretion that is granted to regulatory authorities: the issue of government compensation will normally not arise as long as the regulator exercises only the discretion that it has been granted. Only when regulatory rules are specific enough can it be ascertained that a breach—possibly justifying government intervention—has taken place. Another important point is that breaches of regulatory rules by the regulator might have to be dealt with differently according to the identity of the regulator. If regulatory responsibilities have been conferred on an autonomous entity at arm's length from the government, it might be preferable, in order to safeguard the autonomy and authority of that entity, to rely on appeal mechanisms before an independent body (such as a superior court or another ad hoc group of experts) rather than on intervention by the government to compensate private operators.

6.2.1.4 Breach of contract by public enterprises.

Much will depend in this case on the degree of effective separation between the government and the publicly owned enterprise. For corporatized entities with true commercial autonomy, supply or purchase risks are in fact commercial risks, akin to the risks of dealing with a private firm. Commercial risks should normally be borne by the operator (and in some cases transferred to subcontractors or users if the subcontractors are in a better position to bear those risks). The case of the Côte d'Ivoire water lease, concluded before 1987, clearly illustrates the dangers of leaving commercial risks with the government (box 6.3). On the other hand, public enterprises that lack any type of autonomy are much more likely to default because of political interference in their management. Therefore, the more pervasive the government's control of the enterprise, the greater is the case for considering performance risks as political risks. Whether the government should then bear those risks is an issue we discuss in the next section.

6.2.1.5 Appropriate instrument.

Governments must determine the most appropriate mechanism for mitigating these political risks. A government guarantee designed to protect investors against specifically identified (political) risks is more appropriate than subsidies or financial investments that do not distinguish between different types of risks. The use of such guarantees is not without its costs, limitations, and trade-offs, however.

First, as it is extremely difficult to determine precisely whether some risks are truly beyond the control of the service provider, sovereign guarantees might end up blunting the operator's incentives.

Second, sovereign guarantees can raise acute problems of moral hazard and adverse selection:

- Since the government knows that if a guarantee is called it can finance the liability through taxation, it might be tempted to adopt too lax an attitude in the granting of such instruments (moral hazard). Therefore, unless it is generally assumed that risks should be borne by taxpayers (we return to this topic in section 6.2.3), guarantees should be granted only if the government is willing and able to deal with the source of risk. This means that political risk guarantees should be granted only when they are complemented by genuine efforts to control risks and attempts to reform the underlying causes that give rise to risks, and only with

---

Box 6.3 Government Exposure to Commercial Risk in the Pre-1987 Côte d'Ivoire Water Lease

SODECI is an Ivorian company that is 46 percent owned by SAUR, a French water distributor, and 50 percent by private Ivorian investors and employees of SODECI. Another 3 percent is held by the government and 1 percent by private French interests. Since 1974 it has been responsible for supplying water to Abidjan and other urban and rural centers in the country and for operating the sanitation system in Abidjan. Tariffs collected by SODECI were used to pay revenues to SODECI and to finance two publicly administered funds set up to cover debt service payments and investments in water system infrastructure. SODECI was obliged to maintain and operate any additions made to the existing system by the Water Directorate and the Ministry of Public Works and Transports. SODECI was not consulted on investment decisions but was guaranteed compensation if the amount of water actually consumed was less than forecast, thus shifting most of the commercial risks of the project to the government.

While coverage and efficiency of service improved substantially under the lease, the financial situation of the sector progressively deteriorated during the economic crisis that struck the country in the 1980s. Government investment decisions were based on extremely optimistic consumption forecasts and required extensive borrowing. A continued active investment program in the face of the economic downturn led to a large accumulation of public debt and a low capacity utilization rate. SODECI was insulated against the government's poor investment deci-

sions by its contract. When the forecasts failed to materialize, SODECI was compensated for the shortfall in actual water demand. Between 1982 and 1987 SODECI received some $10 million in compensation taken from the sums that should have been allocated to the construction fund. In 1986 the financial crisis was such that no investment could be made. To make up for this shortfall, the government more than doubled tariffs for industrial water supply, thus causing industrial consumption to fall even further. By 1987 the sector had $330 million of cumulative debts from its ambitious public expenditure program. By 1988 it had arrears to SODECI amounting to $24 million.

A new contract was negotiated in 1987 for a 20-year concession under which SODECI's remuneration was reduced and its revenue guarantee canceled. In addition to operation and maintenance, SODECI is now responsible for projecting demand and planning and executing investments in the urban water supply sector. A portion of the tariffs collected by SODECI are assigned to a development fund for social connections, renewal, and extension works to be executed by SODECI, in accordance with a price schedule set out in the contract and with the approval of the Water Directorate. SODECI also has responsibility for submitting plans for new investments to be financed by the government and is responsible for the execution of works totaling less than 80 million CFA Francs. For larger works SODECI is permitted to participate in a competitive bidding process for the construction contract.

Source: Kerf and Smith (1996) and World Bank staff.

---

respect to the behavior of entities that the government is in a position to influence.

- In addition, there is a risk that the party whose behavior is being insured against might actually behave worse knowing that its contracting partner benefits from government protection (moral hazard). Thus guaranteeing the behavior of publicly owned enterprises might conflict with efforts aimed at increasing the autonomy and commercial orientation of such enterprises.

- Also, investors who benefit from the protection conferred by a guarantee might seek out excessively risky projects (adverse selection). For that reason, guarantees should leave beneficiaries somewhat exposed.

Finally, while the central government can provide guarantees against risks related to the behavior of other entities (decentralized political authorities, for example), it cannot meaningfully guarantee its own behavior. To add credibility to the government's original commitment, other instruments are needed, such as governmental performance bonds or guarantees by multilateral institutions counter-guaranteed by the government. Once again, however, as the government can rely on its taxation powers to replenish the performance bond or to fulfill its counter-guarantee obligations, it is necessary to ensure that such instruments support genuine efforts on the part of the government to limit the risk of breach of contract.

6.2.2 Second Assertion: Some Services Should Be Provided Below Costs

6.2.2.1 Rationale.
There are three main reasons for pricing infrastructure services below costs. First, the provision of some services might create positive externalities, thereby justifying higher levels of consumption than those that would exist if users had to pay the full cost of services. Second, authorities might want to keep prices equal to marginal costs in an industry characterized by increasing returns to scale (which requires that the firm obtain additional sources of revenues to cover its fixed costs). Third, it might be considered desirable to provide public subsidies to some users. As argued in section 3.3, however, exceptions to the principle of cost-covering tariffs should be rare and narrowly defined, especially in developing countries.

6.2.2.2 Appropriate instrument.
In cases where services are indeed priced below cost, government support should take the form of subsidies supplementing the price that users are willing to pay for the service. Subsidies should be provided only for services actually delivered (as in the scheme developed in the Chilean water sector—see box 3.3). Such subsidies directly address the discrepancy between the price that users are ready to pay and the "socially desirable" price. In addition, they fully preserve the incentives for the service provider to perform efficiently.

6.2.3 Third Assertion: The Government Can Bear Risk at Lower Cost

6.2.3.1 Rationale.
The argument that the cost of bearing risks is lower for the government (that is, for taxpayers) than for private investors is based, first, on the fact that individuals tend to be risk-averse and, second, on government's supposedly superior ability to pool and to spread risk. By investing in a wide range of different projects with mutually independent outcomes (pooling risks), the government can reduce the overall risk of its portfolio: underperforming projects will tend to be compensated by overperforming ones. The lower risks represented in a government portfolio will be more attractive to risk-averse investors. In addition, by spreading risk over a large number of people (the taxpayers), the government is able to substantially reduce the risk borne by each individual. This is not only because a given amount of risk is divided among many individuals. It can be demonstrated, in fact, that the sum of the risks borne by all investors will be smaller when the total number of investors is greater (see Arrow and Lind 1970). Once again, such a result will appeal to risk-averse investors.

It is not entirely clear, however, that the government can in fact pool and spread risks better than the private sector.[2] In addition, the above argument overlooks one dimension of the problem: the government has weaker incentives to invest wisely than do private investors. One reason is that, unlike private parties, the government can rely on its taxation powers to raise more capital if its investment decisions prove unwise. Another reason, already mentioned in section 3.1.3, is the fact that civil servants' use of taxpayers' money is usually not as closely and efficiently monitored as the investment decisions of managers of private infrastructure projects.

6.2.3.2 Appropriate instrument.
It is therefore very doubtful that, in terms of investment risks, taxpayers are in a better position than private investors and that they should therefore be satisfied with lower returns. If that were the case, however, it would justify paying lower risk-adjusted returns to the government than to private investors for its loans or equity participation in projects. The difference between public and private returns would, of course, make projects in which the government participates more attractive to private investors and lenders. Indeed, with the government requiring low returns, a larger share of total returns would be available to private parties.

Even if justified on the basis of taxpayers' lower cost of risk bearing, risk-sharing arrangements through loans or equity participations by the government are not without drawbacks, as pointed out in section 3.1.3. With equity contributions, the government shares in losses and profits. The fact that it shares in losses will make the project more attractive to risk-averse investors. The fact that those investors also have to share profits might, on the other hand, reduce their incentives to maximize the performance of the company and induce them to exaggerate their costs (thereby reducing the total amount of profits to be shared). With loans, the government shares downside risks without the upside potential (indeed, the returns on debt are fixed; any returns in excess of what is necessary to reimburse lenders goes to equity holders). Private equity holders can therefore limit their risks without limiting potential profits, which might induce them to pursue excessively risky projects.[3]

6.3 Government Contingent Liabilities

Correct valuation of the different types of government support to infrastructure projects is an essential prerequisite to sound management of government exposure. Valuing direct cash subsidies is straightforward. Valuing the subsidy element of a government loan can be done by comparing the price of government loans with the market price of similar loans.

6.3.1 *Valuation and Budgeting*

The subsidy element of a guarantee can be estimated in the following way: the value of a full credit guarantee (as opposed to a partial risk guarantee covering only certain risks) can be calculated based on the difference between the interest rate of a risk-free loan and that of a normal market loan. The subsidy element equals that difference minus the guarantee fees (box 6.4).

Most governments, however, fail to treat these types of subsidies coherently in their budgets. Indeed, under a cash-based system of budgeting—which is the most common—only cash outlays are recorded. Therefore, while direct cash subsidies are recorded when they are issued, as they should be, the subsidy elements of loans and guarantees are not properly taken into account. The disbursement of a loan is recorded as a cost equal to the full amount of the loan with subsequent repayments represent-

ing offsetting receipts when they are cashed in. As for guarantees, they are simply not recorded as expenses, unless a claim is made in the future. Consequently, the subsidy elements of government loans and guarantees never appear as such. Also, the different forms of government support are treated differently. Policymakers have an incentive to provide guarantees rather than cash subsidies, as they let the fiscal position of the government appear better than it actually is (see Mody and Patro 1995).

Recognizing these problems, the United States changed its budgeting and accounting systems for grants, loans, and guarantees in 1990 in order to record the actual costs of these instruments (see box 6.5). Other countries, such as Canada and New Zealand, have also introduced policies to ensure that guarantees appear in government accounts. New Zealand's Fiscal Responsibility Act of 1994, for example, mandates that the Treasury regularly publish any contingent liabilities of the Crown.

6.3.2 *The Institutional Framework*

Issues of technical capacity and the ability to resist improper pressure, similar to those discussed in chapter 5, are also relevant here. Indeed, issuing guarantees calls for difficult and technical judgments regarding, for example, the extent of coverage. Also, political authorities and investors promoting specific projects might attempt to unduly influence the process.

Box 6.4 Value of a Full Credit Guarantee—A Numerical Example

The loan amount, or government contingent liability (that is, amount covered by guarantee), is $100,000.

- The interest rate on a risk-free loan is 5 percent.
- The interest rate on a normal market loan is 10 percent.
- Guarantee fees are $1,000.

The value of the guarantee = $10\%(\$100,000) - 5\%(\$100,000) - \$1,000 = \$4,000$.

Source: World Bank staff.

Box 6.5 The United States Federal Credit Reform Act of 1990

Prompted by an explosion of loan guarantees issued during the 1980s and a recognition of biases created by the simple cash-based system of budgeting, the United States introduced a new system of budgeting for loans and guarantees, established by the 1990 Credit Reform Act. Under this new method of budgeting each form of credit is valued using a financially equivalent metric—the expected present value of future costs. The budgetary cost of credit is defined as the present value of the expected cash outflows from the government minus the expected cash inflows to the government. If borrower fees, repayments, and interest are not sufficient to cover the principal of a direct loan and the Treasury's cost of borrowing, the shortfall is a cost to the govern-

ment. If guaranteed loan defaults (or interest subsidies) are larger than the fees that borrowers pay to the government, that shortfall is also a cost. These costs, or "subsidies," must compete for budgetary resources on the same basis as other government allocations.

The Credit Reform Act significantly improved the budgeting process in the United States. The issuance of direct loans, guarantees, or grants has the same fiscal implications and requires the same budget discipline. As a result policymakers are able to decide on the form of financial support by looking at the underlying needs of the targeted population rather than on the specific budgetary treatment of alternative financial structures.

Source: Lewis and Mody (1997).

There might be substantial advantages, therefore, to adopting solutions similar to those mentioned in chapter 5. Political authorities would retain the responsibility of determining the budget to be allocated to a central guarantee authority. They could also define the types of projects that could benefit from guarantees. But the central guarantee authority, set up at arm's length from sources of improper pressures, would be responsible for issuing guarantees in each case. The members of the authority could be exempted from civil service salary rules in order to attract and retain high-quality staff. A cross-sectoral mandate might further protect staff against pressures from any single investor or sectoral minister with a stake in a particular project. It might also promote the learning and implementation of coherent solutions across sectors. Finally, it would make maximum use of scarce human resources.

6.3.3 Risk Management

The government can use a variety of tools to ensure that its exposure does not grow excessively or that it supports the wrong project:

- In order to keep track of the extent of government exposure, the exact value of the subsidies provided should be revised regularly. The like-

lihood that a given entity might default on its obligations might vary over time, and this would of course modify the value of government guarantees related to those obligations.

- The government should charge a fee as compensation for the risks it takes and to cover the costs of administering the guarantees. Such fees could rise according to prespecified criteria (such as the downgrading of the guaranteed entity by a rating agency) when the likelihood of default increases.

- If fees are not paid, the government could arrange to seize collateral as compensation.

- Efforts can be made to diversify the overall guarantee portfolio in order to reduce the variance of expected liabilities.

- When the overall portfolio remains correlated with particular variables (the interest rate, for example), the government can purchase appropriate derivatives (such as interest rate derivatives) to hedge its exposure.

- Guarantees should be structured so as to leave the beneficiary with some exposure in order to limit problems of moral hazard.

- In addition to capping the budget of the guarantee authority, the political authorities should put monetary ceilings on total government exposure. Some restrictions might also be put on the use of instruments that severely expose the taxpayer. The types of risks that the government is willing to cover could also be specifically limited. Such rules are often advisable, given the fact that, as discussed in section 3.1.3, government officials decide on the use of tax money rather than their own and might therefore easily abuse the discretionary powers given to them.

Notes

1. Apparently distinct types of support can, in fact, be considered as particular examples of one of these three forms. Complementary investments, such as the rehabilitation of a road leading to a privately concessioned bridge, can be thought of as an in-kind subsidy, for example.

2. The private sector also can pool risks. If the state retains an advantage in this respect because it controls a larger number of diverse projects, that advantage can be transferred to the private sector by privatizing the projects in question. By the same token, large private corporations can also spread risks over a large number of individuals. Those who believe that the government is in a better position to spread risks argue, however, that in order to control a large corporation, some shareholder may hold a large block of stock, which is a significant component of his wealth. Thus from the point of view of such a shareholder, the costs of risk bearing are not negligible, while those costs are negligible for other stockholders. Consequently, in considering prospective investments, the shareholder who controls the company might discount for risk when it is not in the interest of the other stockholders to do so. This problem, the argument goes, would be avoided in government-controlled companies. This line of reasoning is not completely convincing, however. One can point, for example, to the fact that the major shareholder could be an equity fund itself, consisting of a large number of shareholders, thus spreading the costs of risk bearing over an even greater number of individuals. Also, it is far from clear that bureaucratic managers will be less risk averse than corporate managers.

3. For a detailed discussion of whether governments have a lower cost of risk bearing than investors, see Klein (1996c).

Choice of Regulatory Instruments

Basic Options

A variety of instruments can be used to define and regulate concession-type arrangements. They include public law instruments (which form a hierarchy of norms ranging from constitutions to laws and secondary legislation, such as decrees), licenses (unilateral and nonnegotiable acts of the administration that take effect when a private party agrees to their terms), private contracts (negotiated by both parties), and decisions by regulatory authorities. The table below illustrates the range of possible options.

Choosing an Instrument

The choice of instruments will be dictated, in large part, by the legal traditions of the country. Norms of a certain rank might also have to be adopted to modify provisions that would hinder the adoption or implementation of concession arrangements. In addition, the different options can be evaluated against the following criteria:

Ease with which the government can unilaterally change the rules

Laws require the cooperation of the executive and the legislature to effect a change. Decrees or subordinate legislation provide less protection against unilateral modifications, since they can generally be modified by the executive alone. Contracts, for their part, cannot normally be modified unless both parties give their consent. There are some exceptions to that principle, however. In France, for example, concession-type arrangements can be unilaterally amended by public authorities, under certain conditions, provided that appropriate compensation is given to the operator (see box 3.16). Finally, when a separate entity has been entrusted with regulatory responsibilities, much will depend on the degree of insulation it enjoys from political pressures.

Flexibility to tailor commitments to specific investors

General legislation that applies to whole categories of service providers is usually unsuitable when adaptation to specific circumstances is required. Even if there is only one firm (and if a law would apply therefore to only one service provider), contractual agreements can usually be negotiated in a more flexible environment. As to the ability of regulators to tailor decisions to specific investors, that will depend on the degree of discretion that they enjoy. In the United States, for example, the constitution has been interpreted as requiring that investors get a fair rate of return, compared with other industries of similar risk. This leaves the regulators with enormous latitude to make rules and set prices.

Adaptability to changing circumstances

Laws are generally relatively difficult to modify, while decrees can be changed more easily since, as mentioned above, the executive alone can effect a modification. Contracts can be renegotiated by the parties. Regulators' power to modify contracts will depend on the degree of discretion that they enjoy and on the procedural rules that they must follow in that regard. For example, the terms of British Telecom's license can be modified by the regulator with the agreement of the company. Moreover, the regulator can undertake unilateral modifications, against the company's will, but must first seek a recommendation from the Monopolies and Mergers Commission and approval by the secretary of state for trade and industry.

Consistency

General norms, such as laws and decrees, can enhance certainty for investors, especially when they are interpreted by a single forum, such as a cross-sectoral regulator. Use of standard contracts or licenses might promote consistency. Licenses in the U.K. water industry, for example, are fairly standardized. Among the standard provisions are formulas for calculating price limits for service. Each company is required to produce an annual statement for the regulator demonstrating its adherence to the specified limits. The licenses also provide for regular price reviews and adjustments. Standard conditions include service quality requirements and customer relations rules, as well as requirements for the provision of reports and accounting information to the regulator, and the levying of license fees.

Annex Table 1.1 Examples of Instruments Embodying Regulatory Norms

Constitution	The Constitution of *Colombia* provides for proper indemnification for the expropriation of private property (Art. 58). It also specifically gives the state control of the electromagnetic spectrum and the mandate of combating monopolistic practices in the use of the spectrum (Art. 75).
Parliamentary laws	In *Chile* the 1982 Mining, Electric Power Services Law (DFL-1) provided the basis for the regulation of electricity generation, transmission, and distribution and sets out the provisions for rate setting.
Decree-laws	In *Peru* the 1992 Decree-Law of Electric Concessions (Decree-Law 25.844) was adopted by the government (president and cabinet ministers), acting under emergency powers, and replaced previous electricity laws.
Presidential decree	In *Argentina* the creation of the Comisión Nacional de Telecommunicaciónes, the telecommunications regulator, came in a presidential decree (Decreto 1185/90). In addition to the structure of the agency, it described procedures for the award of licenses, control of prices, and interconnection rules.
Ministerial decree	In some cases a decree may be issued by a sector ministry, such as *Costa Rica's* decree by the Ministry of Natural Resources, Energy and Mines in 1989 (Decree No. 18.947), which established parameters for private investor participation in some power projects.
Licenses	In *Jamaica* the license for the national telecommunications operator includes provisions fixing the rate of return to be earned by the company.
Contractual arrangements	A concession contract for the operation and maintenance of the water and wastewater systems in Cancún, *Mexico* sets out service efficiency standards and the tariff regime.
Decisions by regulatory agencies	In *Colombia* the Comisión de Regulación de Energía y Gas, a specialist regulatory agency, plays an active role in implementing competition regulation in the sector. The Comisión imposed a system of free access to the electricity network and issued decisions requiring the state oil company to divest its gas transportation assets.

Source: World Bank staff.

Annex Box 1.1 Transparency of the Policy Framework for the Electricity Sector—Contrasting Indian and Pakistani Approaches

Enron's Dhabol power project in Maharashtra State, India—one of a series of "fast-track projects"—was concluded between Enron and the state government in 1993. The original deal provided for the construction and operation of a 2,015 megawatt, $2.8 billion gas-fired plant. The nationalist Hindu party, which won the subsequent state election, campaigned against the Dhabol project and canceled the agreement when it took power.

The party claimed that the award process lacked transparency and had resulted in a project that was too expensive and a power tariff that was too high. The deal was eventually renegotiated, and the tariff was cut by more than 20 percent, the capital cost reduced by $300 million, and capacity increased to 2,450 megawatts.

In Pakistan, on the other hand, the government approved and published, in March 1994, a Policy Framework and Package of Incentives for Private Sector Power Generation Projects. The power policy framework, considered overly generous by many, promised investors an average tariff of 6.5 US cents per kilowatt-hour and exemption from corporate income tax and import duties on equipment. The policy was successful in attracting almost 2,100 megawatts of new power development. Subsequently, the government moved to tighten its policy and negotiate lower rates, but expressly stated that existing commitments would remain intact.

Source: World Bank staff.

Sustainability

The sustainability of concession arrangements depends on a variety of factors. One important element is the degree of transparency with which such arrangements are devised. Public debate or deliberation will generally reduce the risk of backlash from the legislature or from consumers. The legislative process, for example, usually involves greater transparency than contractual agreements, especially when such contracts are not competitively bid (see annex box 1.1). Concessions might

---

Annex Box 1.2 Regulatory Instruments Used in the Telecommunications Sector in Peru

Multiple instruments of different ranks are used to set up the regulatory framework for telecommunications in Peru: laws are relied on to ensure stability and consistency of the main principles concerning private participation, market structure, and regulatory institutions, while more technical rules are embedded in decrees (or Reglamentos), which also apply to all parties but are easier to modify. Concession contracts and regulatory decisions specify the particular rights and obligations of individual parties. The most important of these instruments are listed below:

• *Decreto Supremo-Ley de Telecomunicaciónes* of April 28, 1993 (decree with rank of law adopted by the president and the minister of transport and communications). The Decreto identifies the different types of telecommunications services, it defines the different instruments that can be used to promote the private provision of

telecommunications services, it lists the functions of the Ministry of Transport and Communication with respect to telecommunications, and it establishes a separate regulatory entity—El Organismo Supervisor de Inversión Privada en Telecomunicaciónes (OSIPTEL).

• *Ley Disponen la Demonopolizacion Progresiva de los Servicios Publicos de Telecomunicaciónes,* adopted by congress on January 12, 1994. This law outlines the progressive demonopolization of local and long distance telecommunications services in the country. It also provides for the award of telecommunications concessions and identifies the main types of information (duration, types of services, coverage, and price regime) that must be provided by such contracts. Finally, it states that OSIPTEL must be autonomous from an "administrative, functional, technical, economic and financial" point of view.

(box continues on next page)

Annex Box 1.2 Regulatory Instruments Used in the Telecommunications Sector in Peru (continued)

- *Reglamento de la Ley de Telecomunicaciónes* adopted by the president and by the minister of transport and communications on February 18, 1994. The Reglamento identifies the different telecommunications services, establishes interconnection rules, and defines the various licenses, permits, or contractual arrangements enabling the private provision of telecommunications services.
- *Reglamento de OSIPTEL,* adopted by the president and by the prime minister on August 5, 1994. The Reglamento defines, in detail, the

legal status, objectives, functions, powers, and organizational structure of OSIPTEL.
- *Concession Contracts with Compañiá Peruana de Teléfonos S.A. and with ENTEL S.A.* These contracts define the scope of the delegated services, the rights and obligations of the concessionaire and the ministry, the price and interconnection regimes, and the rules pertaining to contract modifications and dispute settlement.
- *Various decisions of OSIPTEL,* fixing, for example, maximum prices for various types of telecommunications services.

Source: World Bank staff.

---

also be unsustainable when legal requirements to devise and conclude such arrangements are unclear. This could be the case, for example, when procedural requirements are undefined, or when questions of competency are unresolved. In such situations high-level instruments, such as laws or presidential decrees, might constitute a "safer" option. In Guinea, for instance, the president ratified several privatization agreements, including the water lease. It was not clear, at the time, who was authorized to sign the concessions or, indeed, whether the law allowed concessions of this kind. In effect, the president settled the question by issuing a presidential decree with the force of law. Ultimately, however, it is impossible to make absolutely sure that a given project will not come under attack after conclusion of the agreements. This only underlines the importance of establishing a clear overall legal framework for private participation in infrastructure.

In many cases different rules will be embodied in different types of instruments. This approach can help set up a framework exhibiting more advantages and less disadvantages than any single instrument (see the example of telecommunications in Peru, annex box 1.2).

ANNEX 2

A Guide to Power Purchase Agreements

This annex provides an overview of issues that should be addressed in a Power Purchase Agreement (PPA) between a Purchaser (often a state-owned electricity utility) and a privately owned power supplier (the "Company") constructing a power plant.[1] It emphasizes issues that might be of concern to lenders. The paper does not address all issues that might arise in negotiating a PPA, but provides examples of ways in which they were addressed in existing power projects. In this example, the project is assumed to be a base load thermal plant financed partly with foreign loans and equity (it could be modified to accommodate mid-range or peaking thermal or hydro plants). This example does not cover credit enhancements that might be required if the power purchaser is not creditworthy. The discussion is organized by the section headings that might be found in a typical PPA. Much of the detail of a PPA is often contained in annexes; a list of those commonly found is also provided.

Article I—Definitions

Defines all the capitalized terms used in the PPA and annexes, or cross-references to the section in the PPA where the term is defined. Often, complex terms (for example, force majeure, monthly tariff) are defined in the text of the PPA.

Article II—Sale Of Capacity And Energy

2.1 Obligations to Provide Contract Capacity and Electrical Output. Specifies that the Company must make available to the Purchaser, not later than the specified commercial operation date (COD), the contracted capacity of each unit and deliver energy to the Purchaser in accordance with the PPA.[2] The Company will commit to making each unit available by the COD to ensure that each unit meets specified operating characteristics, to operate and maintain the plant over the term of the PPA, and to comply with the Purchaser's dispatch instructions (see section 8.2).

2.2 Obligation to Pay for Available Capacity and Electrical Output. The Purchaser will be required to pay a monthly tariff for the available capacity and the electrical output generated by the plant. The most common approach is a "two-part" tariff, separated into capacity and energy components. The capacity charge is designed to recover the plant's fixed costs and the energy charge covers fuel costs.[3, 4] Energy costs are usually incurred only if the plant is dispatched by the Purchaser, whereas fixed charges are payable if the capacity is available but not dispatched and, under specified force majeure events, even where capacity is not available. The detailed tariff provisions are often contained in an annex.

The tariff methodology should satisfy several objectives if the PPA is to be bankable: (1) be sufficiently clear to allow potential investors to calculate the project's likely cash flows; (2) generate sufficient revenues to cover the fixed and variable costs of the project, including debt service; and (3) generate sufficient revenue to yield a minimum ratio of earnings to payments of principal and interest to satisfy lenders' criteria. The tariff methodology should also meet the country's regulatory requirements and result in an economically satisfactory and politically acceptable price of electricity.

2.3. Third-party sales. Generally, the ability to make third-party sales, particularly where the Purchaser's creditworthiness is questionable, enhances the financeability of a project.[5] It may benefit both the Purchaser and the Company if the Company were permitted (but not obligated) to sell excess capacity and energy not dispatched by the Purchaser. Because the PPA generally constitutes a take-or-pay obligation of the Purchaser, the proceeds of third-party sales can reduce the Purchaser's monthly tariff payments. Alternatively, the Company, as agent for the Purchaser, might sell available capacity and energy to a third party in return for a negotiated agency fee from the Purchaser.

Another approach would be to allow the Company, after it has delivered a notice of termination to the Purchaser based on the failure of the Purchaser to comply with payment or other obligations under the PPA, to sell part of the plant's contracted capacity and energy to any third party. The revenue would be set off against amounts due to the Company from the Purchaser under the PPA.

2.4 Deemed commissioning; deemed generation. Developers and lenders expect a mechanism in a PPA that enables a deemed commissioning to occur where a unit is ready but cannot be commissioned because of specified events. These events are typically breaches by the Purchaser of its obligations (for example, failure to complete interconnection or transmission facilities or to provide energy for commissioning) and certain force majeure events. The capacity payments are generally determined on the basis of a specified deemed availability. The PPA should set out the point at which deemed commissioning occurs and at which it ceases. These provisions often require an independent engineer to certify when a unit would have passed the relevant test, but for the occurrence of specified events.[6] In addition, PPAs often include a "deemed generation" provision whereby the Purchaser makes capacity payments to the Company for capacity that would have been available, but for specified force majeure events, generally political events.

2.5 Liquidated Damages

2.5.1 Damages for delays. If a unit fails to pass its performance tests by the commercial operation date, the Company may be required to pay the Purchaser liquidated damages of an agreed amount per day up to a cap.[7] Sometimes the damages increase after a specified number of days of delay. Lenders will examine the impact of liquidated damages on debt coverage ratios. The Company should not be required to pay damages if the delay results from events beyond the control of the Company, such as certain force majeure events or failure by the Purchaser to comply with specified obligations.

Another approach is to provide that inordinate delay by the Company, that if not excused, should allow the Purchaser to terminate the PPA. From the independent power developer's point of view, however, the power seller should receive and be required to apply liquidated damages from the contractor to either complete the units or to redeem project debt in order to adjust fixed charges payable thereafter under the PPA.

2.5.2 Damages for underperformance. Liquidated damages are often payable when a plant fails to meet specifications, particularly contracted capacity tests. The relationship between liquidated damages and provisions allowing the Purchaser to terminate the agreement for failure to meet such tests needs to be carefully considered. The parties may wish to consider, for example, whether the

Company's failure to meet a contracted capacity test could lead the Company to terminate the tests and pay liquidated damages to the Purchaser. The liquidated damages could be measured by the difference between contracted capacity and the actual percentage of contracted capacity demonstrated in testing. The Purchaser might prefer an underperforming unit to a termination right, which would require the Purchaser to buy out the project (see section 5.3).

2.6 Testing performance. Testing should be objective and designed to confirm levels of contracted capacity, reliability, and fuel efficiency or heat rate. Testing should be certified by an independent engineer. Receipt of the engineer's certificate should become the trigger for the commencement of capacity payments unless an earlier "deemed" commissioning has occurred (see section 2.4). The PPA should specify the consequences of any inability to complete testing due to unavailability of testing power or transmission facilities.

2.7 Company's purchase of power; precommissioning power. These provisions oblige the Purchaser to provide to the Company energy required for construction, commissioning, maintenance, and start-up. Often the tariff for electricity supplied to generating companies for such purposes is the applicable tariff for industrial companies. In addition, the Company would look to the Purchaser to purchase "pre-commissioning power"—power generated by a unit during testing after its synchronization—generally at a price that would cover the Company's fuel cost associated with producing such pre-commissioning power.

Article III—Conditions Precedent

PPAs often set out conditions precedent to the effectiveness of each party's obligations under the PPA (and certain other obligations may *not* be conditional).[8] Conditions to the Company's obligations under the PPA may include (1) receipt of good, enforceable leasehold interest to the site;

(2) receipt of certain governmental authorizations and clearances; (3) obtaining comfort regarding the receipt of approvals not received as of the date of execution of the PPA; (4) if applicable, government assurances relating to currency convertibility, the availability of fuel and the like (5) if applicable, receipt of government guarantee of the payment performance of the Purchaser; and (6) execution of the construction contract and certain other project agreements. Conditions precedent to the Purchaser's obligations may include receipt by the Purchaser of (1) corporate documents (for example, articles of association and board resolutions) and (2) evidence of the Company's receipt of necessary governmental approvals.

The Company will usually wish to make financial closing a condition precedent to its obligations, whereas the Purchaser will expect that any conditions precedent to the Company's obligations be satisfied within a certain period or the Purchaser shall have the ability to terminate the PPA without liability. Lenders will require that the PPA specify when the obligations of the parties commence. There should be no ambiguity as to whether any provision in the PPA is effective and enforceable. Accordingly, lenders will prefer to make all obligations effective as of the date of execution of the PPA. Open-ended commitments for either party can be avoided by including provisions allowing termination if, after specified dates, certain key events have not occurred (such as financial closing).

Article IV—Pre-operation Period

Pre-operation obligations frequently include a "reasonable efforts" obligation by the Company to obtain necessary consents and approvals, and by the Purchaser to provide reasonable assistance to the Company in obtaining the consents and approvals. The Company's other pre-operation obligations may include (1) appointing the construction contractor and an operator; and (2) providing copies of the construction and O&M contracts to the Purchaser. The Purchaser may be required to provide the Company with title to the site and construction, water, power and other services.

Some advisers have recommended that a Purchaser should have the right, under a PPA, to approve project contracts. Developers and lenders will prefer to avoid this, as the Purchaser may not have sufficient resources to review these agreements in detail. The Purchaser is perhaps better served by clear construction and operational performance criteria in the PPA for the Company to adhere to; the PPA could also include appropriate incentives. It will be the obligation of the Company to contract with construction contractors and operators to see that these criteria are met. The Purchaser's concerns about the enforceability of the Company's obligations can also be addressed through requirements for performance bonds under the PPA in favor of the Purchaser. The pre-operations provisions generally also provide the Purchaser with the right to observe the construction progress of the project.

A PPA will often provide, as part of the pre-operating obligations, for the Purchaser and the Company to agree on operating procedures. These include methods of day-to-day communication, key personnel lists, clearances and switching practices, outage scheduling, and capacity energy reporting. If the parties are able to agree on such operating procedures before the execution of the PPA, they could be included in a schedule to the PPA.

Article V—Term and Termination

5.1 Term. Defines the date on which the agreement becomes effective and the period after which it will terminate. The provision will also provide extensions for specified force majeure events and may also include procedures for a request by either party for an extension (in which case tariff calculations should be defined for the extended term). Lenders will insist that the PPA's term be a few years beyond the period, permitting the Company to generate sufficient cash flow to retire the project's debt.

5.2 Termination. In the event of default, the nondefaulting party will have the right, subject to certain cure rights for the defaulting party and

lenders and other limitations, to terminate the agreement and exercise certain other rights.[9] In addition, continuation of force majeure events beyond a specified period (see Article XI) could also trigger a right of either the Company or the Purchaser to terminate the PPA. Lenders will generally prefer to limit the number of the termination events.

Events giving rise to a termination and/or buyout right for the Company typically include (1) dissolution of the Purchaser; (2) failures by the Purchaser to observe payment obligations and maintain letters of credit or other security; (3) breaches of other obligations by the Purchaser under the PPA; (4) government guarantees (if any) or implementation agreements ceasing to remain in force; and (5) repudiation by the Purchaser of the PPA. The Purchaser typically has the right to terminate the PPA and/or exercise its buyout rights if: (1) the Company fails to achieve financial closing by a specified date; (2) the Company fails to achieve commercial operations of the units by specified deadlines (generally subject to extensions for certain events); (3) the Company abandons the project; (4) the Company breaches its obligations under the PPA; and (5) the Company is dissolved.

Termination provisions generally include requirements for notice by the party wishing to invoke termination and/or buyout, followed by a consultation period between the parties and a period during which the defaulting party may attempt to cure the default. Such a cure right is usually accompanied by a cure period (in addition to the cure period provided to the nondefaulting party) in favor of the lenders if the Company defaults.

5.3 Buyout price. Generally, the termination provisions lead to a buyout by the Purchaser which can be triggered by either party depending on the termination event. Lenders will wish to ascertain that all outstanding debt be included in the buyout price. However, where the Purchaser's credit is in question, buyout will be considered of limited value by developers and lenders, unless supported by government guarantees.

The PPA should provide a methodology for calculating the buyout price. In some PPAs this is specified as a combination of: (1) a discounted cash flow valuation based on the estimated net present value of the Company's expected cash flows over the remainder of the PPA plus a specified residual value of the plant; (2) a construction period evaluation consisting of a specified percentage of equity subscriptions paid into the Company plus an allowed return on the equity at a specified rate; (3) a terminal evaluation set at a specified percentage of the plant's depreciated replacement cost; (4) the Company's outstanding long- and short-term loans and any accrued interest and financing fees; and (5) transfer costs. Each component is scaled according to the reason for termination, with the highest buyout price following a Purchaser default and generally none in the event of expiry of the PPA. Intermediate buyout prices can be negotiated for terminations caused by different force majeure events. An appraiser may be appointed by the parties to calculate the buyout price.

Article VI—Representations and Warranties

The representations and warranties in a PPA typically include the organization and valid existence of the Purchaser and the Company, the legal and binding nature of the obligations constituted by the PPA, the absence of certain legal proceedings that might adversely affect the ability of the parties to meet their obligations, and the due authorization of the PPA by the parties. Sometimes a project might require additional representations and warranties, frequently covering environmental issues, or on land owned by the Purchaser, for example.

Article VII—Undertakings

A PPA generally contains additional undertakings/covenants from each party. The Company's undertakings might include obligations to: (1) use reasonable efforts to obtain financ-

ing for the project; (2) use reasonable efforts to negotiate fuel supply agreements, a construction contract and financing documents;[10] (3) use reasonable efforts to obtain government authorizations; and (4) operate the plant in accordance with the Purchaser's dispatch instructions and prudent utility practices. Typical covenants of the Purchaser include (1) to provide, by or before a specified commercial operation date, interconnection and transmission facilities; (2) to assist in identifying and preparing applications for government authorizations; (3) to assist the Company in negotiating and executing the financing documents; and (4) to cooperate with the Company with respect to the Company's obligations and rights under the PPA. The PPA should set forth the consequences of a failure to comply with any such obligations.

Article VIII—Project Operation

Issues typically include scheduled outages and maintenance outages, operations and maintenance, emergencies and record keeping.

8.1 Scheduled outages and maintenance outages. Prior to the commercial operation date (COD), the Company will be required to submit its desired schedule of scheduled outage periods for the first full maintenance year after commissioning. The PPA should also provide for a date by which the Company must submit its desired schedule of outage periods for each subsequent year. Generally, longer notice is required for years subsequent to the COD. The PPA may also set parameters within which the scheduled outage periods should occur.

The PPA will generally provide for a period during which the Purchaser may object in writing to a requested schedule and propose an alternative schedule. The Company will often insist that scheduled outages should occur only at times determined in accordance with this procedure and that the Purchaser should not require the Company to schedule outages in a manner or time outside the technical limits of the plant, or inconsistent with prudent utility practices or manufacturer recommendations, or which would pose risk of damage to the plant. The Purchaser's maintenance program for interconnection facilities and transmission facilities should also be coordinated with the approved scheduled outages for the plant. Frequently, the Purchaser will also be prohibited from discriminating against the Company in favor of other plants when the Purchaser schedules and reschedules outages.

The PPA will also address "maintenance outages," defined as an interruption or reduction of generating capability (excluding scheduled outages) that cannot be postponed until the next scheduled outage. An abbreviated set of procedures requiring oral notice within 24 hours (or a similar period) to the Purchaser usually is provided for maintenance outages.

8.2 Operation; dispatch. This sets out procedures for issuance by the Purchaser of dispatch instructions to the Company and for the degree of dispatchability allowed to the Purchaser, if any. These provisions usually provide that the plant's dispatch procedures shall be in accordance with dispatch procedures for similar plants on the Purchaser system. Typically the dispatch instructions should take into account the characteristics of the plant, the overall system condition and requirements, and the conditions and characteristics of other power sources available to the purchaser, in setting out appropriate and equitable dispatch instructions. The PPA can also provide the Purchaser with the right to request that the plant be shut down. In turn, the Company will expect limitations on this right as well as indemnification for costs incurred in shutting down and restarting the plant and any increased costs incurred in connection with the shut down. The Company will also reasonably ask for a lead time in which to restart the plant, in accordance with the relevant unit specifications.

These provisions may also provide that the Company shall not be required to operate the plant other than in accordance with prudent utility practices and specified technical limits. The Company may also be asked to use best efforts to employ qualified personnel from the country and to institute training programs for such personnel.

8.3 Emergency plans; supply of power and emergency. The PPA will generally call for each party to establish plans for an emergency, such as local or widespread electric blackout and voltage reduction to effect load curtailment. During an emergency the Company may be required, as soon as possible after a request from the Purchaser, to supply such power as the plant is able to generate, consistent with prudent utility practices and specified technical limits of the plant, and, at the Purchaser's expense, make reasonable efforts to reschedule any outages or to complete work during the outage to restore power as soon as possible. Other limitations and parameters on the ability of the Purchaser to direct the Company to perform emergency-related operations (such as cold starts and emergency maximum loading or deloading) may be included.

8.4 Record maintenance. Each party will be required to keep the records necessary to administer the PPA, including an accurate and up-to-date operation log, at the plant. The provisions will generally require maintenance of such records for an agreed period after their creation.

8.5 Interconnection, metering standards, and testing. The PPA should contain provisions providing for exchanges of information concerning the plant's design, the interconnection and transmission facilities, the allocation of responsibility for construction, and interconnection, easements and rights-of-way, protective devices and the testing of interconnection and transmission facilities. Specifications for the meters to be used for the project should be set forth, as well as responsibility for maintaining the meters, providing regular metering results, checking meter accuracy, and so on.

Article IX—Payment

This specifies procedures for invoicing, the method and amount of payment, resolving disputes relating to invoices, security for payment, and rights to set off.

9.1 Invoicing. This section should establish a payment date by which the Purchaser must pay the Company the monthly tariff payment for a given month. It should also specify the manner in which invoices are to be provided by the Company. Generally, commencing with a month following the date on which synchronization for the first unit occurs, the Company will be required to submit to the Purchaser by a specified date an invoice stating the available capacity, the energy delivered to the Purchaser, the aggregate variable charges, and the total monthly tariff payment. The invoice should include reasonably detailed calculations, in accordance with the PPA; an example of a tariff calculation in a schedule to the PPA is often helpful. Other charges, fees, and reimbursements payable by the Purchaser to the Company are generally billed separately. If the tariff calculation procedures call for an annual adjustment, such as for fluctuations in foreign exchange rates, the provisions will generally provide for invoicing at a specified time(s) each year for such amounts.

The agreement will provide for the form of payment, such as direct payment or wire transfer to an account designated by the Company to the Purchaser.[11] Any delayed payment charges should also be specified. Notice of disputes relating to an invoice should be given promptly. Lenders often expect the agreement to provide that the Purchaser pay the invoice when due, though it may be entitled to a repayment after any invoice dispute is resolved. The waiver of set off rights may also be included.

9.2 Security for payment. The PPA may require the Purchaser to cause a bank acceptable to the Company to issue to the Company one or more irrevocable, unconditional standby letters of credit to ensure short-term liquidity. The PPA will generally provide that the letter of credit shall at all times be in a specified amount, usually tied to projected tariff payments for a specified period, using certain assumptions regarding load factors and other elements of the tariff calculation to calculate the amount. Typically, the Company may draw upon such a letter of credit if the due date for an invoice has passed without payment or if a replacement letter of credit has not been delivered to replace an expiring or partially drawn letter of credit.[12] Failure to replace a letter of credit fully could result in addition of interest to the invoice until such time as the letter of credit is fully restored.

Article X—Liability And Indemnification

These provisions state that neither party shall be liable to the other for damages, except as specified. The Article also requires for each party to indemnify the other for losses resulting from negligent acts of the indemnifying party, except to the extent that (1) such losses are caused by any act of the indemnified party and (2) the indemnified parties are compensated by insurance or specified agreement. The parties may also agree not to assert claims for indemnification until the aggregate amount of all claims exceed a minimum amount. The indemnity provisions will generally provide the indemnifying party with the option to assume and control the defense of claims for which the indemnifying party acknowledges its obligation to provide indemnification.

Article XI—Force Majeure

Treatment of force majeure in PPAs is highly contentious and many approaches have been used. A PPA should clearly classify force majeure events, specifying the impact of each event on the obligations of the parties, in particular on the payment obligations of the Purchaser and the construction, completion, and operational obligations of the Company. The parties might consider the following approach:

11.1 Categories. An event of force majeure is any event that prevents any party in the performance of its obligations under the PPA, but only to the extent that the events are not within the reasonable control of the affected party and could not have been avoided with reasonable care. A nonexhaustive list includes:

(1) *Specified nonpolitical events:* such as natural disasters, labor difficulties, and contractor failure;[13]

(2) *Domestic political events,* including war, revolution, terrorism, political sabotage, changes in the law affecting the project, expropriation, unjustified denials of governmental authorization, and certain interruptions in fuel supply (if fuel risk is borne by the utility);[14]

(3) *Foreign political events,* including generally the same events in category (2) but occurring outside the country concerned.

Generally, the following conditions shall not constitute an event of force majeure unless the existence of such condition is the result of an event of force majeure:

a. late delivery of plant, machinery, equipment, materials, spare parts or consumables for the project, or

b. a delay in the performance of any contractor.

11.2 Notices/duty to mitigate. This provides procedures for notification by the party claiming force majeure to the other party and imposes a duty on the party affected by the force majeure to use reasonable efforts to mitigate the effects of the force majeure.

11.3 Effect on obligations. The Article provides that neither party shall be liable for any failures in complying with its obligations under the PPA (though the obligation to make payments which are payable should be excluded) if the failure was caused by force majeure events.[15] The period allowed for performance by the affected party of its obligations under the PPA is extended day-for-day (plus additional periods to compensate for demobilization and remobilization).

11.4 Buyout consequences of force majeure events. If the construction or operation of the plant is adversely affected, for a certain continuous period, due to the occurrence of a domestic political event, either party can deliver a notice to the other party and, subject to dispute resolution procedures and time limits, terminate the PPA. Upon termination, the Purchaser will be obligated to buy out the project (see Article V).

Article XII—Taxes

Taxes are generally passed through to the Purchaser under the tariff. In addition, there should be provisions addressing administrative matters relating to taxes, including requirements for the Purchaser to support all applications by the Company for exemptions from domestic taxes and an obligation on the part of the Company to take reasonable steps to ensure that its liability on taxes is minimized, and procedures for resolving any dispute of claims by the Company for a payment in respect of taxes under the tariff provisions.[16]

Article XIII—Change In Law

The PPA should address the impact on the tariff in the event of a change in applicable law or its interpretation that affects the Company. "Applicable law" is frequently defined to include any act, decree, regulation, notification, or order having the force of law. "Change in law" is defined to include any new enactment, amendment, modification, or repeal of any applicable law as well as any change in the interpretation of the applicable law (either through decisions by courts or by government). Some PPAs in such circumstances have required an automatic adjustment of the tariff, subject to the approval of the regulatory agencies; other PPAs may require that the parties meet to attempt to amend the PPA to pass on the impact in the tariff payment. In the absence of agreement, the dispute resolution procedures in the PPA would apply. While various approaches to the allocation of risk of change in law are taken in PPAs, lenders will require that the cash flows of a project required for debt service be protected against such changes through tariff modifications.

Article XIV—Dispute Resolution

Dispute resolution provisions should generally provide for good faith negotiations followed by arbitration under internationally accepted rules in a third country.[17] The provision should specify the applicable rules, the number of arbitrators, the place of arbitration, the language of the arbitration proceedings, the nature and enforceability of the award, and the appointing and administrating authority. In addition to arbitration, the PPA may also allow referral of technical matters to an expert for quicker resolution.

Article XV—Notices

This Article sets forth the details for providing notices under the PPA, as well as provisions for changing notice addresses for the parties.

Article XVI—Miscellaneous

These may include an assignment provision restricting assignment by either party to the PPA. Lenders will generally require that the Company assign its rights under the PPA to lenders and that the Purchaser enter into a direct agreement with the lenders relating to such assignment and certain other issues. The Purchaser or the regulatory agencies may wish to provide for an assignment of the PPA to an entity that results from future privatization of the Purchaser. Because of concerns for the privatized entity's operational criteria and credit-worthiness, lenders often attempt to spell out the operational and financial parameters of the privatized entity in hopes of ensuring that the Purchaser's payment obligations under the PPA will be properly assumed and performed. The miscellaneous provisions should also address the governing law of the agreement, a severability clause, a waiver of immunity by the Purchaser, and confidentiality provisions.

Sample Annexes/Schedules

Permits and authorizations
Technical limits and parameters
Interconnection
Commissioning and testing specifications
Metering standards and testing
Buyout price
Insurance

Determination of availability
Outages and emergencies
Tariff calculations

Notes

1. International Finance Corporation. 1996. Financing Private Infrastructure. Washington, D.C., pp. 118–26.

2. The commercial operation date is often based on the financial closing date and should be extended by delays caused by the Purchaser's breach of obligations and certain force majeure events.

3. Fixed charges in a two-part tariff usually include all fixed costs associated with the project, including fixed O&M costs, insurance costs, administrative costs, financial costs, taxes, and return on equity. (The fixed component of fuel transport charges may also be included.) It could be expressed in local currency and/or foreign currency.

4. The energy charge is also known as the "variable charge" and may include variable operating and maintenance costs.

5. Third-party sales also promote the interchange of power, the expansion of transmission systems, and improve overall system efficiency. All such direct sales could be interruptable by the Purchaser, unless the Purchaser notifies the Company of a reduction in the Purchaser's system demand for an extended duration. In such a case, the Company could contract to make its excess capacity available for the corresponding duration.

6. Lenders often require the Company to engage an independent engineer to report on construction progress and to provide certification on construction, testing (usually a condition of loan disbursement), and operations. Sometimes the independent engineer also mediates technical disputes between the parties.

7. If liquidated damages are imposed, they should reflect the actual damages expected to be suffered by the Purchaser (for example, in respect of its outlay on the interconnection and transmission facilities).

8. Such obligations include, for the Company, using its best efforts to achieve financial closing, to obtain consents and approvals, to conduct preliminary studies and the like, and, for the Purchaser, the transfer of title to the site, obtaining consents and approvals and assisting the Company in doing the same.

9. The lenders will expect to enter into a direct contractual relationship with the Purchaser, whereby the Purchaser agrees (i) to make payments to the Company directly into an account designated by the lenders without right of credit or right of set-off; (ii) to provide to the lenders reasonable notice and cure

rights; (iii) to accept in the event of a default, as a substitute for the Company under the PPA, any reasonable agent for the lenders or any reasonable Purchaser of the Company upon a foreclosure sale, provided that such person shall assume all of the Company's obligations under the PPA; and (iv) to afford the lenders an opportunity to remedy the event giving rise to a termination notice prior to termination of the PPA. Also, it may be necessary to negotiate with the Purchaser further provisions to address issues of concern to the lenders arising after the PPA is signed.

10. Lenders will focus on fuel supply risks and how such risks should be managed and mitigated. They will consider the reliability and credit of the fuel supplier, the adequacy of the fuel source, the existence of an alternative fuel supplier, the consequences of non-supply (for example, whether this should be a force majeure event under the PPA), and also transportation, storage, and disposal risks. The liquidated damages payable under the fuel supply agreement will also be relevant. Finally, lenders may investigate whether fuel or alternate fuel could be imported into the country.

11. Lenders will generally require that payments of invoices be made directly to an account controlled by a trustee or security agent or over which the lenders hold some form of security.

12. Some PPAs look to the establishment of escrow accounts funded by the Purchaser's receivables (or liens over such receivables) from specified customers for additional liquidity security.

13. To the extent that insurance is available at a reasonable cost to cover the occurrence of any of the natural events, the Company will be asked to undertake to insure against such risks.

14. Lenders will also examine whether the force majeure arrangement under the fuel supply agreement is properly reflected in the force majeure section of the PPA, in order to leave no gap in the allocation of fuel risks. If, for example, the fuel supplier will be excused from its obligation to supply fuel under the fuel supply agreement due to government actions, the lenders are likely to require that the unavailability of fuel be a political force majeure event for the Company in the PPA.

15. Although the occurrence of a force majeure event may prevent a payment obligation from arising, once a sum does become payable, the payment obligation will not be excused by force majeure.

16. The developers will also be considering the tax implications under their home tax regime.

17. The most often used arbitration rules are those of the International Chamber of Commerce (ICC) and the United Nations Commission on International Trade Law (UNCITRAL). Depending on the parties involved in a dispute, the arbitration rules under the Convention on the Settlement of Investment Disputes between States and Nationals of Other States (through the International Centre for Settlement of Investment Disputes—ICSID) may also be suitable.

ANNEX 3

Organization of American States Members of ICSID, New York, and Panama Conventions

Country	ICSID Convention	New York Convention	Panama Convention
Antigua & Barbuda		X	
Argentina	X	X	X
Bahamas, The	X		
Barbados	X	X	
Belize	*		
Bolivia	X	X	*
Brazil			X
Canada		X	
Chile	X	X	X
Colombia	*	X	X
Costa Rica	X	X	X
Cuba		X	
Dominica		X	
Dominican Republic			*
Ecuador	X	X	X
El Salvador	X	*	X
Grenada	X		
Guatemala	*	X	X
Guyana	X		
Haiti	*	X	
Honduras	X		X
Jamaica	X		
Mexico		X	X
Nicaragua	X		*
Panama	X	X	X
Paraguay	X		X
Peru	X	X	X
St. Kitts & Nevis	X		
St. Lucia			
St. Vincent & the Grenadines	X		
Suriname			
Trinidad & Tobago	X	X	
United States	X	X	X
Uruguay	*	X	X
Venezuela	X	X	X
Total parties/members			
OAS (35)	21	20	16
Global	126	108	16

X denotes parties/members of conventions.
* denotes signatories.
Note: Members of the ICSID and New York Conventions as of April 1, 1997, and of the Panama Convention as of December 19, 1996.
Source: World Bank staff.

ANNEX 4

Lenders' Security Rights

Limited or nonrecourse transactions are typically characterized by the establishment of a special-purpose entity, whereby lenders look to the cash flow and assets of the project company to secure repayment of their loans. A lender's security package consists of a variety of collateral rights pertaining to these assets and cash flow. The various elements commonly included in such packages are listed in the box below.

As defined in the intercreditor agreement, the security package is typically shared pro rata between senior lenders of each individual debt tranche as well as with any currency, interest rate, or commodity swap parties. However, depending on the project's financial structure, some lenders/investors may be subordinated to others regarding security interests in project cash flow and/or assets. Likewise, it is not uncommon for offtake parties, which provide fixed or front-end loaded payments (payments that are expected to be above market), or input providers, which provide their goods at below-market prices, to receive a second lien on project assets. Under such circumstances senior debt providers will have priority with respect to subordinate lenders or third-party contractual participants over project cash flow and/or any proceeds from the liquidation or transfer

---

Annex Box 4.1 Lenders' Security Packages

A lender's security package quite often consists of the following components:
- A first security interest in the borrower's interest on project assets, including a mortgage or fixed charges (that is, charges relating to specific assets without the possibility of substitution) over land, buildings, and other fixed assets.
- Floating charges over moveable assets, including project inventory and receivables, production/work in progress, intangibles, and other personal property and interests.
- A pledge of the shareholders' equity participation in the borrower, including charge over dividend rights.
- Escrow accounts to control and, when necessary, retain cash flow relating to the project, including all monies owing or pending under, for example, the operating, debt service

reserve, and major overhaul account.
- A pledge of the borrower's interest in the major project agreements (for example, partnership/shareholder/joint venture, offtake, construction, input supply, operation and management, technical assistance), including, but not limited to, entitlement to payments, liquidated damages, indemnities, retainage accounts, performance bonds, insurance and brokerage undertakings, and warranty provisions specified under such agreements.
- Assignment of rights underlying major project authorizations, including licenses (such as environmental), permits (such as construction), notices, consents, acknowledgments, and endorsements.
- Specification of the lenders as loss payees on all insurance policies relating to the project.

Source: World Bank staff.

---

of any assets until their loans, pending interest and fee payments and any other costs (such as legal), are paid in full. Also, senior lenders will not allow subordinate lenders to accelerate their loans without their prior written consent.

Lenders will generally require a full collateral assignment of all rights of the borrower. In other words, they will want the right to "step into the shoes" of the borrower in a default situation and have the ability to perform the obligations of the borrower (including curing defaults) and enforce the right of the borrower to transfer the project agreements, in their entirety, to a new company that intends to acquire the project from the borrower. Lenders seek a full collateral assignment in order to bring in a new borrower who assumes the responsibilities and obligations as outlined in the concession agreement without assuming prior liabilities (tax, environment, labor), as would be the case with an assignment of the shares of the borrower. This effectively increases the net value of the concession as transferred/sold to a third party.

As such, lenders will require the parties to the project contracts other than the borrower to execute consents to the collateral assignments. This is required to establish between the lenders and these third-party contractual participants certain rights of the lenders with respect to the contract. This often includes the obligation of the contracted party to notify lenders in the case of a borrower breach/default under the contractual arrangements, lenders' rights (not obligation) to cure defaults by the borrower, lenders' ability to object to amendments or termination of the contract without their consent, and lenders rights to transfer the contract rights to new purchasers (subject to appropriate restrictions as to the qualification and financial capability of the purchasers).

Often, governmental counterparts are unwilling or unable, because of legal restrictions, to grant lenders full collateral rights and seek to limit the rights of lenders to project cash flows. But a collateral assignment limited to the borrower's rights to receive payment under a project agreement does not adequately protect the lenders' interests. Indeed, if the borrower is unable or unwilling to perform as stipulated under the project agreement, its right to receive payment will quickly cease through early termination clauses. In a financing situation in which lenders are providing the majority of the capital for a project on a limited-recourse basis, lenders insist on the right "to become the borrower" in every respect and to operate the project directly or through a transferee without further action. Solutions that have been devised to give satisfaction to lenders have included defining certain quantifiable criteria based on net worth, number of projects of similar size and technology, and so on, against which new "borrowers" would be evaluated or, in certain cases, formulation of lists of automatically approved third-party substitutes. It is in any case essential that lenders be sufficiently comfortable with the security package they are being offered and with the overall legal and regulatory environment in which the project company has to operate. Otherwise, projects will simply not be "bankable" and will not come to financial closure (annex box 4.2).

Annex Box 4.2 "Bankability" of Mexican Power Projects

Under the Carbon II power project a BOT contract for a multiunit, coal-fired plant was awarded to Mission Energy. However, the government refused to give commercial lenders step-in rights and other security interests in the project, which was thus unable to secure financing. The deal eventually fell through over these issues and other disputed matters.

Since then, financing has been closed on the first privately built power plant in Mexico, Samalayuca II,

under a Build-Lease-Transfer (BLT) contract. A BOT contract for the Merida III project was awarded in January 1997. In addition to the passage of a new electricity law and creation of an energy regulator, Mexico has actively sought to encourage private financing for independent power projects by improving the environment for project lenders, including through changes in the Civil Code that facilitate bankruptcy procedures.

Source: World Bank staff.

In addition to payment defaults and remedies allowed for under such circumstances, lenders will also seek to further protect repayment of their loans through:

- The imposition of covenants, both positive (maintaining certain debt-equity and working capital ratios and reporting requirements) and negative (not incurring any additional indebtedness above certain amounts, or not amending or terminating any major project agreement without prior lender consent). Should the borrower not comply with the stated covenants beyond a pre-established cure period (which can vary from 0 to 5 days for payment defaults to more than 180 days for technical problems arising from force majeure events), then, as with a payment default, lenders have the right to declare an event of default, accelerate in full their loans, and exercise any and all of their collateral rights.
- Inclusion of contingent restrictions on dividend distributions should, for example, the borrower not achieve certain debt service coverage ratios. In certain cases, if the borrower falls below the required ratio for an extended period of time (for example, two consecutive quarters), "trapped" cash flow may be applied to prepay debt in inverse order of maturity.
- Lenders will also have certain approval rights, as related, for example, to operating and capital expenditure budgets (approval could be automatic if not above the expected rate of inflation), construction change orders above certain amounts, and the sale or transfer of borrower equity to third parties.
- Likewise, lenders will look to secure their ability to sell off or assign participations in their loans to other debt providers. Issues related to permitted timing of such sale or assignment, minimum amounts to be held by the originating lenders, participating bank voting rights with respect to the borrower, and so on will be outlined in the credit agreement.

Finally, quite often because of problems with registration, perfection, and enforcement of collateral rights, many projects never make it to financial closing (annex box 4.3).

Annex Box 4.3 Legal and Regulatory Issues in Securing Transactions

While collateral is of key importance in enabling private lenders to offer loans and reduce interest rates, legal and regulatory impediments in some countries make it difficult for the lenders to acquire collateral interests. These obstacles are related to the creation, perfection, and enforcement of lenders' security interests in a project.

In order to create a security interest, the collateral pledged must be identified. In some systems, for example in Uruguay, the law requires that the physical property be specifically enumerated and determined, and no substitution is permissible. This creates difficulties and expense in monitoring the loan to ensure that the specified property has not been exchanged or sold. In the United States, by contrast, lenders can obtain a floating security interest for the value of the property rather than identified physical assets and can automatically get a continuing security interest in the proceeds of any sale of the property.

The perfection of a security interest involves obtaining an assurance that no prior superior claims exist on the offered collateral. However, lenders often encounter difficulties in checking which liens may be outstanding on project collateral because of the state of disarray of many public registries. In Bolivia, for example, pledges are filed chronologically, rather than under the name of the borrower or a description of the pledged asset, so that the entire registry must be searched to discover a prior pledge. In addition, there may be unclear procedures for registering government pledges or support agreements to projects. These conditions can result in high transaction costs, including notary costs, relating to the perfection of the lenders' rights.

Enforcement of a security interest involves the ability of the lender to repossess and sell the collateral. In some systems, where private parties and government officials cannot contract to repossess property, this requires a lengthy legal process. In addition, the lenders may not be permitted to attach other property of the borrower, such as proceeds from the sale of collateral.

Source: Fleisig (1995).

ANNEX 5

Investment Insurance Programs

	MIGA	Germany (C&L Deutsche Revision AG)	Japan (EID/MITI)	United States (OPIC)
Eligible investments	New (including expansion, modernization, financial restructuring of existing projects).	New (including expansion and modernization of existing projects).	New (including expansion and modernization of existing projects).	New (including privatization, expansion, and modernization of existing projects).
	Must promote economic growth and development in the host country, be financially, economically, and environmentally sound.	Must be sufficiently legally protected, for example, under a bilateral protection agreement, intensify and foster the relationship with the host country.		Must demonstrate a potential for positive effects on U.S. employment and economy, be environmentally sound, promise significant benefits to the social and economic development of the host country; must not contribute to violations of internationally recognized worker rights.
Types/Forms of Investment	Equity, shareholder loans, shareholder guarantees of third-party loans; loans to unrelated borrowers (project lending); leases, contractual arrangements (licensing, franchising, technical assistance, and management agreements)—minimum 3 years.	Equity investment (shares in foreign enterprises). Loan of an investment type (long-term loan)—shareholder loans or loans to unrelated borrowers (project lending). Capital provided to an overseas branch.	Equity, loans, property rights, surety obligations.	Equity, loans to unrelated borrowers, third-party loan guarantees; construction and service contracts, production-sharing agreements, leases, contractual arrangements (licensing, franchising, technical assistance agreements)—minimum 3 years.

	MIGA	Germany (C&L Deutsche Revision AG)	Japan (EID/MITI)	United States (OPIC)
	Cash, machinery and equipment, consigned inventory, debt-equity swaps, reinvested earnings.	Cash, machinery and equipment, services, licenses, debt-equity swaps, reinvested earnings.		Cash, machinery and equipment, consigned inventory, debt-equity swaps.
Eligible Investors	Natural or juridical person who is a national of a MIGA member country other than host country, or juridical person not incorporated or domiciled in a member country but majority-owned by nationals of MIGA member countries.	German citizens and corporations established under German law and domiciled in Germany.	Japanese citizens and corporations or other institutions established under Japanese law. Domestic investor could be majority-owned by foreign individuals.	Citizens of the United States, corporations, partnerships, other associations created under U.S. law and owned more than 50 percent by U.S. citizens, foreign corporations owned at least 95 percent by U.S. citizens, corporations, and the like.
Eligible Countries	Developing member countries as host countries and industrialized and developing countries as countries of investor.	Host country that ensures the legal protection of the investment, for example, by means of a bilateral investment protection agreement.	Host country's legal system must adequately provide for foreign investment inflows (existence of bilateral agreements not required).	With some exceptions, no insurance if host country's income per capita exceeds US$4,269 (1986); bilateral agreements must exist.
	Host country's approval for the issuance of a MIGA guarantee contract is required.	Some bilateral investment protection agreements require the host country's approval on the investment to be guaranteed as a prerequisite for the applicability of the bilateral agreement, some require a simple notification (or not	Host country's approval for the issuance of a guarantee contract is required.	A Foreign Government Approval (FGA) process is required, which varies, depending on the host country.

(table continues on next page)

Investment Insurance Programs (continued)

	MIGA	Germany (C&L Deutsche Revision AG)	Japan (EID/MITI)	United States (OPIC)
		even this) to the host country.		
Risks covered	Political risks only.	Political risks only.	Political and commercial risks.	Political risks only.
a) Inconvertibility/ nontransfer	Acts that restrict the investor's or lender's ability to convert local currency returns into foreign exchange for transfer outside the host country for more than 90 days.	Acts that restrict the investor's ability to convert amounts paid into a bank account and/or the transfer of such amount to Germany for more than 60 days. In addition: payment prohibition or moratorium.	Acts that restrict the investor's or lender's ability to repatriate funds for more than 60 days.	Acts such as new currency restrictions or failure by exchange control authorities to act on an application for hard currency for more than 60 days (in some cases more than 90 days).
b) Political violence	Damage to, or destruction or disappearance of, tangible assets caused by politically motivated acts of war or civil disturbance, including revolution, insurrection, coups d'etat, sabotage, and terrorism.	Total loss of whole of the investment due to actions such as civil disturbance, war, domestic armed conflicts, revolution, or riots.	Occurrences such as: • Inability to continue business • Bankruptcy or some other reason of similar nature • Suspension of transaction by the bank or some other reason of similar nature • Suspension of business for a period exceeding 6 months attributable to war, revolution, civil war, riot, or civil disturbance.	Two types of loss compensation coverage are available: • Business income coverage • Assets coverage due to war, revolution, insurrection, or politically motivated civil strife, terrorism, and sabotage. Actions undertaken to achieve labor or student objectives are not covered.
c) Expropriation	Partial or total loss of insured investment as a result of acts by host government (outright nationalization and confiscation) causing reduction or elimination of	Total loss of parts or whole of the investment due to nationalization, expropriation, or other events of interventions or noninterventions by	Total loss of insured investment as a result of acts that deprive the investor of the investment by the host government. Creeping expropriation is covered	Total loss of the investment due to acts that i) are attributable to the foreign governing authority, ii) violate international law, iii) deprive the

	MIGA	Germany (C&L Deutsche Revision AG)	Japan (EID/MITI)	United States (OPIC)
	ownership of, or control over, rights to the insured investment and continuing for 1 year. Creeping expropriation is covered if a series of acts, over time, have an expropriatory effect.	the host government whose effects are similar to an expropriation. Creeping expropriation covered if the series of events have the same effect of an expropriation (and lead to a total loss of the investment).	where the insured has objectively assessed an infringement by the host government.	investor of fundamental rights, iv) continue for 6 months. Actions that lead to creeping expropriation such as outright nationalization arising from decrees or a series of events that have the same effect of an expropriation are covered.
		Lawful actions by the host government (exercise of regulatory authority) are not covered.		Coverage excludes losses due to lawful regulatory or revenue actions by the host governments.
d) Breach of contract	Protects against losses arising from the host government's breach or repudiation of a contract with the investor. In the event of an alleged breach or repudiation, the investor must be able to invoke an arbitration clause in the underlying contract and obtain an award for damages. If the investor has not received payment, MIGA will compensate.	Breach of commitments by the host government or government-controlled entities of a contractual (bilateral) or noncontractual (unilateral) obligation is covered if it is politically motivated. The bi- or unilateral "commitments" must be stated in the guarantee document.	Breach by the host government of a contractual obligation is covered. Suspension of the insured business operations has to occur for more than 6 months.	In some cases OPIC may cover the breach by the host government of a contractual obligation if it meets the requirements for expropriation (total loss) and either i) the insured must have successfully demonstrated that the actions could not have been justified under the terms of the underlying commercial arrangement, or ii) the failure to perform must be the subject of an arbitral award in favor of the investor that remains unpaid for a period of 3 months.
Commercial insolvency			Bankruptcy of the party in which the insured investment was made and which	

(table continues on next page)

Investment Insurance Programs (continued)

	MIGA	Germany (C&L Deutsche Revision AG)	Japan (EID/MITI)	United States (OPIC)
			cannot be imputed to the insured.	
Scope of Coverage **a) Duration**	Minimum 3 years and maximum 15 years for equity (20 years under certain circumstances). For loans, leases, and transactions the term is generally equal to the duration of the under-lying contract or agreement.	Up to 15 years, with gradual roll-overs of 5 years.	Minimum 3 years and up to 15 years, with possible extension for projects with long construction periods.	Maximum 20 years (equity). For loans, leases, and transactions the term is generally equal to the duration of the underlying contract or agreement.
b) Limits/ ceilings	Maximum amount of coverage for a single project is US$50 million. Maximum coverage ratio of debt (to unrelated borrowers) to shareholder invest-ment in the same project is 6:1. Country ceiling US$225 million per country.	No written limits of coverage or country ceiling restrictions (case-by-case).	Per-project limit is 50 billion Yen. No country ceilings.	Maximum amount of political risk insurance for a single project is US$200 million. No country ceiling but per-country exposure is limited to 15 percent of global portfolio.
c) Maximum percentage of coverage	Although to date MIGA has maintained a 90 percent limit, it can insure up to 95 percent of the invest-ment. For equity investments: up to 95 percent of invest-ment and up to an additional 450 percent to cover future earnings. For loans and loan guarantees: up to 95 percent of principal and up to an additional 150 percent of the principal for interest to accrue over the term of the loan. For technical assistance	Ninety-five percent. Earnings are eligible up to 10 percent per year, but limited to a maximum of 50 percent on the value of the equity/capital investment and 100 percent of the shareholder loans; if reserves are transferred into shares, the coverage can be increased to 300 percent of original investment.	Ninety-five percent for political and 40 percent for commercial risks. Ninety percent of earnings up to 10 percent of invested amount up to 100 percent of principal in total are insured.	Ninety percent of eligible invest-ment. Loans and leases from financial institutions to unrelated third parties may be insured for 100 percent of principal and interest.

	MIGA	Germany (C&L Deutsche Revision AG)	Japan (EID/MITI)	United States (OPIC)
	contracts, and the like: 95 percent of the total value of payments due.			
Risk premium	Premiums are determined on predefined "base rates" in relation to the type of industry such as: 1) Manufacturing and Services 2) Natural Resources (including agribusiness and forestry) 3) Oil and Gas/Infrastructure and the type of coverage (currency transfer, expropriation, breach of contract, war and civil disturbance) and range from 0.25 percent to 1.25 percent per year. No differentiation between equity and debt. Base rates may be adjusted depending on project's risk profile (economic and political conditions of host country). Application fee: US$5,000 investment< US$25million, US$10,000 investment >US$25million (fee is credited against first year's premium). Optional processing fee of US$25,000 depending on complexity of the project and/or the environmental sensitivity to cover unusual MIGA underwriting costs. Unused portion of the processing fee	For all types of coverage 0.5 percent per year on total insured amount. Handling fee 0.1 percent flat investment < DM10 million plus 0.05 percent flat for amounts exceeding DM10 million (capped to DM20,000).	Combined premium rate of 0.55 percent-1.75 percent per year (depending on host country)is charged for all risks.	Premiums are determined based on the characteristics of the coverage provided, the project, the host country, and the type of industry period. Base rates are defined in relation to the type of industry such as: 1) Manufacturing and Services 2) Institutional Loans and Leases 3) Oil and Gas 4) Natural Resources 5) Contractors and Exporters, and the type of coverage (inconvertibility, expropriation, political violence) and range from 0.20 percent to 1.50 percent per year. Base rates can be adjusted up or down by 30 percent, depending on the risk profile of the project.

(table continues on next page)

Investment Insurance Programs (continued)

	MIGA	Germany (C&L Deutsche Revision AG)	Japan (EID/MITI)	United States (OPIC)
	will be deducted from the first-year premium.			

Indeminification/ recovery: Inconvertibility/ nontransfer

	MIGA	Germany (C&L Deutsche Revision AG)	Japan (EID/MITI)	United States (OPIC)
	Compensation paid upon receipt of blocked local currency and in the currency stated in the guarantee contract.	Compensation is based on the gross amount of the loss of an investment. The gross amount of the loss on an investment is with respect to a participation or, in the event of total loss, the actual value of the investment at the time of the occurrence of the guarantee contingency but not more than the contribution value. With respect to partial loss, the decrease in value calculated as the difference between the actual value of the participation at the time of the occurrence of the guarantee contingency but not more than the contribution value on the one side and the residual value of the participation on the other. Compensation on the insured portion of earnings is paid on the payments of earnings outstanding.	Compensation is paid up to the insured amount limit (actual-loss) and based on the following formula: loss x 95 percent (political) < contracted insured amount < uncollected portion of total investment.	Compensation is paid on the basis of the prevailing rate of exchange for the blocked local currency.
	Recovery: Local currency to be transferred to MIGA or sold to World Bank or other international financial institutions.	Recovery: C & L Deutsche Revision AG may require the subrogation of rights to the investment.	Recovery: MITI may require the subrogation of rights to the investment.	Recovery: Local currency to be transferred to OPIC.

	MIGA	Germany (C&L Deutsche Revision AG)	Japan (EID/MITI)	United States (OPIC)
Political violence	Equity: compensation is paid on the lesser of the book value of the assets or the cost to repair or replace the damaged assets. Loans/ loan guarantees: compensation is paid on the insured portion of the principal and interest payments in default as a direct result of damage to the assets of the project.			1) Business Income Coverage: Compensation is based on what the project would have realized in net income but for the damage, plus the project's continuing, normal operating expenses, which must be paid during the time the damage is being repaired (renting a temporary facility is included). 2) Asset coverage: Compensation is based on the investor's share of the adjusted (least of the original cost of the item, fair market value at the time of loss, or the cost to repair the item) cost of the property or replacement cost. Replacement costs are paid up to twice the investor's share of the lost or damaged property's original cost, provided the property is replaced within 3 years.
	Recovery: Subrogation of any claims to MIGA			Recovery: Subrogation of any claims to OPIC.
Expropriation (including breach of contract)	Equity: Compensation is paid on the net book value of the insured investment. Loans/loan guarantees: compensation is paid on the outstanding principal and any accrued and unpaid interest on the loan.			Equity: Compensation is based on the book value of the investment. Loans/loan guarantees: compensation is based on outstanding principal and accrued interest.

(table continues on next page)

Investment Insurance Programs (continued)

	MIGA	Germany (C&L Deutsche Revision AG)	Japan (EID/MITI)	United States (OPIC)
	Recovery: Assignment to MIGA of the investor's or lender's right, title, and interest in the expropriated investment (for example, equity shares or loan agreement).			Recovery: Assignment of all rights, titles, claims, and so on, together with all securities evidencing the insured investment.
Waiting periods: Inconvertibility/ nontransfer	90 days	60 days	60 days	60–90 days plus (depending on host country).
Political violence	None (for direct physical damage); 365 days (if war/civil disturbance prevent the project from operating for at least 365 consecutive days).	None	None (unless suspension of business is concerned, which has to last for a period of 6 months).	Equity: None Debt: 1 month
Expropriation: (including breach of contract)	365 days 180 days for funds	None	None	Equity: 6 months Debt: 3 months
Dispute settlements between host country and the insured	Local or international court judgments/ arbitral awards not required if claim is valid. Except for breach of contract, the arbitral award must be be given by a local or international court, depending on the provision in the breached contract.	If claim is valid and came into existence without any objection, a court judgment is not required. In the case of any objection or unfair justice, the bilateral investment protection agreements provide for the investor or the federal government to choose immediate international arbitration.	Local or international court judgments/ arbitral awards not required if claim is valid.	Local or international court judgments/ arbitral awards not required for filing a claim. Except for breach of contract, arbitration under the dispute mechanism in the contractual arrangement is required.

Sources:
1. Responses to questionnaires, compiled by Anita Hellstern.
2. MIGA *Investment Guarantee Guide.*
3. MIGA *Financial Institution Guide,* second edition, February 1996.
4. *Allgemeine Bedingungen für die Übernahme von Garantien für Kapitalanlagen im Ausland* (Fassung November 1993).
5. *Merkblatt für die Übernahme von Bundesgarantien für Kapitalanlagen im Ausland* (Fassung November 1993).
6. *Trade and Investment Insurance in Japan,* EID/MITI; *Program Handbook,* OPIC.
7. Malcom D. Rowat, 1992, *"Multilateral Approaches to Improving the Investment Climate of Developing Countries: The Cases of ICSID and MIGA," Harvard International Law Journal* 33(1): 103–44.

References

Alexander, Ian, Colin Mayer, and Helen Weeds. 1996. "Regulatory Structure and Risk and Infrastructure Firms—An International Comparison." Policy Research Working Paper 1698. World Bank, Private Sector Development Department, Washington, D.C.

Amador, F.V. Garcia. 1992. "The Calvo Doctrine, Calvo Clause." In Rudolph Bernhardt, ed., *Encyclopedia of Public International Law*. New York: Max Planck Institute for Comparative Public Law and International Law.

American International Underwriters. 1997. "Building Toward the Future: Insuring Infrastructure Projects in the Next Millennium." http://aiu.aig.com/aiu/aiu24.htm#infra-broch.

Antonmattei, Paul-Henri. 1996. "Ouragan sur la Force Majeure." *Jurisclasseur Périodique II*, 3907.

Armstrong, Mark, Simon Cowan, and John Vickers. 1994. *Regulatory Reform—Economic Analysis and British Experience*. Cambridge, Mass: MIT Press.

Arrow, Kenneth J., and Robert C. Lind. 1970. "Uncertainty and the Evaluation of Public Investment Decisions." *American Economic Review* 60(3): 364–78.

Bauer, Johannes. 1996. "Principles of Cost-Based Regulation." Paper presented at the Latin American and Caribbean Department and International Finance Corporation joint seminar, September, World Bank, Washington, D.C.

Bezançon, Xavier. 1995. *Les Services Publics en France: Du Moyen Age à la Révolution*. Paris: Presses de l'école nationale des ponts et chaussées.

Bitran, E., and P. Serra. 1994. "Regulatory Issues in the Privatization of Public Utilities—The Chilean Experience." *Quarterly Review of Economics and Finance* 34(0), special issue: 179–97.

Broches, Aron. 1990. *Arbitration Under the ICSID Convention*. Washington, D.C.: International Centre for Settlement of Investment Disputes.

Brown, Stephen, and David Sibley. 1986. *The Theory of Public Utility Pricing*. New York: Cambridge University Press.

Cakmak, Zeynep. 1996. "Turkey's BOT Law: The Effects Of Amendments, Court Rulings." *Middle East Executive Report* 19(6): 8.

Carbajo, José, and Antonio Estache. 1996. "Railway Concessions—Heading Down the Right Track in Argentina." *Viewpoint 88*. World Bank, Finance and Private Sector Development Department, Washington, D.C.

Cavers, David, and James Nelson. 1959. *Electric Power Regulation in Latin America*. Baltimore: Johns Hopkins University Press.

Chadwick, Edwin. 1859. "Results of Different Principles of Legislation in Europe: of Competition for the Field as Compared with Competition within the Field of Service." *Journal of the Royal Statistical Society*, series A22, London.

De Laubadère, André, Jean-Claude Venezia, and Yves Gaudemet. 1995. *Traité de Droit Administratif*. Paris: Librairie Générale de Droit et de Jurisprudence, 13e edition.

Department of Treasury and Finance. 1994. *Infrastructure Investment Policy for Victoria*. State of Victoria, Australia.

———. 1996. *Investment Evaluation—Policy and Guidelines*. State of Victoria, Australia.

Dnes, Antony W. 1995. "Franchising and Privatization." *Viewpoint 40*. World Bank, Finance and Private Sector Development Department, Washington, D.C.

Ekelund, Robert B., and Robert F. Hébert. 1981. "The Proto-History of Franchise Bidding." *Southern Economic Journal* 48(2): 464–74.

Engel, Eduardo, Ronal Fischer, and Alexander Galetovic. 1996a. "Highway Franchising in Chile." Santiago: Universidad de Chile, Center for Applied Economics.

———. 1996b. "A New Method to Franchise Highways." Santiago: Universidad de Chile, Center for Applied Economics.

Escobar, Alejandro. 1997. ICSID Counsel. Personal communicaton, April.

Fishbein, Gregory, and Suman Babbar. 1996. *Private Financing of Toll Roads*. Resource Mobilization and Cofinancing (RMC) Discussion Paper Series 117. Washington, D.C.: World Bank.

Fleisig, Heywood. 1995. "The Power of Collateral: How Problems in Securing Transactions Limit Private Credit for Movable Property." *Viewpoint 43*. World Bank, Finance and Private Sector Development Department, Washington, D.C.

Folsom, Ralph, and Minan. 1991. "The Chinese Legal System: Reform and Conflict Since the Cultural Revolution." In Ralph H.Folsom, Michael W. Gordon, and John A. Spanogle, Jr. eds., *International Business Transactions*. St. Paul: West Publishing Co.

Folsom, Ralph H., Michael W. Gordon, and John A. Spanogle, Jr. 1991. *International Business Transactions*. St. Paul: West Publishing Co.

Foreman-Peck, James, and Robert Millward. 1994. *Public and Private Ownership of British Industry, 1820–1990*. Oxford: Clarendon Press.

Fouchard, Philippe, Emmanuel Gaillard, and Berthold Goldman. 1996. *Traité de l'arbitrage commercial international*. Paris: Editions Litec.

Freshfields. 1995. *Project Finance*. Third edition.

Glynn, D.R. 1992. "The Mechanisms of Price Control." *Utilities Policy* 2 (April): 90–99.

Guislain, Pierre. 1997. *The Privatization Challenge: A Strategic, Legal, and Institutional Analysis of International Experience*. Washington, D.C.: World Bank.

Guislain, Pierre, and Michel Kerf. 1995. "Concessions—The Way to Privatize Infrastructure Sector Monopolies." *Viewpoint 59*. World Bank, Finance and Private Sector Development Department, Washington, D.C.

Helm, Dieter. 1994. "British Utility Regulation: Theory, Practice and Reform." *Oxford Review of Economic Policy* 10: 17–39.

Her Majesty's Treasury. 1994. *Competition and the Private Finance Initiative: Guidance for Departments*. London: Private Finance Panel.

———. 1995. *Private Opportunity, Public Benefit: Progressing the Private Finance Initiative*. London: Private Finance Panel.

———. 1996. *Private Finance Initiative: Guidelines for Smoothing the Procurement Process*. London: Private Finance Panel.

ICSID (International Centre for Settlement of Investment Disputes). 1965. *Convention on the Settlement of Investment Disputes Between States and Nationals of Other States*. Washington, D.C.: World Bank.

———. 1996. ICSID Cases. Doc. ICSID/16/Rev. 5 November 30, as revised at March 1997. Washington, D.C.

IFC (International Finance Corporation). 1996. *Financing Private Infrastructure*. Washington D.C.

Inter Press Service. 1997. "World Bank Head Turns Up Heat on Energy Scandal." February 25.

Irwin, Timothy. 1997. "Price Structures, Cross-Subsidies, and Competition in Infrastructure." *Viewpoint 107*. World Bank, Finance and Private Sector Development Department, Washington, D.C.

Jacobson, Charles D., and Joel A. Tarr. 1995. "Ownership and Financing of Infrastructure: Historical Perspectives." Policy Research Working Paper 1466. World Bank, Office of the Vice President Development Economics, Washington, D.C.

Kerf, Michel, and Warrick Smith. 1996. *Privatizing Africa's Infrastructure: Promise and Challenge*. Technical Paper 337. Washington D.C.: World Bank.

Kholi, Harinder, Ashoka Mody, and Michael Walton. 1996. "Frontiers of the Public-Private Interface in East Asia's Infrastructure." Report on a high-level conference held in Jakarta, Indonesia. World Bank, Washington, D.C.

Klein, Michael. 1996a. "Economic Regulation of Water Companies." Policy Research Working Paper 1649. Private Sector Development Department, World Bank, Washington, D.C.

———. 1996b. "Managing Guarantee Programs in Support of Infrastructure Investments." World Bank, Private Sector Development Department, Washington, D.C.

———. 1996c. "Risks, Taxpayers and the Role of Government in Project Finance." Policy Research Working Paper 1688. World Bank, Private Sector Development Department, Washington, D.C.

Klein, Michael, and Neil D. Roger. 1994. "Back to the Future: the Potential in Infrastructure Privatisation." In Richard O'Brien, ed., *Finance and the International Economy*. New York: Oxford University Press.

Klein, Michael, and Warrick Smith. 1994. "Infrastructure Regulation: Issues and Options for East Asia." World Bank Private Sector Development Department, Washington, D.C.

Klein, Michael, Jae So, and Ben Shin. 1996. "Transaction Costs in Private Infrastructure Projects—Are They Too High?" *Viewpoint 95*. World Bank, Finance and Private Sector Development Department, Washington, D.C.

Kwoka, John E. 1996. "Privatization, Deregulation, and Competition: A Survey of Effects on Economic Performance." Private Sector Development Department Occasional Paper 27. World Bank, Washington, D.C.

Laffont, Jean-Jacques, and Jean Tirole. 1993. *A Theory of Incentives in Procurement and Regulation.* Cambridge, Mass.: MIT Press.

Levy, Brian, and Pablo T. Spiller. 1993. "Regulation, Institutions, and Commitment in Telecommunications: A Comparative Analysis of Five Country Studies." In Michael Bruno and Boris Pleskovic, eds., *Proceedings of the World Bank Annual Conference on Development Economics 1993.* Washington, D.C.: World Bank.

Lewis, Christopher M., and Ashoka Mody. 1997. "The Management of Contingent Liabilities: A Risk Management Framework for National Governments." In Timothy Irwin, Michael Klein, Guillermo W. Perry, and Mateen Thobani, eds., *Dealing with Public Risk in Private Infrastructure.* Washington, D.C.: World Bank.

Mandelker, Jeannie. 1996. "The Change in Power." *Infrastructure Finance.* 5(7): 11–16.

McAfee, R. Preston, and John McMillan. 1988. *Incentives in Government Contracting.* Toronto: University of Toronto Press.

McConnaughay. 1995. "Dispute Resolution." Thomas A. Pyle, ed., *The Life and Death of an Infrastructure Project.* Hong Kong: Asia Law and Practice Ltd.

McMillan, John. 1992. *Games, Strategies, and Managers.* New York: Oxford University Press.

———. 1994. "Selling Spectrum Rights." *Journal of Economic Perspectives* 8(3): 145–62.

Milgrom, Paul, and John Roberts. 1992. *Economics, Organization and Management.* Englewood Cliffs, New Jersey: Prentice Hall.

Mitchell, Brigitta, and Karim-Jacques Budin. 1997. "The Abidjan-Ougadougou Railway Concession." *Infrastructure Notes, Transport RW-14.* World Bank, Transport, Water, and Urban Development Department, Washington, D.C.

Mody, Ashoka, and Dilip Patro. 1995. *Methods of Loan Guarantee Valuation and Accounting.* Cofinancing and Financial Advisory Services (CFS) Discussion Paper 116. Washington, D.C.: World Bank.

Myers, James J. 1996. "Developing Methods for Resolving Disputes in World-Wide Infrastructure Projects." *Journal of International Arbitration* 13(4): 101.

Nelson, Steven C. 1989. "Alternatives to Litigation of International Disputes." *International Lawyer* 23(Spring): 187–206.

Nevitt, Peter K. 1989. *Project Financing.* London:

Euromoney Publications PLC.

OECD (Organisation for Economic Co-operation and Development). 1987. *Pricing Water Services.* Paris.

OFWAT (Office of the Water Services). April 5, 1997. http://www.open.gov.uk:80/ofwat.

Oxford Analytica. 1996. *Latin America Daily Brief.* "Ecuador: Water Provision." August 21.

———. 1997. *Asia Pacific Daily Brief.* "Dams Controversy." March 26.

Parra, Antonio. 1996. "ICSID and the Americas." ICSID presentation September 2–3, Costa Rica.

Paulsson, Jaul. 1996. "Dispute Resolution." In Robert Pritchard, ed., *Economic Development, Foreign Investment and the Law: Issues of Private Sector Involvement, Foreign Investment and the Rule of Law in a New Era.* International Bar Association Series. Boston: Kluwer Law International and International Bar Associaton.

Peters, Paul, and Nico Schrijver. 1992. "Latin America and International Regulation of Foreign Investment: Changing Perceptions." *Netherlands International Law Review.* XXXIX: 355–83.

Petrei, A. Humberto. 1987. *El Gasto Público Social y sus Efectos Distributivos.* Rio de Janeiro: Estudios Conjuntos de Integração Econômica da America Latina.

Pritchard, Robert, ed. 1996. *Economic Development, Foreign Investment and the Law: Issues of Private Sector Involvement, Foreign Investment and the Rule of Law in a New Era.* International Bar Association Series. Boston: Kluwer Law International and International Bar Associaton.

Pyle, Thomas A., ed. 1995. *The Life and Death of an Infrastructure Project.* Hong Kong: Asia Law and Practice Ltd.

Redfern, Alan, and Martin Hunter. 1991. *Law and Practice of International Commercial Arbitration.* Second edition. London: Sweet & Maxwell.

Republic of the Philippines. 1994. Implementing Rules and Regulations of R.A. No. 6957, "An Act Authorizing the Financing, Construction, Operation and Maintenance of Infrastructure Projects by the Private Sector and for Other Purposes," as Amended by R.A. No. 7718.

République Française. 1980. *Décret du 17 mars 1980 portant approbation d'un cahier des charges type pour l'exploitation par affermage d'un service de distribution publique d'eau potable.* Paris.

Reynolds, Lloyd G. 1985. *Economic Growth in the Third World, 1850–1980.* New Haven: Yale University Press.

Rivera, Daniel. 1996. *Private Sector Participation in the Water Supply and Wastewater Sector—Lessons from Six Developing Countries.* Washington, D.C.: World Bank.

Shaikh, Hafeez, and Maziar Minovi. 1995. *Management Contracts: A Review of International Experience.* Cofinancing and Financial Advisory Services (CFS) Discussion Paper Series 108. Washington, D.C.: World Bank.

Siebert, Horst, and Michael J. Koop. 1993. "Institutional Competition versus Centralization: Quo Vadis Europe?" *Oxford Review of Economic Policy* 9(spring): 15–30.

Skadden Arps Slate Meagher and Flom. 1996. *Project Finance, Selected Issues in Choice of Law.* London: Euromoney Publications PLC.

Smith, Warrick, and Ben Shin. 1995a. "Regulating Brazil's Infrastructure—Perspectives on Decentralization." Latin American and the Caribbean Economic Notes 6. World Bank, Washington, D.C.

———. 1995b. "Regulating Infrastructure—Funding Regulatory Agencies." Latin American and the Caribbean Economic Notes 5. World Bank, Washington, D.C.

St.-John-Needham, Virginia. 1994. "The Law of the Land." *Latin Finance* December.

Stewart-Smith, Martin. 1995. "Industry Structure and Regulation." Policy Research Working Paper 1419. World Bank Legal Department, Legal Reform and Private Sector Development Unit, Washington, D.C.

Train, Kenneth E. 1991. *Optimal Regulation: The Economic Theory of Natural Monopoly.* Cambridge, Mass.: MIT Press.

White and Case. 1995. "Memorandum to IFC on China."

Wilson III, William A., Stuart Solsky, and Nicholai J. Sarad. 1997. "Private Power Momentum." *Independent Energy* March 27(2): 34.

World Bank. 1989. "Environmental Assessment." *Operational Manual.* Operational Directive 4.00-Annex A, A1, A2, A3. Washington, D.C.

———. 1990. "Involuntary Resettlement." *Operational Manual.* Operational Directive 4.30. Washington, D.C.

———. 1995. "Bureaucrats in Business." Policy Research Report. Washington, D.C.

———. 1996. "Procurement for Private Infrastructure Projects." Washington, D.C.

———. 1997. "What a Private Sector Participation Arrangement Should Cover." In *Toolkits for Private Participation in Water and Sanitation.* Washington D.C.

Ziadé, Nassib G. 1996. "ICSID Conciliation." *News from ICSID* 13(2): 3–8.

Zupan, Mark A. 1989. "The Efficacy of Franchise Bidding Schemes in the Case of Cable Television: Some Systematic Evidence." *Journal of Law and Economics* 32(2): 401–56.

Distributors of World Bank Publications

Prices and credit terms vary from country to country. Consult your local distributor before placing an order.

ARGENTINA
Oficina del Libro Internacional
Av. Cordoba 1877
1120 Buenos Aires
Tel: (54 11) 815-8354
Fax: (54 11) 815-8156

AUSTRALIA, FIJI, PAPUA NEW GUINEA, SOLOMON ISLANDS, VANUATU, AND WESTERN SAMOA
D.A. Information Services
648 Whitehorse Road
Mitcham 3132
Victoria
Tel: (61) 3 9210 7777
Fax: (61) 3 9210 7788
E-mail: service@dadirect.com.au
URL: http://www.dadirect.com.au

AUSTRIA
Gerold and Co.
Weihburggasse 26
A-1011 Wien
Tel: (43 1) 512-47-31-0
Fax: (43 1) 512-47-31-29
URL: http://www.gerold.co/at.online

BANGLADESH
Micro Industries Development Assistance Society (MIDAS)
House 5, Road 16
Dhanmondi R/Area
Dhaka 1209
Tel: (880 2) 326427
Fax: (880 2) 811188

BELGIUM
Jean De Lannoy
Av. du Roi 202
1060 Brussels
Tel: (32 2) 538-5169
Fax: (32 2) 538-0841

BRAZIL
Publicações Tecnicas Internacionais Ltda.
Rua Peixoto Gomide, 209
01409 Sao Paulo, SP.
Tel: (55 11) 259-6644
Fax: (55 11) 258-6990
E-mail: postmaster@pti.uol.br
URL: http://www.uol.br

CANADA
Renouf Publishing Co. Ltd.
5369 Canotek Road
Ottawa, Ontario K1J 9J3
Tel: (613) 745-2665
Fax: (613) 745-7660
E-mail: order.dept@renoufbooks.com
URL: http://www.renoufbooks.com

CHINA
China Financial & Economic Publishing House
8, Da Fo Si Dong Jie
Beijing
Tel: (86 10) 6333-8257
Fax: (86 10) 6401-7365

COLOMBIA
Infoenlace Ltda.
Carrera 6 No. 51-21
Apartado Aereo 34270
Santafé de Bogotá, D.C.
Tel: (57 1) 285-2798
Fax: (57 1) 285-2798

COTE D'IVOIRE
Center d'Edition et de Diffusion Africaines (CEDA)
04 B.P. 541
Abidjan 04
Tel: (225) 24 6510;24 6511
Fax: (225) 25 0567

CYPRUS
Center for Applied Research
Cyprus College
6, Diogenes Street, Engomi
P.O. Box 2006
Nicosia
Tel: (357 2) 44-1730
Fax: (357 2) 46-2051

CZECH REPUBLIC
National Information Center
prodejna, Konviktska 5
CS – 113 57 Prague 1
Tel: (42 2) 2422-9433
Fax: (42 2) 2422-1484
URL: http://www.nis.cz/

DENMARK
SamfundsLitteratur
Rosenoerns Allé 11
DK-1970 Frederiksberg C
Tel: (45 31) 351942
Fax: (45 31) 357822
URL: http://www.sl.cbs.dk

ECUADOR
Libri Mundi
Libreria Internacional
P.O. Box 17-01-3029
Juan Leon Mera 851
Quito
Tel: (593 2) 521-606; (593 2) 544-185
Fax: (593 2) 504-209
E-mail: librimu1@librimundi.com.ec
E-mail: librimu2@librimundi.com.ec

EGYPT, ARAB REPUBLIC OF
Al Ahram Distribution Agency
Al Galaa Street
Cairo
Tel: (20 2) 578-6083
Fax: (20 2) 578-6833

The Middle East Observer
41, Sherif Street
Cairo
Tel: (20 2) 393-9732
Fax: (20 2) 393-9732

FINLAND
Akateeminen Kirjakauppa
P.O. Box 128
FIN-00101 Helsinki
Tel: (358 0) 121 4418
Fax: (358 0) 121-4435
E-mail: akatilaus@stockmann.fi
URL: http://www.akateeminen.com/

FRANCE
World Bank Publications
66, avenue d'Iéna
75116 Paris
Tel: (33 1) 40-69-30-56/57
Fax: (33 1) 40-69-30-68

GERMANY
UNO-Verlag
Poppelsdorfer Allee 55
53115 Bonn
Tel: (49 228) 949020
Fax: (49 228) 217492
URL: http://www.uno-verlag.de
E-mail: unoverlag@aol.com

GREECE
Papasotiriou S.A.
35, Stournara Str.
106 82 Athens
Tel: (30 1) 364-1826
Fax: (30 1) 364-8254

HAITI
Culture Diffusion
5, Rue Capois
C.P. 257
Port-au-Prince
Tel: (509) 23 9260
Fax: (509) 23 4858

HONG KONG, MACAO
Asia 2000 Ltd.
Sales & Circulation Department
Seabird House, unit 1101-02
22-28 Wyndham Street, Central
Hong Kong
Tel: (852) 2530-1409
Fax: (852) 2526-1107
E-mail: sales@asia2000.com.hk
URL: http://www.asia2000.com.hk

HUNGARY
Euro Info Service
Margitszgeti Europa Haz
H-1138 Budapest
Tel: (36 1) 111 6061
Fax: (36 1) 302 5035
E-mail: euroinfo@mail.matav.hu

INDIA
Allied Publishers Ltd.
751 Mount Road
Madras - 600 002
Tel: (91 44) 852-3938
Fax: (91 44) 852-0649

INDONESIA
Pt. Indira Limited
Jalan Borobudur 20
P.O. Box 181
Jakarta 10320
Tel: (62 21) 390-4290
Fax: (62 21) 390-4289

IRAN
Ketab Sara Co. Publishers
Khaled Eslamboli Ave., 6th Street
Delafrooz Alley No. 8
P.O. Box 15745-733
Tehran 15117
Tel: (98 21) 8717819; 8716104
Fax: (98 21) 8712479
E-mail: ketab-sara@neda.net.ir

Kowkab Publishers
P.O. Box 19575-511
Tehran
Tel: (98 21) 258-3723
Fax: (98 21) 258-3723

IRELAND
Government Supplies Agency
Oifig an tSoláthair
4-5 Harcourt Road
Dublin 2
Tel: (353 1) 661-3111
Fax: (353 1) 475-2670

ISRAEL
Yozmot Literature Ltd.
P.O. Box 56055
3 Yohanan Hasandlar Street
Tel Aviv 61560
Tel: (972 3) 5285-397
Fax: (972 3) 5285-397

R.O.Y. International
PO Box 13056
Tel Aviv 61130
Tel: (972 3) 5461423
Fax: (972 3) 5461442
E-mail: royil@netvision.net.il

Palestinian Authority/Middle East
Index Information Services
P.O.B. 19502 Jerusalem
Tel: (972 2) 6271219
Fax: (972 2) 6271634

ITALY
Licosa Commissionaria Sansoni SPA
Via Duca Di Calabria, 1/1
Casella Postale 552
50125 Firenze
Tel: (55) 645-415
Fax: (55) 641-257
E-mail: licosa@ftbcc.it
URL: http://www.ftbcc.it/licosa

JAMAICA
Ian Randle Publishers Ltd.
206 Old Hope Road, Kingston 6
Tel: 876-927-2085
Fax: 876-977-0243
E-mail: irpl@colis.com

JAPAN
Eastern Book Service
3-13 Hongo 3-chome, Bunkyo-ku
Tokyo 113
Tel: (81 3) 3818-0861
Fax: (81 3) 3818-0864
E-mail: orders@svt-ebs.co.jp
URL: http://www.bekkoame.or.jp/~svt-ebs

KENYA
Africa Book Service (E.A.) Ltd.
Quaran House, Mfangano Street
P.O. Box 45245
Nairobi
Tel: (254 2) 223 641
Fax: (254 2) 330 272

KOREA, REPUBLIC OF
Daejon Trading Co. Ltd.
P.O. Box 34, Youida, 706 Seoun Bldg
44-6 Youido-Dong, Yeongchengpo-Ku
Seoul
Tel: (82 2) 785-1631/4
Fax: (82 2) 784-0315

MALAYSIA
University of Malaya Cooperative Bookshop, Limited
P.O. Box 1127
Jalan Pantai Baru
59700 Kuala Lumpur
Tel: (60 3) 756-5000
Fax: (60 3) 755-4424
E-mail: umkoop@tm.net.my

MEXICO
INFOTEC
Av. San Fernando No. 37
Col. Toriello Guerra
14050 Mexico, D.F.
Tel: (52 5) 624-2800
Fax: (52 5) 624-2822
E-mail: infotec@rtn.net.mx
URL: http://rtn.net.mx

NEPAL
Everest Media International Services (P) Ltd.
GPO Box 5443
Kathmandu
Tel: (977 1) 472 152
Fax: (977 1) 224 431

NETHERLANDS
De Lindeboom/InOr-Publikaties
P.O. Box 202, 7480 AE Haaksbergen
Tel: (31 53) 574-0004
Fax: (31 53) 572-9296
E-mail: lindeboo@worldonline.nl
URL: http://www.worldonline.nl/~lindeboo

NEW ZEALAND
EBSCO NZ Ltd.
Private Mail Bag 99914
New Market
Auckland
Tel: (64 9) 524-8119
Fax: (64 9) 524-8067

NIGERIA
University Press Limited
Three Crowns Building Jericho
Private Mail Bag 5095
Ibadan
Tel: (234 22) 41-1356
Fax: (234 22) 41-2056

NORWAY
NIC Info A/S
Book Department, Postboks 6512 Etterstad
N-0606 Oslo
Tel: (47 22) 97-4500
Fax: (47 22) 97-4545

PAKISTAN
Mirza Book Agency
65, Shahrah-e-Quaid-e-Azam
Lahore 54000
Tel: (92 42) 735 3601
Fax: (92 42) 576 3714

Oxford University Press
5 Bangalore Town
Sharae Faisal
PO Box 13033
Karachi-75350
Tel: (92 21) 446307
Fax: (92 21) 4547640
E-mail: ouppak@TheOffice.net

Pak Book Corporation
Aziz Chambers 21, Queen's Road
Lahore
Tel: (92 42) 636 3222; 636 0885
Fax: (92 42) 636 2328
E-mail: pbc@brain.net.pk

PERU
Editorial Desarrollo SA
Apartado 3824, Lima 1
Tel: (51 14) 285380
Fax: (51 14) 286628

PHILIPPINES
International Booksource Center Inc.
1127-A Antipolo St, Barangay, Venezuela
Makati City
Tel: (63 2) 896 6501; 6505; 6507
Fax: (63 2) 896 1741

POLAND
International Publishing Service
Ul. Piekna 31/37
00-677 Warzawa
Tel: (48 2) 628-6089
Fax: (48 2) 621-7255
E-mail: books%ips@ikp.atm.com.pl
URL: http://www.ipscg.waw.pl/ips/export/

PORTUGAL
Livraria Portugal
Apartado 2681, Rua Do Carmo 70-74
1200 Lisbon
Tel: (1) 347-4982
Fax: (1) 347-0264

ROMANIA
Compani De Librarii Bucuresti S.A.
Str. Lipscani no. 26, sector 3
Bucharest
Tel: (40 1) 613 9645
Fax: (40 1) 312 4000

RUSSIAN FEDERATION
Isdatelstvo <Ves Mir>
9a, Kolpachniy Pereulok
Moscow 101831
Tel: (7 095) 917 87 49
Fax: (7 095) 917 92 59

SINGAPORE, TAIWAN, MYANMAR, BRUNEI
Ashgate Publishing Asia Pacific Pte. Ltd.
41 Kallang Pudding Road #04-03
Golden Wheel Building
Singapore 349316
Tel: (65) 741-5166
Fax: (65) 742-9356
E-mail: ashgate@asianconnect.com

SLOVENIA
Gospodarski Vestnik Publishing Group
Dunajska cesta 5
1000 Ljubljana
Tel: (386 61) 133 83 47; 132 12 30
Fax: (386 61) 133 80 30
E-mail: repansekj@gvestnik.si

SOUTH AFRICA, BOTSWANA
For single titles:
Oxford University Press Southern Africa
Vasco Boulevard, Goodwood
P.O. Box 12119, N1 City 7463
Cape Town
Tel: (27 21) 595 4400
Fax: (27 21) 595 4430
E-mail: oxford@oup.co.za

For subscription orders:
International Subscription Service
P.O. Box 41095
Craighall
Johannesburg 2024
Tel: (27 11) 880-1448
Fax: (27 11) 880-6248
E-mail: iss@is.co.za

SPAIN
Mundi-Prensa Libros, S.A.
Castello 37
28001 Madrid
Tel: (34 1) 431-3399
Fax: (34 1) 575-3998
E-mail: libreria@mundiprensa.es
URL: http://www.mundiprensa.es/

Mundi-Prensa Barcelona
Consell de Cent, 391
08009 Barcelona
Tel: (34 3) 488-3492
Fax: (34 3) 487-7659
E-mail: barcelona@mundiprensa.es

SRI LANKA, THE MALDIVES
Lake House Bookshop
100, Sir Chittampalam Gardiner Mawatha
Colombo 2
Tel: (94 1) 32105
Fax: (94 1) 432104
E-mail: LHL@sri.lanka.net

SWEDEN
Wennergren-Williams AB
P. O. Box 1305
S-171 25 Solna
Tel: (46 8) 705-97-50
Fax: (46 8) 27-00-71
E-mail: mail@wwi.se

SWITZERLAND
Librairie Payot Service Institutionnel
Côtes-de-Montbenon 30
1002 Lausanne
Tel: (41 21) 341-3229
Fax: (41 21) 341-3235

ADECO Van Diemen EditionsTechniques
Ch. de Lacuez 41
CH1807 Blonay
Tel: (41 21) 943 2673
Fax: (41 21) 943 3605

THAILAND
Central Books Distribution
306 Silom Road
Bangkok 10500
Tel: (66 2) 235-5400
Fax: (66 2) 237-8321

TRINIDAD & TOBAGO AND THE CARRIBBEAN
Systematics Studies Ltd.
St. Augustine Shopping Center
Eastern Main Road, St. Augustine
Trinidad & Tobago, West Indies
Tel: (868) 645-8466
Fax: (868) 645-8467
E-mail: tobe@trinidad.net

UGANDA
Gustro Ltd.
PO Box 9997, Madhvani Building
Plot 16/4 Jinja Rd.
Kampala
Tel: (256 41) 251 467
Fax: (256 41) 251 468
E-mail: gus@swiftuganda.com

UNITED KINGDOM
Microinfo Ltd.
P.O. Box 3, Alton, Hampshire GU34 2PG
England
Tel: (44 1420) 86848
Fax: (44 1420) 89889
E-mail: wbank@ukminfo.demon.co.uk
URL: http://www.microinfo.co.uk

VENEZUELA
Tecni-Ciencia Libros, S.A.
Centro Cuidad Comercial Tamanco
Nivel C2, Caracas
Tel: (58 2) 959 5547; 5035; 0016
Fax: (58 2) 959 5636

ZAMBIA
University Bookshop, University of Zambia
Great East Road Campus
P.O. Box 32379
Lusaka
Tel: (260 1) 252 576
Fax: (260 1) 253 952

10/09/97